The European Competitive Environment

The European Competitive Environment

Text and cases

Leigh Davison, Edmund Fitzpatrick and Debra Johnson

Butterworth-Heinemann Ltd
Linacre House, Jordan Hill, Oxford OX2 8DP

 A member of the Reed Elsevier plc group

OXFORD LONDON BOSTON
MUNICH NEW DELHI SINGAPORE SYDNEY
TOKYO TORONTO WELLINGTON

First published 1995

British Library Cataloguing in Publication Data
A catalogue record for this book is available from the British Library

ISBN 0 7506 2278 4

Typeset by Datix International Ltd, Bungay, Suffolk
Set in 10/12pt Monophoto Photina
Printed and bound in England by Clays Ltd, St Ives plc

Contents

List of contributors   vii

Preface   ix

Acknowledgements   xi

Part One: Introducing the European Competitive Environment

1   The single market: competition in context
   Debra Johnson   3
2   The distortion of competitive forces: state aids
   Ian Barnes and Pamela M Barnes   26
3   Articles 85 and 86: control of restrictive practices and abuses of
   dominant positions
   Edmund Fitzpatrick   44
4   Brussels and the control of merger activity in the European Union
   Leigh Davison and Edmund Fitzpatrick   60
5   Competition policy in the Member States: a case of convergence?
   Colin Turner   77
6   Social policy and competition
   Campbell McPherson and Sue Stacey   92
7   The external dimension of EU competition policy
   Lee Miles   109

Part Two: Case Studies

Case 1   Open skies over the European Union?
     Leigh Davison   125
Case 2   Competition in European financial services: the banking
     industry
     Max E Good   143
Case 3   Competition policy: the Hungarian experience
     Pal Majoros and Laszlo Nyusztay   156
Case 4   Transforming competition policy: the case of Sweden
     Lee Miles   176
Case 5   Let the Euro 'phone wars' begin
     Andrew Mearman and David Gray   193
Case 6   Europe's energy sector
     Debra Johnson   214
Case 7   EU railways: open access or natural monopoly?
     Brian Milner   231

Index   251

Contributors

Ian Barnes is Dean of Economics, School of Economics, University of Humberside.

Pamela M Barnes is a Senior Lecturer in European Studies, School of Economics, University of Humberside.

Leigh Davison is Head of Economics, School of Economics, University of Humberside.

Edmund Fitzpatrick is Joint Dean, School of Finance and Law, University of Humberside.

Max E Good is a Lecturer in Economics, School of Economics, University of Humberside.

David Gray is a Lecturer in Economics, School of Economics, University of Humberside.

Debra Johnson is a Senior Lecturer in Economics and European Studies, School of Economics, University of Humberside.

Pal Majoros is a Professor in the Department of Foreign Trade Policy at the College for Foreign Trade, Budapest, Hungary.

Andrew Mearman is a Lecturer in Economics, School of Economics, University of Humberside.

Campbell McPherson is a Senior Lecturer in European Studies, School of Economics, University of Humberside.

Lee Miles is a Lecturer in European Studies, School of Economics, University of Humberside.

Brian Milner is a Senior Lecturer in Quantitative Methods and Quality Management in the School of Systems and Information Sciences, University of Humberside

Laszlo Nyusztay is an Associate Professor in the Department of Foreign Trade Policy at the College for Foreign Trade, Budapest, Hungary.

Sue Stacey is a Lecturer in Economics, School of Economics, University of Humberside.

Colin Turner is a Lecturer in Economics and European Studies, School of Economics, University of Humberside.

Preface

Competition is the underlying theme in the evolution of European integration. Increased competition via the removal of non-tariff barriers between Member States was the method chosen to create the single market. Enhanced competition serves the EU in two ways. First, it stimulates greater efficiency and helps improve Europe's competitiveness. Secondly, by breaking down barriers between Members States and granting access to each other's markets, it increases the economic interdependence of Member States and thereby deepens the integration process in Europe. The movement of trans-European networks to the top of Europe's policy agenda and the attempts to liberalize heavily regulated utilities, such as energy and telecommunications, reinforce this second effect.

This book explores these issues by combining chapters on the theory and practice of competition policy with case studies. A broad working definition of competition policy has been used. In other words, the scope of the book extends beyond an examination of Articles 85–94 and the Merger Control Regulation, although these are covered in some depth, and examines European Commission initiatives to embed the principles of competition into the maximum number of its sectoral policies. These latter attempts are explored in more detail in the case studies on airlines, banking, energy, telecommunications and railways.

The book is also forward looking. It contains chapters on the impact of enlargement – one of the great challenges facing the EU at the end of the twentieth century – and on the need for applicant countries to prepare themselves for membership by amending their own competition policy. Case studies deal with the January 1995 EFTA enlargement and the later Central and Eastern European enlargement.

The book should be useful to a wide range of students. It is aimed at the increasing number of students who are following courses on European integration. The use of case studies ensures that the study of competition is taken beyond legal and economic theory and related to the practical impact on and experience of European businesses. Thus, the book will also be valuable to business students and will help law students relate the legal details of competition to policy considerations and to their impact on the real world of the business environment. In other words, the book will help law students understand why competition law is central to the study of EU law.

Although designed to be used on its own, the text also complements and builds upon another book in this series, *European Business: Text and Cases*.

The European Competitive Environment

This earlier book looks at some of the major issues within the European business environment and introduces the student to procedures and decision making within the EU. The two books can therefore be used in conjunction with each other. This volume provides a logical progression from the material in the first text and explores the various aspects of competition and the regulatory framework in more depth. Taken together, the two volumes provide an extended range of case studies which provide a comprehensive and topical consideration of the impact of European Union policy on a wide range of business sectors.

Leigh Davison
Edmund Fitzpatrick
Debra Johnson

Acknowledgements

We would like to take this opportunity to thank each author who has contributed to a case and/or a chapter. Namely, Ian Barnes, Pamela M Barnes, Max Good, David Gray, Pal Majoros, Andrew Mearman, Campbell McPherson, Lee Miles, Brian Milner, Laszlo Nyusztay, Sue Stacey and Colin Turner.

**Part One   Introducing the European Competitive
Environment**

1 The single market: competition in context

Debra Johnson

The single market programme, which was introduced by the 1985 White Paper *Completing the Internal Market*, is a significant landmark in the development of the European Union. Prior to the publication of the White Paper and the European Commission's subsequent energetic campaign to implement the proposals, the European Community appeared stagnant, obsessed with budgetary disputes and the problems of reform of the Common Agricultural Policy. The single market campaign served to revitalize the Community and raise it from its torpor.

Interpretations vary as to the longer term role of the single market. One view is that the single market is no more than a reaffirmation of the aspirations of the Treaty of Rome which had, after all, spoke of 'establishing a common market' (Article 2). This included the 'abolition, as between member states, of obstacles to freedom of movement for persons, services and capital' (Article 3c) and sought 'the approximation of the laws of Member States to the extent required for the proper functioning of the common market' (Article 3h). In other words, the single market simply served to put the European Community back on course. This interpretation contains no assumptions about the future of the European Community after the achievement of the single market.

Closely linked to this is the view of the governments of Margaret Thatcher and John Major which welcomed the single market as an extension of domestic economic policies. They regarded the single market, for the most part, as supply side economics writ large on a European scale. For them, the creation of the single market – a large barrier-free trading area in which market forces hold sway and the freeing up of the forces of competition results in a more efficient and competitive European economy – was an end in itself. Therefore, although the British governments of the 1980s and the first half of the 1990s acquired a reputation for disruptive behaviour in relation to the European Community, the UK government was often the member state which was most supportive of the Commission's attempts to pass single market measures.

For others, the single market represented a means to an even more ambitious end – the achievement of European Economic and Political Union. In line with neo-functionalist theory, the single market would reveal other areas in which the European Community needed to take action to achieve its aim of a truly single market. To a certain extent this view has been borne out by the development of flanking policies such as environment and social policy, which have been introduced in part to support single market objectives, and ultimately by the Maastricht Treaty. This Treaty was negotiated when enthusiasm about the single market was at its peak and partly in response to the view that the single market would be incomplete without the introduction of a single currency. The provisions of the Maastricht Treaty, particularly in relation to economic and monetary union, represent the triumph of neo-functionalist spillover – that is, a seemingly technocratic, economic programme has snowballed and become the catalyst for European Union.

Whatever the motivations of the supporters of the single market, all its advocates recognize competition as the motor force for attainment of the single market goal. Through Articles 85–94 of the Treaty of Rome, the European Commission has always possessed instruments which it could use to ensure that competition within the Union's borders is fair and non-discriminatory. The single market not only demonstrated the need to enforce these Articles more vigilantly and to strengthen the Commission's specific competition powers via means such as the Merger Control Regulation, but was also, in a much broader sense, an extension of competition policy in its own right.

The Single Market White Paper is made up of almost three hundred proposals to remove non-tariff barriers among member states. The removal of each barrier was designed to free up the forces of competition within the Community's borders. Taken separately, each measure represented only a tiny increase in competition but taken altogether it was anticipated that the full implementation of the single market programme would have a fundamental impact on the Community's economy. Soon after the introduction of the single market programme, it became clear that other measures were needed to capture the full benefits of the single market and that the Programme needed to be extended into areas such as energy, environmental and social policy which were not anticipated by the White Paper.

In short, the theme of competition in the single market can be interpreted in several ways. A narrow interpretation would look at the implications for the European Community's competition policy of the implementation of the White Paper. A more literal interpretation would concentrate on the implications of the White Paper itself for the strength of competition within the European economy. A wider interpretation would see the single market as a series of objectives which extend beyond the confines of the White Paper. If policies need to be introduced to achieve the objectives of the White Paper but which were not in the White Paper itself, then so be it. The single market is an idea which extends beyond the bounds of a single policy document, however ambitious. This and subsequent chapters encompass both the narrow and the broader, more dynamic view of competition within the single market and the European Union.

Background to the single market

The development of the European Community has taken place in phases. During times of buoyant growth and economic optimism, European integration tends to make significant progress. Conversely, the process of integration has always faltered and stalled during periods of economic recession.

Growth in Europe was rapid and unemployment low during the first fifteen years of the European Community's existence. The Treaty of Rome had anticipated the establishment of a customs union within twelve years of the foundation of the Community. In fact, spurred on by the confidence in Europe at the time, the original six members created a customs union by 1968 – two years ahead of schedule.

The development of a common market alongside that of a customs union was also on the agenda of the founding fathers. Work towards a common market was expected to continue after the customs union was in place. This was not to be. The unprecedented prolonged period of uninterrupted economic growth did not last. International financial instability during the late 1960s resulted in the 1971 collapse of the Bretton Woods system which had been in operation since 1944. The oil price crisis of 1973 accentuated the inflationary pressures which were already present in the system. Such catalysts helped trigger off an international recession which resulted in high levels of inflation and unemployment.

The deterioration of the economic climate coincided with and brought about a slowdown in the momentum of European integration. By the early 1980s, the integration process appeared moribund. Concern was also growing about Europe's competitive position relative to the United States and Japan. Although the economic crisis was general throughout the industrialized world, Europe appeared to be faring worse than these two main rivals. Trend growth rates fell in all countries but the European Community's growth was down more than that of the US and Japan (Table 1.1).

During the period 1968–1973, Europe's average growth rate was 1.7 percentage points above that of the United States. The situation rapidly altered. In the six years following the first oil shock in 1973, the growth rates of Europe and the United States were broadly similar. By the 1980s, European growth was averaging 0.4 percentage points less than that of the United States.

The European Competitive Environment

Table 1.1 *GDP growth rates (% p.a. – average)*

	1968–1973	1973–1979	1979–1990
United States	3.2	2.4	2.6
Japan	8.6	3.6	4.1
EEC	4.9	2.5	2.2

Source: OECD

The two economic indicators giving the most cause for concern in the early 1980s were inflation and unemployment. Inflation contributed to Europe's poor competitive performance and unemployment was the result. The European Community, Japan and the United States all experienced an acceleration of prices following the 1973 and 1979 oil price shocks. Once again the inflationary performance of Europe, where the average rate of price increases during 1973–1979 was double that of the previous five years, was worse than that of the US and Japan. Inflation rates were also much higher in Europe during the 1980s (Table 1.2).

Table 1.2 *Inflation (% p.a. – average)*

	1968–1973	1973–1979	1979–1990
United States	5.0	8.5	5.5
Japan	7.1	9.9	2.6
EEC	6.1	12.1	7.3

Source: OECD

The European Commission identified inflation as a major drain on Europe's economy, both in terms of its negative impact on competitiveness and in terms of 'its negative effect on investment decisions. Inflation has discouraged investment by reducing profit margins, raising nominal interest rates and fostering uncertainties as to future capital costs, the long-term outlook for demand and the real rate of return' (Fifth Medium Term Economic Policy Programme: European Economy – March 1981).

A similar pattern emerged in relation to unemployment. Joblessness grew steadily from 1973 throughout the OECD area but the problem was at its greatest in the European Community. Unemployment averaged 9.5 per cent in the European Community during the 1980s, 2.5 percentage points above jobless rates in the US and almost four times greater than in Japan. Until 1979, European unemployment had been markedly lower than in the United States. Deterioration in the employment situation was most noticeable in Belgium, the Netherlands and Spain but the problem was general throughout the Community (Table 1.3).

Table 1.3 *Standardized unemployment rates (% p.a. – average)*

	1968–1973	1973–1979	1979–1990
United States	4.6	6.7	7.0
Japan	1.2	1.9	2.5
EEC	2.9	4.8	9.5

Source: OECD

It was against this background of sluggish and poor relative economic performance that the European Commission began to draw up a strategy for revitalising the Community's economy. The Fifth Medium Term Economic Programme, published in 1981, contains the germs of the 1985 Single Market White Paper which set out the detailed proposals to implement the Single Market.

The Programme acknowledged Europe's fundamental economic difficulties and concluded that 'the countries of the Community have been unable to adapt sufficiently to these changed circumstances. Our competitive position in relation to Japan, the United States and the newly industrialized countries weakened.'

The Commission criticized the economic policy of many member states which had 'given inadequate weight to supply considerations as opposed to the management of demand . . . And inadequate attention has been given to structural changes while government interventions in this area have sometimes tended to delay rather than to foster the adjustment of our economic structures.' The solution, according to the Commission, lay in:

> reducing costs and promoting investment to improve the structural position and international competitivity of our economies . . . In many countries, there must be a recovery of profitability, improved expectation of sales and greater freedom for investors to react to market forces. There needs to be greater freedom for the market to produce relative price changes, to provide the necessary incentives for investment. Competition should be promoted and distortion of competition controlled. Public intervention must be clearly defined in its limits and its aims.

Such intervention in the private sector should stimulate regional equilibrium, technical innovation and a reallocation of resources from declining to competitive activities.

In other words, the key to the Community's economic problems lay in freeing up the supply side of Europe's economy and in releasing the forces of competition. The European Community already had competition policy tools within the Treaty of Rome. The 1985 Single Market White Paper marked a more direct onslaught on non-tariff barriers to trade within the Community. This has led to further initiatives to bring the principles of competition into areas not originally envisaged in the single market such as social and environmental policy. Competition considerations also underpin the current campaign to develop trans-European networks.

The remainder of this chapter covers competition policy in general terms; looks at the single market in more detail; examines the assumptions underpinning it; identifies its achievements to date and discusses the initiatives which are under way to develop the principles of the single market still further.

What is a single market?

The single market programme, also referred to as the 'internal market', the 'common market' and '1992', the latter because of the deadline of 31 December 1992 for completing the project, was initially set out in the 1985 White Paper *Completing the Internal Market*. The origins of this programme lay in the Treaty of Rome but its timing and the immediate impetus for it were attributable to Europe's economic crisis and the belief that Europe's poor relative economic performance was due to the continuing fragmentation of Europe's market. These divisions increased industry's costs and discouraged exploitation of economies of scale – a factor which particularly hindered the development of Europe's high technology industries. Consequently, in March 1985, the Internal Market Council called for 'action to achieve a single large market by 1992 thereby creating a more favourable environment for stimulating enterprise, competition and trade.'

The resulting White Paper identified three categories of barriers – physical, technical and fiscal – for removal. Many of the proposals in isolation would have a tiny impact on the creation of the single market. For example, the proposal for 'a system of certification in reproduction materials for decorative plants' was hardly going to transform the structure of the European economy. However, taken together, the almost three hundred proposals contained in the White Paper were expected to deliver a significant kickstart to Europe's economy. The Cecchini Report, published in 1988, anticipated that implementation of the programme would contribute an additional 4.5–7 per cent to Community GDP, depending on whether appropriate accompanying economic measures were taken; reduce inflationary pressure; and, after a short-term increase in unemployment as industries adjusted to the more competitive environment, create at least 1.8 million additional jobs and possibly more.

Physical barriers to trade arose from the existence of frontier controls and the associated stoppages and paperwork. Border controls were necessary because of differences in indirect taxes, monetary compensatory amounts in relation to the Common Agricultural Policy, transport controls, public security, immigration, and drug control.

The removal of frontier controls would lessen border delays, reduce bureaucratic costs and provide a clear indication of the commitment of the Community towards further integration. The Cecchini Report calculated that the direct cost to business of customs-related administrative activities on intra-Community trade was equivalent to about 1.5 per cent of an average consignment's value. The addition of the cost of delays increases this figure to almost 2 per cent – a significant burden to companies on tight margins. Businesses in the US and Japan did not incur similar costs.

The removal of technical barriers to trade provided the biggest boost to the single market and refers to regulations and rules which inhibited the free flow of goods and services within the Community. For example, the existence of twelve different technical standards, one for each member state, within the Community, required firms wishing to market their products throughout the Community to adapt them to twelve different national standards. This imposed significant additional and, according to the Commission, unnecessary costs on European business, therefore harming the ability of the Community to compete with Japan and the United States which had large, unified domestic markets. Competition within the Community itself was also inhibited, thereby adding to x-inefficiency and affecting overseas competitiveness as well. Such barriers were particularly damaging to high technology industries in which European business was prevented from reaping the full benefits of economies of scale in relation to research and development.

Previously the Commission had tried to eradicate different technical standards to trade by harmonising standards. This had proved a drawn-out, cumbersome process which had limited success and had resulted in European standards which were often obsolete by the time member states had agreed to them. The single market programme, reinforced by the Cassis de Dijon decision of 1979, moved away from harmonization towards the use of mutual recognition, that is, goods which were legally sold in one member state could legally be sold in another. The Commission has not abandoned the idea of European standards but reserves them for the establishment of 'essential requirements', particularly health, safety and environmental protection.

The use of mutual recognition and selective harmonization to prevent the erection of trade barriers has been reinforced by the Mutual Information Directive which requires member states to notify the Commission of new regulations and standards before their implementation. The Commission has the power to freeze the introduction of these national regulations if it judges that a Union initiative would be more appropriate. This system allows the existence of regulatory diversity provided it does not give rise to new trade barriers.

Restrictions on the ability to supply services to other member states were analogous to those on goods and were, therefore, also included in the White Paper. Mutual recognition of standards was adapted to all types of services and to the recognition of professional and educational qualifications. The development of a single banking licence and home country control (Case Study 2), for example, paralleled the policy in relation to manufactured goods. The Second Banking Directive established the principle that the granting of a licence to operate in one member state acted as a passport to operate in all other member states. In other words, only one banking licence rather than twelve was required to enable a bank to operate throughout the European Union. Common rules were also established in relation to prudential controls. This reflected the 'essential requirements' element of the new approach to standards. The case also considers some of the ways in which individual banks have responded to the challenge of the changes.

The White Paper also proposed the completion of the Common Transport Policy which had been an important part of the Treaty of Rome but which had been so neglected in the interim that the European Parliament had brought a case against the Council of Ministers for failure to act. The European Court of Justice agreed with the Parliament and the White Paper gave added impetus to the introduction of competition in what had been a heavily regulated market.

Case studies on the airline (Case Study 1) and rail (Case Study 7) sectors highlight some of the problems inherent in introducing competition into transport. The airline case demonstrates that, even with the introduction of a liberal legal framework, significant obstacles remain to the introduction of competition in the form of state aid to national airlines. Attempts to remove such aid have resulted in litigation and require difficult decisions on the part of the Commission.

The rail case discusses attempts to introduce competition into the EU's rail network by separating infrastructure from the supply of rail services. This approach corresponds with that taken by the British government in its campaign to privatize British Rail. The case explores the British experience in some depth. It also examines some of the technical obstacles which lie in the way of developing a truly European network in which there is competition between rail services and enhanced competition between rail and other forms of transport.

The liberalization of public procurement was an important part of the single market programme. The supply of goods to public purchasing bodies is equivalent to approximately 15 per cent of Community GDP but an overwhelming proportion of public contracts went to companies from the awarding country. The Single Market White Paper set out a schedule for specific measures to open up this large and previously closed market throughout the Community.

A crucial element in the single market has been the liberalization of capital movements within the Community. If goods, services and people were to be free to move throughout the Community, free movement of finance was essential. Without this, the benefits of the freeing of goods and services markets would be seriously reduced or even lost. Legal restrictions on capital movements have been lifted. A priority of the European Commission in the 1990s is to lessen the cost, and improve the speed and efficiency of cross-border transfers of money. As the 1985 White Paper stated, 'the task is to set up an attractive and competitive integrated financial system for both Community and non-Community business circles.'

The removal of fiscal barriers, especially in relation to different levels of indirect taxation, has always been regarded as an essential arm of the single market. The importance of fiscal measures is twofold.

First, the need for fiscal checks figures prominently among the reasons for the need to maintain the existence of frontier controls.

Secondly, the existence of big differences in tax levels can, in itself, lead to distortions of competition. A transitional agreement on the VAT regime has been reached but, in the mid-1990s, there are a number of examples of continuing trade distortions in the EU arising from differences in indirect taxation. Since 1 January 1993, for example, large numbers of British citizens have been crossing the Channel to France to take advantage of their new right to buy unlimited quantities of alcohol and tobacco for their own personal use. Significantly lower French excise duties provide a strong incentive for this activity. Accurate estimates of the extent of this trade are difficult to generate but the likely losses to UK brewers, distillers, retailers and the Treasury run into millions of pounds.

Single market mechanisms

The single market represents a belief in the efficacy of competition. The introduction of market forces through the removal of barriers which have been shielding sectors from competition will, according to this belief, unleash the benefits of competition in terms of greater efficiency, technological progress and improved competitiveness. In the case of the single market, the barriers in question were the non-tariff barriers which remained among member states after the completion of the customs union (Figure 1.1).

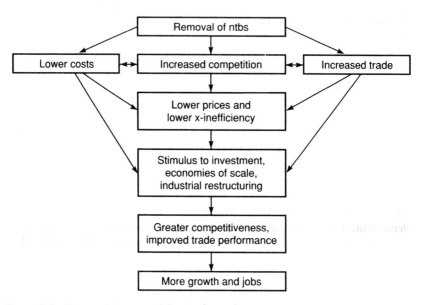

Figure 1.1 Economic impact of the single market

Yet how specifically does the removal of non-tariff barriers work through and improve the overall performance of the European economy? The following analysis reflects the underlying assumptions of the architects of the single market programme. These assumptions are set out in more detail in the Cecchini Report, published in 1988, which also attempted to estimate quantitatively the benefits which would accrue from the introduction of the single market.

The following major consequences for companies were anticipated as the combined impact of the removal of remaining barriers to trade. First, there would be a significant reduction in costs as firms, no longer having to adapt their operations to twelve national markets, were able to take advantage of economies of scale in both production and business organization.

Secondly, the removal of non-tariff barriers brings additional competition into a firm's member state and, by granting unfettered access to the other member states of the European Union, increases competition throughout the Union. This stimulates the drive to increased efficiency and encourages industrial reorganization. Industrial restructuring also encourages exploitation of economies of scale. In the longer term, industrial reorganization may be even more far reaching as the reallocation of resources in line with the principles of comparative advantage becomes a possibility.

Thirdly, increased competition and the exploitation of economies of scale also results in increased innovation and stimulates investment – essential developments if Europe is to compete effectively with the US, Japan and other Far Eastern rivals.

The effect of the single market on economic operators will vary. Consumers, whether individuals or businesses, will be better off. Pressure on prices will be downward. The quality of products and service should increase and consumers should be offered a wider choice of products.

The benefits for goods and service providers are not so unreservedly positive. There will be winners and losers in the liberalization process. The single market heralds the end of a cosy life behind national barriers. Most companies, to a greater or lesser extent, have had to take measures to adjust to the new business environment as margins are squeezed as a result of the increased competition. However, the increased size of the 'domestic' market also means greater opportunities and lower costs. A positive response to this challenge leads to optimal use of resources and enhances a firm's competitiveness. The least efficient firms will not survive this supply side shock. The most efficient will help re-establish Europe's position among the world's leaders in technology.

The ambitious and all-encompassing nature of the single market programme leads to macroeconomic as well as microeconomic implications. Some job losses were anticipated in the short term as companies adapted to the changes but in the medium term the macroeconomic effect of the single market was expected to be positive and include a boost in GDP growth and employment. In addition, the opening of public procurement will, when the liberalization is fully implemented, help reduce the strains on public finances throughout the Union. The revenue-raising side of government finance will also be helped by the extra taxes resulting from the additional economic activity.

Overall, the supply side effects of lower prices and enhanced productivity acts as a stimulus to demand, both domestic and from third countries. This should manifest itself in an improved European trade performance and result in additional growth and jobs.

A full, in-depth study of the extent to which the single market has

13

delivered the goods is being prepared by the European Commission for presentation to the Council of Ministers in 1996. Even then, four years after the single market deadline, the effects of the programme will not have fully worked their way into Europe's economies. Several important measures are being phased in over a number of years and the structural adjustment of specific sectors to the new competitive environment will continue for some time after the implementation of liberalization measures.

The above analysis is relatively simplistic. The telecommunications case study (Case Study 5) introduces some of the complexities involved in introducing competition into a highly complex, technically sophisticated and rapidly evolving industry. The case discusses some of the potential contradictions between the competition imperative and other objectives such as innovation through cooperation, public service obligations (also an issue in energy markets) and the push for scale economies. The case concludes that, although the thrust of the legislation is geared towards the introduction of competition, the Commission allows for deviations from this aim provided other benefits are clearly demonstrable. Contradictions between competition and other legitimate objectives, notably protection of the environment and security of supply, are also explored in the energy case study (Case Study 6).

Competition policy and the single market

European policy makers recognized the importance of a strong competition policy in the construction and management of the single market. There was a real danger that the destruction of public barriers to competition, which lay at the heart of the single market programme, would be replaced by private barriers erected by companies who prefer to protect themselves from the effects of competition rather than embark upon the adjustments necessary to meet the challenges of increased competition. Consequently, in order to support the objectives of the single market, the White Paper and subsequent policy documents emphasized the need for the European Commission to enforce and enhance competition policy in a vigorous, transparent and non-discriminatory fashion.

The founders of the European Community anticipated the need for a European-wide competition policy to ensure that trade among member states took place on a fair basis and included Articles 85–94 in the Treaty of Rome to deal with potential competitive distortions. These Articles continue to form the legal base of the European Union's competition policy in the 1990s and, as Chapter 5 demonstrates, are increasingly shaping the formulation of competition policy in individual member states. The degree of convergence upon the supranational norm is variable, however, and is most marked within the smaller member states. Larger member states, with the exception of Italy which introduced a national competition law for the first time in 1990 (based, for the most part, on Articles 85 and 86 of the Treaty of Rome), have done much less to realign their national competition laws. In the longer term, the logic of integration will make it increasingly difficult to maintain national competition policies.

Article 85 deals with restrictive practices and aims to prevent 'all agreements ... which may affect trade between member states and which have as their object or effect the prevention, restriction or distortion of competition within the common market.' Prohibited agreements include price fixing, market sharing among competitors, tie-in clauses between suppliers and buyers, information sharing which leads to collusion and establishment of quotas.

Not all agreements between economic operators are prohibited. Under the *de minimis* rule, agreements adjudged to result in insignificant economic effects are allowed to proceed. Also allowed are agreements in which any harmful effects are more than compensated for by particular benefits, especially benefits shared by consumers in the form of lower prices or increased quality of goods and services. Group exemptions from the provisions also exist for agreements relating to specialization, exclusive distribution, exclusive purchasing, patent licensing, research and development, franchising and know-how licensing.

Article 86 prohibits the abuse of a dominant position. Dominance itself is not prohibited but abuse of it is if it affects trade between member states. Examples of abuse of dominance include unfair selling prices; limits to production or market and technical development to the detriment of the consumer; discriminatory pricing; contracts which contain obligations which have no obvious link with the subject of the contract such as fidelity rebates; and the acquisition of firms which results in a significant deterioration in the competitive structure of the EU's market. Chapter 3 deals with the application of Articles 85 and 86 and discusses the role of institutions and enforcement in this process.

Article 90 charges public undertakings and undertakings which have been granted special or exclusive rights by member states to conduct themselves in line with the competition rules of the Treaty insofar as the observance of these rules does not hinder them from performing the particular tasks assigned to them. In other words, state monopolies and enterprises should respect Articles 85–94, although there may be certain circumstances (such as provision of electricity, telephone services or transport) where public service obligations may lead to exceptions.

Sectors dominated by state monopolies include energy, transport, postal services and telecommunications. Within the context of achieving the objectives of the single market, the European Commission has embarked up-on campaigns to eliminate state monopolies in these sectors. As a result of the absence of competitive pressure, prices in countries which maintain such monopolies tend to be higher than those in countries where there is an element of competition. There is also little consumer choice and no incentive to inno-vate. This ultimately damages the overall competitiveness of a country.

The Treaty of Rome, under Article 90(3), gives the European Commission the power to use the Treaty directly to open up these markets to competition. In the early days of telecommunications liberalization, the Commission tried to use Article 90 to demonstrate its commitment to ending state monopolies. This approach was resented by member states but served to demonstrate the seriousness of the Commission's intentions when it came to the matter of eliminating state monopolies. Subsequently, the Commission has chosen to liberalize these sectors through a more consensual, gradual approach. The success of such approaches can be assessed from the cases which deal with airlines, telecommunications and energy. Limited success in the energy sector, however, has resulted in renewed warnings from the Commission that failure to reach agreement on liberalization proposals will result in the Commission using its existing but more inflexible powers under the Treaty of Rome to open up energy markets.

Once liberalization is complete, strong application of the competition rules will be necessary to ensure that the benefits of competition are secured and especially to ensure that member states are not subsidising their industries. Article 92 forbids member states from granting any form of aid to enterprises which could threaten competition and trade among member states. The Treaty catalogues those forms of state aid which are deemed acceptable. These include aid to areas with 'abnormally low' living standards or serious employment problems; aid to promote projects of 'common European inter-est'; aid to rectify damage caused by natural disasters or unusual events; and aid of a social character granted to individual consumers without discrimination related to the origin of the product concerned.

The Single Market White Paper stressed the need for rigorous enforcement of provisions against state aids on the grounds that they distort competition and, in the long run, damage Europe's competitiveness. State aids come in many forms but figures suggest that there has been some decline in direct financial aid over recent years. However, state aids remain controversial and the European Commission has had far from its own way in trying to stamp down on them. Chapter 2 assesses the European Commission's role and success in controlling state aids. Case Study 1 discusses the state aids situation in the airline industry where state aids and heavy losses continue to bedevil the attempts of the Commission to free up this sector.

Although the Commission already had many potential instruments to control competition within the European Community, these were deemed insufficient on their own to regulate the single market which was expected to stimulate sectoral restructuring and encourage the search for mergers and joint ventures. Articles 85 and 86 could have been used to control cross-border mergers. However, it was decided to press ahead with a longstanding proposed regulation on merger control. The Regulation was eventually adopted in 1989 and implemented in 1990. The advantage of this approach lay in the degree of transparency and certainty which a customized merger regulation gave to European companies. Chapter 4 considers key issues surrounding the issue of European merger control, such as thresholds, dominance and distinct markets and the way the Regulation has been interpreted to date.

Achievements of the single market

As the deadline of 31 December 1992 approached, assessments were made of the degree to which the proposals within the 1985 White Paper had been adopted and enforced. The extent to which additional measures had been taken to reinforce single market objectives and the measures which would need to be taken in the future both to manage, up-date and extend the range of the single market were also considered.

The first such report was the so-called Sutherland Report, formally entitled *The Internal Market After 1992 – Meeting the Challenge*, prepared in 1992 by a team headed by former Competition Commissioner, Peter Sutherland. The Sutherland Report formed the basis for a Commission communication, *Communication on the Operation of the Internal Market After 1992 – Follow-up to the Sutherland Report*. These reports confirmed the intention of the Commission to ensure the implementation and enforcement of White Paper legislation and to extend the operation of the single market.

The Sutherland Report and its follow-up made major contributions to three key policy documents which were first published and discussed in 1993. The first two were the Commission Communication *Reinforcing the Effectiveness of the Internal Market* and the working document *Towards a Strategic Programme for the Internal Market* which were published in June 1993 and which set out a detailed programme to protect the achievements of the single market and to build on them further. The third document was the White Paper *Growth, Competitiveness, Employment – the Challenges and Ways Forward into the 21st Century* which was published in December 1993 in response to Europe's growing unemployment problem and the need to do something about it. A key part of the 1993 White Paper was recognition of the need to draw maximum benefits from the single market and to develop

17

it further. This aspect of the White Paper entails significant overlap with the prescriptions of the Strategic Programme.

Success of the 1985 White Paper

The above documents all comment on the degree to which the single market has been achieved and on the need to develop it further. The first annual report on the single market, published in March 1993, noted that, in view of the fact that 95 per cent of the measures in the 1985 White Paper had been adopted by the Council of Ministers, the basic legal framework for the single market was in place. Decisions in the areas of intellectual property, company law, VAT and company taxation still need to be taken before the work of the Council of Ministers is complete on the single market.

The next phase of the implementation of the single market programme is the transposition of directives adopted by the Council of Ministers into the national law of member states. The performance of individual member states in the transposition process varies widely. Ironically, the two countries with reputations as the two most reluctant member states in the integration process, Denmark and the United Kingdom, have the best record when it comes to implementation of single market legislation. By the end of 1993, Denmark had carried out 93 per cent of all the required transpositions and the UK 90 per cent The greatest delays in transposition were in Greece (82.3%), France (82%), Spain (82%) and Ireland (81.4%).

The subject areas in which transposition of directives into national laws is complete or above average include free movement of capital, the removal of border controls, liberalization of financial services (with some exceptions in the insurance sector), the removal of technical barriers, company taxation and indirect taxes. Areas in which transposition into national law has been relatively slow include public procurement (only 59% of the national transposition measures had been taken by the time of the 1993 single market progress report), company law (60%), intellectual and industrial property (61%) and insurance (73%).

The Commission lacks any evidence that the areas in which national transposition is below average has caused any problems in the operation of the single market. However, it is very early to draw any conclusions from the operation of the single market programme as economic operators have had little time to adjust to the new environment. The implementation of the single market programme has also coincided with the development of economic recession in Europe which has reduced the opportunities for expansion into the wider market.

Transposition of directives into national law does not guarantee that the full benefits of competition are secured. This requires that those laws which are agreed are implemented in an appropriate manner, enforced and, where appropriate, efficiently managed through cross-border administrative cooperation.

Developing the single market

The legislation in the 1985 White Paper represents not the end but the beginning of the process of the construction of the single market. The development of the single market is a dynamic process. It has already been noted how it quickly became apparent after the publication of the White Paper that certain key policy areas had been omitted from the single market programme. Such omissions are hardly surprising in view of the highly ambitious nature of the single market programme.

Further omissions may become apparent as assessments of the effectiveness of the single market are made. Technological development will also highlight the need to launch new initiatives to ensure that the integrity of the single market is maintained and that competition operates throughout the widest possible range of sectors.

The Strategic Programme identifies the following areas as important to develop in the future to ensure that the objectives of a market in Europe without frontiers will be reinforced and developed.

The remainder of this chapter discusses some of the major policy areas which were not included in the original Single Market Paper but have subsequently become important in the campaign to achieve single market objectives.

1 Relations with third countries

A major oversight of the 1985 White Paper was the absence of consideration of the impact of the single market on the exports of third countries to the European Union. Fears of the emergence of a 'Fortress Europe' were commonplace amongst the EU's trading partners in the late 1980s. The realization of such fears would have resulted in the loss of the benefits expected from the creation of the single market: competition would have increased among member states of the EU but the stimulus to perform better from third-country presence would have been removed. EU companies could also have found themselves excluded from important third country markets. In the event, the fears of Europe's trading partners were unfounded and products from third countries are free to circulate around the Union according to the same rules as domestically produced goods.

However, certain trade policy matters did need reassessment. Although the European Commission has responsibility for trade policy generally, member states have had autonomy in some areas. Some member states, for example, operated their own quotas against imports of cars produced in

19

Japan. National quantitative restrictions also occurred in other sectors and played a part in the Multi-Fibre Agreement and the Generalized System of Preferences. Such quotas served to refragment the market and were against the principles of the single market.

The question of reciprocity also rang alarm bells among Europe's trading partners. Early drafts of the Second Banking Directive contained a strict reciprocity article which would have required partner countries to extend exactly the same rights to European Union banks as their banks received in the European Union. In some cases, this would have resulted in European banks receiving more favourable treatment in third countries than the domestic banks of those countries. The principle of national treatment (i.e. that EU banks should receive the same treatment in the domestic markets of third countries as do the domestic banks themselves) has, however, been adopted as the appropriate approach to reciprocity.

The more direct relationship of the impact of competition policy on third countries is becoming increasingly topical. This is a result of the more dynamic agenda of the EU; the preparation of EFTA members and the countries of Central and Eastern Europe for EU membership; and the growing debate about the possible need to harmonize competition policy on a wider scale. Initially, this is most likely to occur among OECD members and perhaps later within the framework of the new World Trade Organisation. Chapter 7 considers the competition issues involved in relations with third countries in more detail.

Enlargement of the European Union, and the changes required by it, will constitute one of the key themes of European integration for the remainder of this century. Accordingly, two cases deal with the adjustments required in new and potential member states. Sweden, which became a member of the EU on 1 January 1995, took speedy action, as Case Study 4 shows, to bring its competition policy in line with that of the European Union. Accession to the EU provided the ideal opportunity to reform Swedish competition policy at a time when serious doubts had been raized about the ability of Sweden's large public sector and heavily regulated private sector to compete without reform. Hungary (Case Study 3), which will enter the EU five to ten years after Sweden, is nevertheless preparing for its eventual accession by ensuring that all the laws which are being introduced to oversee and police the transition from a command to a market economy are consistent with the laws of the Union. Competition policy, as the case demonstrates, is no exception to this trend.

2 Social policy

The single market programme implied radical changes in business practices but had very little to say about labour market regulations. Not long after the publication of the 1985 White Paper, Commission President Jacques Delors and others began to express concerns that the single market held out the prospect of very tangible benefits for business but that, without some corresponding benefits for Europe's workforce, support for and ultimately the success of the single market could be jeopardized. The Social Charter of Fundamental Social Rights, which was launched in 1988, was the Commission's answer to these anxieties and forms the basis for the Social Protocol of the Maastricht Treaty.

The Social Charter and the proposals which subsequently ensued from it were fully in line with the objectives of the single market. That is, differences in labour market regulation should not be allowed to act as a barrier to trade. In a Community with different regulations covering issues like safety, working hours, paid holidays, etc., countries with lower standards could gain a competitive advantage over companies from member states with higher standards. This could encourage firms from high standard, and therefore higher cost, countries to relocate in member states with lower standards – a practice known as 'social dumping'. This in turn would put pressure on. member states with higher standards to reduce their standards. This was regarded by many as a potentially undesirable by-product of the single market.

The debate has not been one-sided. The British government strongly resisted moves towards harmonization of labour market regulation; refused to sign the Social Charter and only signed the Maastricht Treaty after gaining an opt-out from the Social Protocol of the Treaty. The UK position stresses labour market flexibility and maintains that the imposition of the Social Charter and Protocol would impose heavy costs on British industry and significantly impair the competitiveness of British goods and services. The issues raized by this debate are explored more fully in Chapter 6 on social policy.

3 Environmental policy

Environmental policy was not included within the original single market programme but it has quickly become clear that environmental issues have a direct bearing on the single market and hence on competition. The Strategic Programme identifies the vetting of national environmental measures to ensure compatibility with the single market. Article 130t of the Maastricht Treaty allows member states to adopt more stringent measures to protect the environment than those adopted through the Council of Ministers provided such measures are compatible with the Treaty. In other words, stricter measures are allowed provided they do not act as new non-tariff barriers between member states, thereby restricting competition.

The emergence of environmental non-tariff barriers could easily happen.

A member state which introduced regulations requiring that all soft drinks sold in its territory had to be sold in containers made of glass, for example, or which banned the use of particular materials in packaging would effectively refragment the European market. Manufacturers using plastic or banned materials from outside such a member state would have to make special arrangements to sell their goods in the member state with the more stringent regulation. In other words, the company would be unable to adopt a single strategy for selling its product throughout the European Union, as the logic of the single market requires. Not only this, but enterprises in companies with higher environmental standards will face higher costs and therefore could be placed at a competitive disadvantage when seeking to place their products in other member states of the European Union. Companies which face a significantly higher additional burden from differential environmental standards may ultimately decide to relocate in parts of the Union with lower environmental costs or outside the Union altogether. The upshot of a policy to bring about higher environmental standards may not therefore be higher but lower standards as companies take action to avoid additional costs.

4   Trans-European networks

The single market initiative to date has concentrated on the removal of regulations and the enforcement of the legislative framework. It has become increasingly apparent that the benefits of a barrier-free Europe may be endangered by the absence of an appropriate physical infrastructure which will enable economic operators to exploit the full potential of the single market.

A successful single market will stimulate trade and increase the amount of traffic on roads, railways, inland waterways and on air routes. The European Union's transport system is becoming increasingly congested and, as a result of a national rather than a European focus on the development of transport systems, there are missing links and bottlenecks in the Union's transport networks. Problems also arise from the lack of interoperability between different modes of transport and between countries. Some of the issues raized by trans-European networks in the transport sector are touched upon in the rail case study.

The energy sector (see Case Study 6), like transport, plays an important supporting role to other industrial and service sectors. Competitiveness of industry depends on reliable, efficient and cheap supplies of energy. Not all member states are connected to the European Union's gas and electricity networks and grid-interconnections are inadequate for the potential trade in gas and electricity.

The telecommunications sector is undergoing rapid technological development. Europe's telecommunications industry is hampered by continuing fragmentation of markets and problems arising from inadequate interconnection and interoperability. Given the size of the annual market of telecommunication services in the European Union at ECU 84 billion and an equipment market of ECU 26 billion and the growing contribution of information and communications to successful and competitive businesses in all sectors, it is essential that the European Union overcomes its problems in this area.

In order to ensure that the benefits of the single market will not be lost, the European Union has built in the completion of trans-European networks (i.e. a genuine European infrastructure) into its planning for the future. Not only were networks included in the Maastricht Treaty (Articles 129b to 129d), but they have an important place in the Strategic Programme and figure prominently in the White Paper *Growth, Competitiveness and Employment*.

The attainment of trans-European networks will reinforce the single market goal of increasing competition within the European Union by facilitating trade and speeding up communication. The dismantling of bottlenecks and the extension of networks to all operators in the Community will bring more businesses into direct competition with each other. This applies not only to enhanced competition within the transport, energy and telecommunications sectors but also to all other sectors of economic activity. In the area of transport, the prospect of getting goods to the consumer more quickly and more cheaply will make it possible for producers in the Union's peripheral regions, for example, to compete with those located more centrally within the Union. In relation to the rest of the world, cheaper energy and more efficient communications and transport will increase the competitiveness of Europe's industry and help Europe's business community to fulfil one of the original objectives of the single market – an enhanced ability to compete with the United States and Japan.

The TENS initiative is in its early stages. The Commission has identified projects of common interest and is seeking to establish a partnership between itself, member states and the private sector to develop the networks. The problems of developing the network vary from sector to sector. The Growth White Paper estimates that investment expenditure of ECU 400 billion by 1999 is required in order to meet the initial TENS objectives. However, no additional funding will be available from the Community's budget. Therefore efforts are under way to find new forms of finance from the private sector. Funding will be a particular problem for the transport sector where the investment required is higher than in the other two sectors, projects have a long life and returns are low. The challenge for the energy sector is not so much financial but ensuring that the regulatory environment allows enterprises access to the gas and electricity grids. In other words, the completion of the internal energy market as outlined in the case study is crucial. A trans-European network in energy would be meaningless without this. Similar considerations apply to telecommunications.

Summary

The aim of boosting competition within the European Union is fundamental to the single market. The Commission's 23rd Competition Policy Report succinctly summarized the link between competition and the single market:

> increased competition was seen as the mechanism by which many gains of this programme [i.e. the single market programme] would be realized once the fiscal, administrative and other barriers were eliminated.

The strength of this relationship implied a renewed and vigorous competition policy to ensure that the benefits of the single market are not lost. In fact, it is accurate to describe the single market programme as an extension of traditional competition policy and therefore as part of competition policy itself.

It quickly became clear that in order for the objectives of the single market to be fulfilled, it was necessary to take measures in areas not included in the single market programme such as energy and environmental policy. This reflects the fact that the goal of the single market itself is not a static concept but an ongoing process which needs constant attention and modernization.

The close connection between competition policy and European Union goals was reconfirmed by the 1993 White Paper *Growth, Competitiveness and Employment*. This document stressed that the forces of competition would enhance Europe's competitiveness by introducing flexibility and eliminating rigidities in markets; by encouraging efficient allocation of resources and much-needed restructuring and by stimulating research and development, innovation and investment. The push, therefore, to achieve a single market, i.e. a market without barriers to competition, did not end on 31 December 1992 but continues into the 1990s and beyond.

Key Documents

Cecchini, P. (1988) *The European Challenge*, Wildwood House.
Commission of the European Communities (1985), *Completing the Internal Market*, Com (85) 310.
Commission of the European Communities (1993) *Making the most of the Internal Market; Strategic Programme*, Com (93) 632.

Commission of the European Communities (1993) *Growth, Competitiveness, Employment – the Challenges and Ways Forward into the 21st Century*, Com (93) 700.
Commission of the European Communities (1994) *The Community Internal Market – 1993 Report*, Com (94) 55.

Questions

1 Describe the main impact of the removal of non-tariff barriers on businesses within the European Union.
2 How will the introduction of trans-European networks increase competition within the European Union?
3 Identify areas in which action still needs to be taken to fulfil the objectives of the single market. Which do you think is most important and why?

25

2 The distortion of competitive forces: state aids

Ian Barnes and Pamela M Barnes

Despite the fact that state aids are an aspect of most countries' industrial policy, there is no consensus as to whether they are harmful or not. State aids can be broadly defined as a transfer of resources from the public sector to the commercial and industrial sector, for which there are no goods or services provided to the same value in return. Help can either be given directly by cash payments or via other help given by the public sector.

Very often state aids are targeted at specific industries (either in the public or private sector) which face difficulties, or which the state wishes to help. The subsidies change the cost structure of industry, and as a consequence resource allocation is altered. The market outcome should move in favour of the industry if the state aids is a success. State aids can therefore be used to:

1   Preserve the current structure of an economy.
2   Facilitate change to adapt to current market conditions.
3   Promote change in an industry in order to gain an overall advantage in the wider market place.

Whilst aid may be justified in a number of cases, the actions of a state helping its industry can cause problems elsewhere. If the state aids change the cost structures of firms, then others not receiving the help may be disadvantaged. With the completion of the single market, there is a danger that help given in one state may seriously damage the competitive position of firms in another. State aids may cause resources to be wasted, as the member states endeavour to outbid each other in an attempt to establish dominance in a particular industry, or to attract inward investment from outside the EU. In response to this problem, the EU has attempted to develop a strategy for containing the use of state aids, in those cases which distort the market.

All European states combine elements of the market economy with political intervention to assist the process of change. There is some evidence that intervention can retard development, and slow down much-needed change, for example in the steel industry and civil aviation. As a result of subsidies, there is less incentive to innovate and become efficient. Despite this, governments regard intervention as a sovereign right, and distrust attempts by the EU to restrict this. The only control over state subsidies that is likely to be fully acceptable is that which is imposed on other states.

One simplistic solution would be to ban the use of state aids to industry within the EU. This would leave the adaptation process to market forces. Free-market enthusiasts might well favour this view, but the reality is that, even after offering assistance to overcome pressing social problems, there is a need to take account of the political agendas of the member states.

Transferring the responsibility for industrial policy to the EU is a possible solution to the problem of unequal treatment towards industry in the EU. However, the EU has only limited resources to conduct an independent industrial policy. It is therefore important that member states' activities are not contradictory. That is, there should be a sharing of common goals, given the degree to which industry depends upon the single market. There are many examples of useful intervention by the member states, such as the investment in modern transport systems. This has become a priority for the EU, given the wish to see the development of trans-European networks, which involve the linking of national transport networks to create an integrated European network.

A new emphasis on policy emerged in the mid-1990s. The need to address the issue of international competitiveness became even more apparent. This now overlays the reaction of the EU to the completion of the single market. It means that the EU needs to think of ways of going beyond overcoming the negative effects of restructuring its industries, and now must look for ways in which it can compete globally. As yet, this aspect of policy needs to be further developed.

The purpose of this chapter is to analyse the way that the EU can deal with the problem of state aids to industry, in order to meet the challenges of the single market and global competition. In particular it seeks to analyse three issues:

1   The reasons why the member states subsidize their industry.
2   How state aids cause conflict within the EU.
3   The EU's contribution towards the development of a more coherent state aids policy at European level.

The political economy of state aids

The member states of the EU have a surprising number of mechanisms to influence the activities of their businesses. Many of these fall under the heading of state aids and include:

1   Influencing the distribution of resources between industry, for example by the manipulation of energy prices.
2   Manipulating the location of industry, by the use of regional assistance.
3   Giving direct cash grants to industry.
4   Using public ownership to maintain industry which might not be viable in the market economy.
5   Offering tax concessions or adjusting the taxation system to assist particular industries.
6   Making soft loans available at preferential rates of interest.
7   Direct investment by the government.
8   Offering the use of land or facilities at preferential rates.
9   Buying of shares in companies.
10 Not expecting a return on public investments in what would normally be a market-oriented exercise.

Economic theory has normally been hostile to state subsidies of all kinds in closed economies operating under perfect competition. However, there may be cases where state aids are justified, where the market fails to give the optimum result. The justification for state aids is that:

1   There are some goods where there is a problem of 'free riding'. In these cases, the state needs to provide the goods or services if they are considered desirable. 'Free riding' occurs where there is an incentive for people to wait for others to pay for goods and services, or to consume the goods themselves free of charge. Perhaps the best commercial example of this would be the case of information, where there is a reluctance to pay for it, where it is widely available free of charge.
2   Some products generate significant externalities (overspill effects). A number of products generate either good or bad side effects. In some cases the market either overproduces or underproduces these products. The result is a gap between the market-based outcome, and what is desirable for society. Examples of underproduction are to be found in the area of education and training, where there are frequent problems of employers 'free riding', in the hope that others will train their labour force. Examples of bad externalities are most evident in areas of environmental concern, where the state may feel the need to support industry in its efforts to reduce pollution.
3   The size and risk involved in major projects may be too great for the private sector of an economy to easily undertake.
4   There is a need to promote competition. Some markets are not contestable, because the cost of entering them is too high. An example of this was the market for large passenger aircraft. The Airbus consortium

involved collaboration between companies across national borders, and was supported by direct state aids. There was also indirect help, because the French and German national airlines were expected to purchase the aircraft, so offering an assured market. It led to the creation of a major competitor to the dominant American company Boeing.

5 There are cases where there is a need to help an industry, either to obtain the required technology, or to gain sufficient size to attain economies of scale. This may be particularly the case where there are high fixed costs involved.
6 There is a need to create or maintain employment.
7 They will alleviate balance of payments problems by encouraging exports or reducing imports.

The case against state aids is that they lead to an inefficient allocation of resources. The history of many member states has shown that attempts at industrial intervention can result in expensive failures. Even where an outright disaster is avoided, the cost of giving the aid can exceed the benefits gained. This can happen because of misallocation of resources.

The idea that resources might be misallocated depends on finding an answer to what is the ideal allocation of resources. For many economists, it is the combination of resources which maximizes output. If a subsidy reduces the cost of capital, this may cause more capital to be employed and less labour. If this leads to less production than previously, this would reduce allocative efficiency. On the other hand if the cost of skilled labour is reduced by state provision of training programmes, this might lead to an excessive amount of labour being employed. State aids may also have an impact on technical efficiency, although if a firm is operating at its most efficient with the best technology, it is unlikely that state intervention will have an impact on this. Resource allocation arguments concerning state aids tend to be inconclusive. This is because they do not take account of social costs and benefit to society of the production.

Finally, there may be a case against state aids, based upon 'x-inefficiency' [1]. In a practical sense this amounts to what most people would regard as inefficiency, and includes problems such as lazy managers. It is concerned with the internal process of the firm, rather than the microeconomics of resource allocation. X-inefficiency is far more likely to be tolerated within organizations which are cushioned from the full effect of market forces.

If the above arguments are inconclusive, at a practical level, there are major problems associated with the impact of national state aids on an open economy. As the single market becomes a reality, so state aids spill over from one state to another. The problem of state aids in the wider context of the EU is that they do not act in isolation. The further that an economy moves away from autarky towards openness, the greater the likely overspill effect of industrial support. For many economists the ideal situation is one where there is free trade, which would imply that there would be no subsidies. Few subsides operate in isolation: if prices fall in one country, they may impact on industry in another.

Once one state starts to subsidize its industry to a significant degree, other countries will try and counteract this by offering aid to their industries. On occasions this has led to an almost indecent auction to attract the limited amount of footloose international investment available. On other occasions, the level of state aids to assist an ailing industry in one state has led wastefully to similar measures being adopted elsewhere in the EU.

The politics of state aids

The reasons for states giving aid to industry cannot always be explained solely by the use of economic rationality. There are a number of ways of analysing the political rationality for giving state aids. The giving of state aids may be seen as part of a political calculation, designed to win the support of a region or a particular class of voters. It may be an aspect of coalition building, where the support of a particular faction within parliament has to be won, in order to carry through a package of measures.

Support for state aids may come from elites within the dominant political party, or because of the activities of interest groups. Some groups are clearly more successful than others, for example farmers. Generally, producer groups tend to dominate at the expense of the consumers. There is a danger that elected politicians can become dependent upon interest groups for funding, publicity and for information. Politicians may not have adequate information on which to base their decisions, and therefore become further reliant on interest groups, who push for further state spending

Moreover once aid is given to an industry, it is difficult to remove, for the following reasons:

1   Support has tended to come as a result of a crisis facing the sector, or because of the need to maintain employment. Once the crisis has passed, support is difficult to remove.
2   Any removal of support reduces the profitability of the sector, and makes valuable investment redundant, because the returns on investment fall.
3   It is often difficult to reallocate resources to other uses, particularly where an area is highly dependent on an industry.

4   The fact that the state has assumed responsibility for an industry means that it is a burden that has to be shared by all of society. The budgetary cost will be widely distributed and not well understood by the general population.

The role of an EU-wide policy

In a situation where there are competing national objectives with regard to state aids, there is a role for an organization like the EU to ensure that state aids are organized on an orderly basis. An EU policy should:

1   Eliminate many of the conflicting rival national policies.
2   Reduce the unfairness of national policies, where the stronger states gain at the expense of weaker states, on competition based upon subsidies.
3   Create a European-wide strategy for the use of state aids, based upon improving international competitiveness.

The intervention by the EU in state aids policy is not universally welcome. As the EU has gained powers, this has reduced the role of national parliaments in controlling economic affairs. This has caused concerns to many who might actually see technical merits in proposals to limit state aids. These include:

1   A lack of democratic control at the EU level.
2   Integration is being taken further than is desirable.
3   A loss of national control over policy related to industry.

However, it might reasonably be noted that state aids policy in many member states often lacks democratic accountability. This is because of the tendency of governments to be highly secretive about these activities.

It is difficult to see the EU, in the short term, being able to replace the role of the member states, because it lacks the resources and a mandate to intervene at the micro level. Detailed involvement may also not be desirable for technical reasons, including the fact that at the EU level:

1   The detailed information which is required to conduct policy may not be available.
2   There may be too many parties involved.
3   Policy cannot be constructed to suit the local need.

Under these circumstances, the EU's role is restricted to trying to set an overall framework for industry to operate within. This may involve either dealing with industries facing a European-wide crisis, or encouraging industries with the potential to expand.

The Treaties and state aids

Within the EU there are a variety of administrative structures, and many of these have the ability to assist industry. The definition of what constitutes the state is a wide one, given these differing administrative arrangements. This means that in Germany, financial assistance given to industry by the Länder, (Germany's regional governments) would be considered to be state aids, as is help given by regional authorities in other countries.

The EU has a unique competency with regard to the control and monitoring of state aids. Within countries, it is not normal to review the process of giving state aids. Internationally, no group of countries is so committed to the task of evaluating the process as is the EU.

The granting of state aids can give a substantial competitive advantage to domestic producers, and as a consequence many are regarded as being incompatible with the Common Market. Under Article 92(1) of the EC Treaty, state aids *are not* permitted if they affect the EU in any way. It states that:

> Save as otherwise provided in this Treaty, any aid granted by a Member State or through State resources in any form whatsoever which distorts or threatens to distort competition by favouring certain undertakings or the production of certain goods shall, so far as it affects trade between Member States, be incompatible with the common market.

Many firms are involved in activities which are largely concerned with national markets. Governments may well wish to assist with their development on the basis of social goals such as maintaining employment. However, the aid may have an impact on producers in other EU states attempting to enter the market. The Court of Justice has ruled that Article 92(1) applies if the firm is in competition for the home market with producers from other Member States[2].

The Treaty then declares that the following state aids *are* compatible with the common market:

(a) Aid having a social character granted to consumers, as long as it does not discriminate as to the origin of the product. An example might be free milk given to schoolchildren.

(b) Aid given to make good the damage caused by natural disasters or exceptional circumstances.

(c) Aid granted to certain areas of the Federal Republic of Germany affected by the division of Germany, so far as that aid is required to compensate for the economic disadvantage caused by that division.

This last provision will undoubtedly be the subject of review in the future, if there is reasonable progress in restoring the economy of Eastern Germany. In the 1990s, Article 92(2 C) was used to deal with problems post-unification. In 1994, the Commission approved aid, given by the German state of Bavaria, to support the maintenance of a wagon-carrying trailer connection between Tettau and the railway station in Steinbach am Wald (the rail connection had been disrupted in 1952, when the infrastructure network of Germany was divided). Transitional payments of DM 363,000 per year were allowed until the end of 1995. These were then to be replaced by alternative, self-financing arrangements[3].

Article 92(3) states that certain aid given by the member states *may be* compatible if they:

(a) Promote economic development in areas of abnormally low living standards or serious underemployment. (There is no specific heading for regional policy.)
(b) Promote projects of common European interest, or remedy a serious disturbance in the economy of a member state.
(c) Help industry facing a crisis, although the aid should not be regarded as permanent.
(d) Promote cultural and heritage conservation as long as it does not affect trading conditions. (Added by the Treaty on European Union.)

Other categories of aid could be granted, subject to the council acting by qualified majority, upon a proposal from the Commission.

The Commission, working in cooperation with the member states, is given the task, under Article 93, of reviewing all systems of aid. Member states should inform the Commission of any aids being given to industry, and these aids must conform to the requirements of the Treaty. If they do not conform, the Commission can issue a Decision requiring the member states to either amend or abolish the scheme. In theory, the aids should be transparent, that is their effects on industry should be easily understood. In practice, many of the effects of policy are difficult to understand, and states seek to muddy the waters in order to win an advantage.

The problem of state aids being used to gain markets outside the EU is covered by Article 112. This aims to prevent an escalation in the use of subsidies in the competition between the member states for third markets. Article 112(1) calls for Member States to:

> ... harmonize the systems whereby they grant aid for exports to third countries
> to the extent necessary to ensure that competition between undertakings of the
> Community is not distorted.

This provision is, however, very difficult to implement, given the variety of ways that aid of this kind can be given. So, for example, the process of export guarantees is not harmonized to any significant extent, neither is the link between indirect help given by foreign aid budgets.

The EC Treaty gives special mention to state aids given to particular sectors of the economy. They are as follows.

Agriculture

Agriculture is a special case, in that it is in the most highly protected and regulated of the EU industries. As such, it is hardly surprising that it is not subject to normal market forces. Article 42 of the EC Treaty states that the rules for competition in production and trade in agricultural products shall only apply to the extent that is determined by the Council of Ministers.

Help is given in a number of forms by the member states, including the use of tax concessions and a range of grants. It is usual to have a ministry which is dedicated to supporting the industry, and which offers a range of free services to farmers. The completion of the single market should have led to a reduction of assistance given to the industry, as this removed many of the barriers to free movement of agricultural products. However, the problems associated with currency instability have maintained the level of involvement by the member states in the agricultural sector.

Transport

The efficient operation of transport services is an essential element of all the economies of the EU. In some areas, subsidies are of vital importance, for example in the maintenance of the railway system. Commercial criteria cannot be fully applied, because of the need to offer an alternative to road transport. Article 77 of the EC Treaty covers transport; and this states that:

> Aids shall be compatible with this Treaty if they meet the needs of coordination
> of transport or they represent reimbursement for the discharge of certain
> obligations inherent in the concept of a public service.

Coal and steel

Special powers are available to the EU under the European Coal and Steel Community Treaty. These refer to the particular industrial sector and call for the prohibition of:

subsidies or aids granted by States, or special charges imposed by States, in any form whatsoever;

This is not as restrictive as it appears in the sense that it refers to direct subsidies. The history of this sector is full of examples of aid being given for restructuring the industry.

Public enterprises

The relationship between the governments of the member states and public enterprises is a particular problem. Article 90, makes it clear that public enterprises are subject to competition rules; however, this is one of the most difficult areas of state aids to police. In many of the member states, public enterprises have received very significant levels of support, often by means of indirect assistance. This can cause severe problems for that part of the industry which is not in state hands, either within the national market, or elsewhere within the EU. This has been a particular problem of the steel industry and civil aviation.

In order to promote clarity in the financial relations between the member states and their publicly owned industry, the EU adopted a directive 'on the transparency of financial relations between member states and public undertakings.'[4].

Monitoring state aids

Around 1 000 cases of state aids per year are dealt with by the European Commission. Over half relate to transport, agriculture, fisheries and coal mining, while the rest are concerned with industry and the service sector. Typically only about one per cent of decisions related to industry is negative, although a number of cases are investigated. Table 2.1 gives a fuller picture of the trend.

Table 2.1 *Notified state aid (excluding aid to agriculture, fisheries and transport)*

Type of decision made (%)	1991	1992	1993	1994*
No objection	81%	87%	88%	88%
Procedure initiated	11%	5%	7%	8%
Positive final decision	5%	6%	4%	3%
Negative final decision	2%	1%	1%	1%
Total number of decisions	470	537	457	475

* Estimated figures based upon 356 cases to September 1994

Source: Commission: reported in *Europe Documents* No 1909, 16 November 1994

The Commission is only concerned with those cases where public funds are involved, which have been of benefit to the business. If normal market conditions apply, then aids can go ahead. The Commission is generally seeking to ensure that the rules set out in the Treaties are applied. Where there is ambiguity, as in the case of soft loans, then rules have been clarified by the Court of Justice. In this case the Court has applied the 'commercial investors principle'. According to this criterion, loans are normally meant to be given by the state on the same terms as would be found in the capital markets. If more favourable terms are on offer, this is a state aid. This is a picture which becomes very cloudy, however, when there is substantial state ownership of the banking sector, for example in France.

A clear picture of the extent of state aids is not available on an up-to-date basis. The reasons for this are related to poor reporting procedures, and a reluctance of the Member States to declare all their interventions. Many countries still break or bend the rules either by not informing the Commission, or by giving the aid first and asking for permission afterwards (although the Commission can demand that illegal payments are refunded). This is despite the fact that Article 93(3) makes it clear that:

> The Commission shall be informed, in sufficient time to enable it to submit its comments, of any plans to grant or alter aid.

At any time, a number of cases will be subject to detailed investigation by the Commission's investigators into state aids. The number of staff in this area is, however, nowhere near adequate for the task which it faces.

The EU has produced surveys of state aids, and makes comment on its success in monitoring them in its reports on Competition Policy. In the period 1988 to 1990, an average of ECU 89 billion per year was given, with about 40 per cent of this going to manufacturing. Some countries have an active state aids policy, as is illustrated in Table 2.2. This shows that Italy has given the greatest amount of aid in monetary terms, both in respect to the total amount of aid offered, and the aid per employee. However, it was Greece which gave the largest amount of aid as a percentage of value added. In contrast to this, the UK was generally reluctant to commit large amounts of resources to assist industry.

State aids is a sensitive area of activity for the EU. All the member states find it easier to see the purpose behind the giving of aid within their own country. There is generally considerable political support for many of the national decisions. The EU has therefore to move carefully. There is no specific maximum amount of aid that states are allowed to give; indeed, the member states have very different philosophies with regard to state involve-

Table 2.2 *State aids to manufacturing industry 1988–90*

	As a percentage of value added	ECU per person employed	Million ECU
Italy	6.0	2175	11,027
Ireland	4.9	1734	368
Belgium	4.1	1655	1211
Greece	14.6	1502	1072
France	3.5	1380	6106
Netherlands	3.1	1327	1225
Luxembourg	2.6	1270	48
Germany	2.5	984	7865
Spain	3.6	936	2499
Portugal	5.3	758	616
Denmark	2.1	634	333
UK	2.0	582	3133
EURO 12	3.5	1203	35,503

Source: Commission (1993) *Third Survey on State Aid*, quoted in Commission of EC (1993) *XXIInd Report on Competition Policy 1992*, p. 214

ment in their economies. The member states are free to decide on the level of aid they give, within EU rules. The Commission monitors the aid being given. In 1993, Karel Van Miert, the Commissioner in charge of Competition, suggested that the approval process involves trying to determine an overall common interest. He stated that:

> . . . if the Commission wants to approve the granting of aid, it must ultimately be able to argue plausibly to the eleven other Member States that the aid awarded in the twelfth Member State is in the true interest of all, even if competition in the common market is affected. Ultimately, therefore, and this is much too rarely recognized, the Commission plays the role of the referee, a role which is quite important for the completion of the single market[5].

The Commission seeks to avoid permitting aid which gives particular firms a competitive advantage. Community intervention should therefore only occur where state aids is likely to be a distortion of trade flows between the member states. The Commission does not require monitoring of small amounts of aid. The size limit was set in 1993 at ECU 50,000 per item of aid, with an overall limit of ECU 100,000 over a three-year period.

State aid is considered acceptable if:

- The desired changes could not happen without assistance.
- The amount of assistance is finite and in proportion to the task it is meant to assist with.
- It is meant for restructuring, and is not to meet the running costs of the business.
- It will be of benefit to the EU as a whole.
- It fits coherently with the policies of the EU. Aid given to businesses in an industry where there is already overcapacity should be carefully monitored.

In addition to these criteria, as a result of the problem of repeated claims for aid from some of the airlines such as Air France, the EU now insists that aid cannot be repeated (see Case Study 1). Aid is given for the last time on the basis that it must be made to work, and move the airlines concerned towards long-term viability. In theory there should be no more payments permitted, and if a further crisis hits the business, it should be allowed to fail.

State aids and the national political process

The giving of state aids to industry tends to be a highly political issue. The existence of EU rules is generally taken into account when the Member State makes a decision to grant aid; however, once a political commitment to a project has been made, interference from the EU is generally resented. There are, however, advantages to the member states from the EU's role in monitoring the process. The EU:

- Helps to reduce the competitive element in state aids, where countries are encouraged to bid against one another for mobile investment by transnational enterprises.
- Protects the Member States from lobbyists who seek to gain ever higher levels of subsidy.

There are, however, many spectacular examples of where the Commission has had to give in to the political realities of the situation. Projects have gone ahead which did not meet with a strict application of the rules. In such circumstances the regional needs of the area receiving the aid, or the social consequences of very high unemployment, are taken into account. The Commission decision to approve £61 million of state aids in 1994 to be granted to Hualon Corporation is an example of this. This was to build a £157 million synthetic fibres plant in Northern Ireland. The plant was to supply the materials to low-cost clothing producers in Europe. As the synthetic fibres industry in Europe was already suffering from considerable excess capacity, the addition of 23,500 tonnes of potential production did not appear to make sense. There was no economic reason to offer aid to a mature industry, especially as the increased production in Northern Ireland was unlikely to be a substitute for synthetic fibres from outside the EU. Any EU-approved policy initiative in this area should normally have been directed towards reducing excess capacity.

The state aids was justified on the grounds that the factory would employ 1800 people, with an extra 500 associated jobs. This was a politically important project, as it was in an area of extremely high levels of unemployment, where wages were 20 per cent below those of the UK average. (Wages were not as low as many of the Asian producers, for example in Taiwan, Malaysia and Vietnam, they were 57%, 12% and 4% of UK rates.) The decision to permit the aid was granted on the basis that the manufacturing process in Northern Ireland was labour intensive, and therefore did not compete with the output of what was a high technology industry in the rest of Europe[6]. Underlying this was of course a view that industrial investment was an essential element in any peace process in Northern Ireland.

The EU, despite the all-too-frequent examples of misapplying aid, has managed to gain agreement to cut the area where regional aid is permitted throughout the EU. The privatization of certain industries has resulted in a reduced potential for soft loans being available to nationalized industries.

State aids and the international economy

In contrast to the wish of the EU to reduce Member State involvement in industry which distorts the single market, there is less concern about the subsidy of European champions to meet the challenge of global competition. Global competition is less well regulated than that within the EU, although the World Trade Organization may eventually change this. If any one state appears to be gaining an advantage because of subsidy to its domestic industry, the likelihood is that the source of pressure for reform will be bilateral rather than multilateral. Trade disputes and the threat of retaliation are frequently the outcome, with anti-dumping duties or other sanctions being taken against those products suspected of benefiting from unreasonable state assistance.

The dispute between the USA and EU concerning the manufacture of large passenger aircraft is a significant example. The Airbus consortium was created with the assistance of the German, French, British and Spanish governments. By combining the national efforts of these states, a viable alternative competitor was created to US Boeing. Without this aid it is unlikely that a viable manufacturer of commercial airlines would have existed within the EU. The USA and EU agreed in May 1992 to limit the extent of help that was to be given in the future[7]. This was to be reviewed as part of the Uruguay GATT Round, but no agreement was reached on a permanent solution. Issues of further conflict included the need to restrict the extent of indirect support, control on subsidies given to aero engines and parts, and the exempting of aid being given to current projects[8].

The control of state aids: the case of shipbuilding

The shipbuilding industry is a useful example of how collective action on the part of the EU has helped to reduce excessive competition between the Member States via the use of state aids. Shipbuilding is a typical industry in decline. In the early stages of contraction there was a tendency for state aids to cancel each other out. Generally the EU showed a degree of tolerance, recognising that this was an industry which required time to adjust from a social point of view. Table 2.3 shows the situation in the 1980s.

Table 2.3 *State aid to shipbuilding as a percentage of gross value added*

	1986–88	1981–86
France	68.0	56.6
Italy	28.2	45.9
UK	25.0	21.6
Spain	17.5	–
Germany	16.6	12.3
Belgium	12.3	27.7
Denmark	7.8	33.8
Netherlands	3.8	10.7
Luxembourg	0	0
Ireland	0	0
Greece	0	0
Portugal	n/a	n/a

Source: Commission (1990) *Second Survey on State Aid*, p. 21

Despite the subsidies offered by the Member States, the EU was not able to halt the decline of the industry. In 1975 208,833 people were employed in the industry. By 1980, this had dropped to 124,229 people and had fallen further to 77,152 in 1992[9]. The competition in subsidies could not stop the closures of yards, and Europe losing ground to non-EU competitors. Very fierce international competition saw the EU share of the world market drop from 25 per cent in 1988 to 20 per cent in 1990. By 1992 this share had dropped to 18 per cent. The problem for the EU was that their yards were 20 per cent more expensive than those in the Far East[10].

The high levels of fixed capital required for a modern shipyard mean that if they close they cannot easily be reopened. However, if the subsidies continue, there is no incentive to modernize and this will hold back structural change. If Europe wishes to make the industry viable perhaps the policy might be widened, and a maritime policy be created which links the building of vessels with a policy of European carriers having to use domestically built vessels. It would only work if there was also a sharing of cargoes destined for EU ports, and this suggestion would carry a risk of retaliation from other maritime nations[11].

The only long-term schemes that the EU has envisaged for shipbuilding are related to reduced capacity. The EU has also attempted to reduce the level of aid, which stood at over 25 per cent of contract value in the 1980s, to 9 per cent in the early 1990s, and eventually to 6 per cent. Perhaps the best hope for the industry is to get the costs of shipbuilding down, by high levels of investment. In this way the EU can meet its obligations to reduce subsidies in preparation for the introduction of an agreement on subsidies negotiated between all the major industrial countries via the OECD. This will come into force in January 1996, and will end direct subsidies to the industry. It will, however, permit the granting of aid of up to 100 per cent of shipyards' research costs. This is not a significant concession, because shipyards only spend 1 to 2 per cent of their turnover on research. It will not compensate for the loss of direct subsidies[12]. The competitive nature of the shipping industry means that there is little sentiment about purchasing. If national yards are not competitive, they will lose orders. The future of EU shipyards does not look good, and this is an industry that may decline further. However, there is a consolation, in that vast amounts of state aids will not be wasted slowing down the process.

Conclusions

The use of state subsidies to assist with the process of industrial development has been a important feature of the European industrial landscape, particularly since the end of the second world war. There has been a realization that this may not always be an appropriate strategy in an increasingly open European economy, enjoying the competitive benefits of the single market. Certainly, if the use of state aids is directed solely at maintaining market share at the expense of other rivals within the EU, there can be little justification for it.

Despite many brave pronouncements about the need to be competitive, in some sectors attempts to create a truly European-wide policy have failed. An example of this was the attempt to restructure the EU steel industry in 1993–94, which failed due to the unwillingness of the member states to reduce excess capacity. However, there have been successes. A combination of tougher action at the EU level, combined with budgetary constraints within the Member States, should lead to state aids being better employed. What is missing from the policy agenda is how the EU can realistically redirect the enthusiasm to assist industry to the task of creating global competitiveness.

Further Reading

Bangemann, M. (1992) *Meeting the Global Challenge*, Kogan Page.
Barnes, I. (1994) The single market after 1992. In I. Barnes and L. Davison (eds), *European Business: Text and Cases*, Butterworth-Heinemann.
Commission of the EC (1993) *Growth, Competitiveness, Employment – the Challenges and Way Forward into the 21st Century* Com (93) 700 final.
Cowling, K. (1990) In H. Tomann (ed.), *Industrial Policy After 1992*, Anglo German Foundation.
Jacquemin, A. (1993) In D. Wright (ed.), *The European Challenges Post– 1992: Shaping Factors, Shaping Actors*, Edward Elgar.

References

1 Liebenstein, H. (1966) Allocative efficiency and 'x'-efficiency *American Economic Review*, Vol. 56, pp. 392–415.
2 *European Economy* (1991) Fair competition in the internal market: Community state aid policy, No. 48, September, p. 51.
3 *Europe*, 16/17 May 1994, p. 13.
4 Directive 80/723/EEC amended by 85/413/EEC.
5 Karel Van Miert (1993) in a speech to economists in Bonn, quoted from *Europe*, Document, 9 July 1993.
6 *Financial Times*, 31 May 1994, p. 8.
7 For further information see Barnes, I., Chadburn, D. and Jones, R. (1994) European collaboration in aircraft manufacture. In I. Barnes and L. Davison (eds), *European Business: Text and Cases*, Butterworth-Heinemann.
8 *Financial Times*, 19 May 1994, p. 5.
9 Commission of the EU (1994) *Panorama of EU Industry 1994*.
10 *European*, 17 June 1993, p. 40.
11 Bangemann, M. (1992) *Meeting the Global Challenge*, Kogan Page. p. 98.
12 *Financial Times*, 18 November 1994, p. 6.

Questions

1 Under what circumstances can state aids be considered to be beneficial?
2 Why did moves to complete the single European market highlight the state aids problem within the EU?
3 What are the crucial elements of a successful EU-wide state aids policy?
4 Why is it difficult to assess the extent of state aids being offered by the Member States of the EU?

3 Articles 85 and 86: control of restrictive practicesand abuses of dominant positions

Edmund Fitzpatrick

Introduction

The maintenance of effective competition is one of the fundamental activities of the Community. The original Treaty of Rome charged the Community with the creation of a system to ensure that competition in the common market is not distorted. This responsibility has grown in significance with expanded Community membership and the movement towards greater integration which eventually led to the single european market. Even so, as member states have committed themselves in treaty obligations and Council agreements to the removal of trade barriers and the pursuit, through collective action, of such goals as growth and increased employment, there nevertheless remain strong temptations for them to frustrate allocative efficiency by protecting national industries through subsidies and other forms of state aid. Even where member states have been prepared to abandon the practice of subsidising certain industries, there is still consider-able potential for firms in the private sector to erect barriers to trade by adopting various forms of anti-competitive behaviour. This chapter will consider how Community law and policy seeks to deter organizations – both in the private and public sectors – from distorting competition in the common market by entering into cartel and other arrangements based on anti-competitive agreements (proscribed by Article 85 of the EC Treaty) or by abusing market dominance (proscribed by Article 86 of the EC Treaty). Article 90 applies the Treaty's competition rules to public undertakings.

The scope of Article 85

Article 85 targets the kind of market behaviour whereby firms which ought to be competing in a particular market choose instead to collaborate in some way. Article 85(1) sets out the kinds of behaviour which are covered by its provisions:

The following shall be prohibited as incompatible with the common market: all agreements between undertakings, decisions between associations of undertakings and concerted practices which may affect trade between member states and which have as their object or effect the prevention, restriction or distortion of competition within the common market . . .

The manner in which Article 85 has been interpreted and applied by the Court of Justice (ECJ) and the Court of First Instance (CFI) will be discussed in more detail below. The effect of the Article is that any arrangement which is covered by its provisions is automatically void and the infringing parties may become liable to a fine of up to ten per cent of their previous year's turnover. The level of fines is aimed at deterring cartel arrangements and other forms of anti-competitive agreements which may involve such things as price fixing, market sharing, setting limits on production or discriminating against trading partners who are not party to the agreement. In applying Article 85, the ECJ is frequently called upon to make an economic assessment of the parties' conduct.

Under Article 85(3), the Commission may exempt firms from the application of the article, but such exemptions are given on strictly limited grounds.

The scope of Article 86

Article 86 provides

Any abuse by one or more undertakings of a dominant position within the common market or in a substantial part of it shall be prohibited as incompatible with the common market in so far as it may affect trade between Member States.

The article does not prohibit the acquisition of market power; rather it proscribes the abuse of their market positions by dominant firms. In so doing, the Article lists examples of the kinds of behaviour which may constitute an abuse. These are explained below. A breach of Article 86 makes the wrongdoer liable to the same level of fine as for breach of Article 85. Unlike Article 85, there is no possibility of exemption under Article 86.

Current policy issues affecting the regulation of restrictive practices and abuses of dominant positions

Before considering the manner in which Articles 85 and 86 have been legally interpreted and applied it is appropriate to consider some of the current policy issues affecting the application of the articles.

45

Generalized application of Articles 85 and 86

In its White Paper *Growth, Competitiveness, Employment – the Challenges and Ways Forward into the 21st Century*[1], the Commission argues for the need for a fundamental restructuring of the European economy if the goals of growth and increased employment are to be achieved. In attaining these goals, there has to be a resolute application of competition rules if pre-existing market rigidities are to be eliminated. The fact that firms are now more willing than ever to abandon anti-competitive practices when challenged by the Commission indicates a change in business culture brought about by the operation of Articles 85 and 86 for more than thirty years. However, there are many sectors which, in the past, have been excluded by the Commission from the operation of the Articles. Financial services, telecommunications, transport and energy are all sectors which have traditionally been given privileged treatment. But there is little point in insisting on productive efficiency in certain sectors while allowing access to others – particularly infrastructure – to be hampered by practices which, strictly speaking, are incompatible with Community law. The Commission is now moving towards a generalized application of Articles 85 and 86 in all sectors of economic activity. For example, in 1992 the Commission took enforcement action for the first time against sea transport operators. In **French/West African Shipowners' Committees** decision[2], the Commission fined the members of a shipping cartel ECU 15m for abuse of market dominance and operating a restrictive agreement. Similar actions have been taken in the railway, airline and telecommunications industries.

Looking to the future, it is likely that enlargement poses one of the greatest threats to the generalized application of Articles 85 and 86. At present, many of the poorer member states have accepted the need for increased competitiveness in return for regional and structural support. The pressures that a future membership of twenty or more States will put on these budgets, as well as the need for significant reform of the Common Agricultural Policy, may mean that the trade-off that the Union can offer in return for accepting the discipline of competition will be substantially reduced. Without the economic fillip of spending from Brussels, it may be that the temptation, particularly for new businesses in the former COMECON states, to set up market barriers may be too strong to resist.

Increased alignment of national and Community law

In its 23rd Competition Report, the Commission welcomes the application of Articles 85 and 86 as a manifestation of subsidiarity. The Commission also notes the tendency of Member States, on their own initiative, to redraft their national rules to make them more consistent with Community law. For example, in 1993 Belgium enacted new national legislation along the lines of Articles 85 and 86. Moreover, intending Member States are adopting the Community model for their competition regulation (See Case Studies on Sweden and Hungary). However, realignment is not universal. In the UK, draft legislation, which was prepared in 1989, to reform the restrictive Trades Practices Act 1976 along the lines of Article 85 has not been presented to Parliament. Nor has the UK government plans to significantly amend its monopolies legislation – which dates from the time of the UK's accession and relies heavily on formal definitions of monopolies and a public interest test – to make it consistent with Article 86 (considered in more detail in Chapter 5).

Another aspect of alignment is the fact that Articles 85 and 86 are 'directly effective', meaning that they can be the subject of adjudication in national courts when relied upon by citizens seeking to enforce their rights under Community law. Being able to bring proceedings based on European competition law in national courts has considerable advantages both for litigants and for the Commission. As far as the parties are concerned, their grievances are dealt with locally with concomitant savings in costs. As far as the Commission is concerned, it is able to restrict its workload to cases of major importance. Indeed, in **AUTOMEC v Commission (No 2)** [1992] 5 CMLR 431, the CFI ruled that the Commission is entitled to prioritize its enforcement activities and can refuse to make a final decision in an area where national courts are also competent to make decisions.

Tolerance of certain forms of anti-competitive behaviour

Here, there are at least two situations where the Commission may be prepared to show a degree of tolerance of market cooperation. First, where parties to an agreement operate in a worldwide market and are, therefore, faced with global competition then their collaboration may be exempted from the strict application of competition rules where their activities promote global competitiveness of European industry. The **Philips/Thompson/Sagem** (see Chapter 4) cooperative joint venture decision illustrates this approach. Secondly, where competitive pressure can be increased on a market, the Commission will welcome collaboration in research and development and product innovation. In recognition of the potential benefits of certain kinds of collaboration, the Commission introduced in 1993 an expedited procedure for dealing with joint ventures seeking exemption under Article 85(3).

The interpretation of Article 85

In order for Article 85 to apply to the conduct of firms, their activities must fall within the scope of the wording of the Article. For example, it is inevitable that the operation of a cartel will involve an agreement or some other form of collaborative arrangement. Where however, the impact of such an agreement is limited to the markets in one member state so that the arrangement does not have the potential to affect trade between member states, then Article 85 will not apply and any anti-competitive practice on the part of the cartel will not be within the jurisdiction of the Community institutions (although, of course, the competition rules of the individual member states may still apply). It is inevitable, therefore, that the development and application of the Article has revolved around the interpretation of the words and phrases used in the Article itself. The following examines how certain parts of the Article have been interpreted by the Commission and the ECJ.

Agreements between undertakings, decisions by associations of undertakings and concerted practices

Article 85 prohibits consensual arrangements between undertakings. The prohibited arrangement may take the form of a formal contactual agreement between the participating firms. It is more likely, however, that firms who enter into anti-competitive agreements will prefer to operate on an informal, often covert, basis. For this reason, the Article covers a range of possible conduct which can constitute market collusion.

Examples of how the Commission and the ECJ have dealt with informal arrangements can be seen in the **Quinine Cartel** decision[3] and the **BMW** decision[4]. In the former, the Commission dealt with the situation where a group of companies who produced quinine had become concerned that the world markets were becoming flooded with cinchona bark, the raw material of their product. In order to discourage cinchona producers from switching their production to some other crop, the quinine producers entered into a price and export fixing arrangement. This arrangement was described by the cartel members as a 'gentlemen's agreement' to signify that it was not intended to be legally enforceable. The Commission nonetheless considered the arrangement did bring the cartel's conduct within the provisions of Article 85, particularly as the parties had arranged for alleged breaches of the agreement to be remedied by arbitration.

In **BMW**, the Commission took exception to an attempt by the Netherlands' BMW Dealers' Advisory Committee to deter Dutch BMW dealers from exporting cars to other member states. The advisory committee wrote to the dealers, purporting to give them advice in the following fashion: 'The

Dealers' Advisory Committee considers that its most important function is to give good advice to the distribution network and the only advice it has to offer in this case is: No more sales outside Belgium!' Construing this statement in the context of the other correspondence that had been received by the dealers, the Commission found that Article 85 had been infringed.

From the above, it can be seen that the application of Article 85 relies on an analysis of the substance and effects of firms' behaviour, not on the strict legal form of their mutual undertakings. This can be further seen in cases involving the refusal to admit businesses to exclusive distribution networks. In **AEG Telefunken**[5], the German electrical goods producer argued that its refusal to admit certain retailers to its distribution network, such as those with aggressive discounting policies, could not infringe Article 85 as their behaviour was a form of unilateral conduct, and, therefore, the element of mutuality of behaviour required by the Article was absent. The ECJ did not agree. The refusal to approve a new distributor was an act which took place in the context of the contractual expectations of those distributors who had already been admitted to the network.

AEG Telefunken is an important indication of the way the Commission and the ECJ will view the whole operation of distribution networks. Clearly, at least from a superficial point of view, the greater the number of wholesalers and retailers admitted to a producer's distribution system the more likely it is that strong competition will benefit consumers. However, many producers are keen to restrict supplies to certain kinds of distributors and it may be that they have good reasons for this. For example, it is in the interest of a firm producing complicated goods such as hi-fi equipment and computers to ensure that customers receive the right kind of skilled technical sales assistance, both before and after a purchase. In such a case, it may be in the interests of the consumer that producers insist on supplying only those who are technically competent to deal in the product. On the other hand, a producer may simply seek to use a selective distribution network as a means of maintaining artificially high prices; which may frequently be a shared interest with those who have already been admitted to the network.

The **AEG Telefunken** decision makes a clear distinction between selective distribution agreements which restrict admission on qualitative grounds which can be objectively justified (such as the technical competence of the dealers or the suitability of trading premizes) and agreements which restrict admission on quantitative grounds (such as the fact that the number of approved distributors already operating in an area is sufficient for local demand). Generally, the applicant for admission may be refused where the qualitative criteria cannot be met; but where qualitative criteria can be satisfied, producers cannot impose quantitative criteria. This is not to say that it will always be contrary to Article 85 to maintain a distribution network in which the outlets charge high prices. Where qualitative criteria require specialist outlets, the higher expenses associated with the provision of these may justify the charging of higher prices. The Article may not be infringed where there remains scope for competition in areas other than price, such as the quality of service provided to customers.

In its recent decisions, the Commission and the CFI has applied the distinction between qualitative and quantitative restrictions fairly strictly, though not without being criticized for doing so[6]. In **Givenchy**[7], the Commission regarded certain terms in the perfume manufacturer's selective distribution contract as infringing Article 85 on the grounds of their quantitative nature. The offending terms included the requirement that approved retailers made minimum purchases and a stipulation that they participated in advertising and promotional campaigns. There was also an admissions procedure which was relatively slow and therefore delayed the entry into the network of new retailers. Korah has observed that in the perfume market, which is very competitive (Givenchy had only 3.1% of the luxury market and no producer had more than 5%), it is difficult to see how quantitative selection criteria can lead to a distortion of competition, especially as there are too many producers for there to be effective collusion between any of them.

Nonetheless, the CFI has recently treated quantitative criteria as an infringement without considering the impact of the agreement on the market as a whole. In **YSL**[8], a perfume manufacturer's refusal to supply its luxury brands to outlets other than pharmacies was regarded as a potential breach of Article 85, as in some member states the number of pharmacies is controlled by law. This decision, however, did not pay particular attention to the fact that the luxury perfume market is very competitive.

Article 85 also makes specific provision for concerted practices. Frequently, the detection of these will not lie in uncovering some form of mutual undertakings between those operating the practice. Rather, there will have to be an analysis of what is happening in the market and an investigation into the motives for why firms have behaved in a particular way. In **Dyestuffs**[9], the ECJ defined a concerted practice as a course of conduct in which undertakings, without going so far as entering an agreement, coordinate their activities in a way which 'knowingly substitutes a practical cooperation between them for the risks of competition.'

In **Dyestuffs**, the Commission alleged that a number of independent producers had operated a price-fixing ring. The Commission based its allegations on uniform price increases made by members of the cartel. The Court was clear that parallel market behaviour was not, in itself, evidence of a concerted practice, but concluded that parallelism could be a strong indication of concertation when it produced conditions of competition which were not normal for a particular market. In this respect, the Court suggested that price could be particularly relevant in seeking to establish concertation, especially if parallel conduct 'permits the parties to seek price equilibrium at a level different from that which would have resulted from competition.'

The Court in **Dyestuffs** also stressed the importance of examining market structure in seeking to establish the existence of a concerted practice. This was recently further developed in **Woodpulp**[10], where the Court examined the implications of an oligopolistic market structure in determining whether Article 85 had been infringed by concertation. In **Woodpulp**, a number of non-EU producers who exported the raw material for paper to the Community were found by the Commission to have engaged in concerted practices by – among other things – making price announcements. The Court, although upholding the Commission's findings in relation to other breaches of Article 85, quashed the Commission's decision in relation to the price announcements.

The particular problem which faced the Court was how to interpret the parties' conduct when they operated in a tightly oligopolistic market. The Court noted that in such markets parallel behaviour may in fact be a rational response to price changes rather than evidence of a desire to act anti-competitively. It emerges from the opinion of the Advocate General and from the judgement of the Court that the activities of the operators in an oligopolistic market must be scrutinized with considerable care (the Court itself commissioned independent economic assessments of the actions of the alleged wrongdoers). In the final analysis, it is clear from the judgement that a finding of concertation can only be supported where there is an element of collusion which reduces the uncertainty and risks associated with acting in a market. In the words of the Advocate General, 'the concept of concerted practices refers to reciprocal communications between competitors with the *aim* [emphasis added] of giving each other assurances as to their conduct on the market.' In other words, Article 85 will not apply where conduct is dictated by market structure rather than by anti-competitive intent.

Which may affect trade . . .

Article 85 only applies to agreements (etc.) which have the potential to affect trade between member states. In **Societie Technique Miniere v Maschinenbau Ulm GmbH**[11], the ECJ identified this feature of Article 85 as promoting the creation of a sole market among the member states. In the Court's judgement, determining whether an agreement might affect inter-state trade would involve an examination of the agreement's ability to partition a particular market between member states and therefore 'render more difficult the economic interpenetration desired by the Treaty.'

The idea of potential to hinder economic interpenetration has been applied in situations where an agreement is intended to operate solely in a national market. In **Vereeniging van Cementhandelaren v Commission**[12], it was alleged that an agreement between members of a cement producers' trade association which involved price fixing infringed Article 85. The trade association denied that its agreement was covered by the Article as the agreement operated exclusively in the Netherlands and accordingly, the agreement would not affect trade between member states. The agreement in fact covered 400 wholesalers whose commercial activity accounted for 67 per cent of the Dutch market. On this basis, the ECJ concluded that the agreement had the potential to affect trade. The agreement had the effect of consolidating national partitioning and protecting national production. To this extent, parallel imports and exports of cement would be reduced and economic interpenetration diminished.

In order to be caught by Article 85, it is not necessary that the agreement should have the potential to affect the volume of trade adversely. It is enough that the normal patterns of trade are disturbed in some way. In **Consten & Grundig v Commission**[13], Grundig had granted Consten the sole distributorship of its goods in France and had given Consten the exclusive right to market goods under the GINT trade mark. Consten tried to prevent other distributors from selling Grundig goods which they had imported into France. In the ECJ, it was argued by Consten and Grundig that the agreement did not infringe Article 85 as, as a result of the agreement, the volume in trade in Grundig's goods had actually increased. The ECJ, however, was clear that under normal trade conditions there would be a number of parallel importers and wholesalers and it was this normality which had been disturbed by the agreement.

Object or effect the prevention, restriction or distortion of competition

The competition protected by Article 85 is normal competition taking into account imperfect markets. In **Consten & Grundig**, the agreement had anti-competitive potential because it eliminated intra-brand competition at the wholesale level.

In **Societie Technique Miniere**, the ECJ suggested how the anti-competitive nature of the agreement should be assessed. First, it is necessary to ask whether the *object* of the agreement was to distort competition. This can be decided by examining the clauses of the agreement itself. Would the economic effect of the agreement be to bring about 'changes in the play of competition'? If this can be answered affirmatively, then there may be an infringement of the Article. Second, where it is not the object of the agreement to distort competition, can this nonetheless be said to be the *effect* of the agreement? The question of effect on competition is a question of fact and is asked in the context of what would be the competitive situation in a market if the agreement did not exist. Therefore, in the situation where one party had granted another exclusive rights of sale – as was the case in **Societie Technique Miniere** – the economic and market context for deciding issues of object or effect include a consideration of:

> ... the nature and the quantity, whether limited or not, of the products which are the object of the agreement, the position and size of the grantor and concessionaire on the market for the products concerned, the isolated nature of the agreement in question or, on the contrary, its position in a series of agreements, the severity of the clauses aiming at protecting the exclusive right or, on the contrary, the possibilities left for other commercial currents upon the same products by means of re-exports and parallel imports.

Exemption

When an agreement infringes Article 85(1) it is automatically void, and operating such an agreement can render the parties liable to a fine, as explained above. There are some agreements which the Commission will not normally proceed against as they are covered by the so-called *de minimis* rule. That is, they are of minor importance. Such agreements were identified in a Commission notice in 1986 [(1986) OJ C 231/02] as agreements where the undertakings do not account for more than 5 per cent of the market affected by the agreement and where the aggregate turnover of the under-takings does not exceed ECU 200m. If an agreement is not protected as *de minimis*, then the parties can only give it effect if it has been exempted under Article 85(3), which provides that Article 85(1) may be disapplied where an agreement contributes 'to improving the production or distribution of goods or to promoting technical or economic progress, while allowing consumers a fair share of the resulting economic benefit, and which does not:

(a) impose on the undertakings concerned restrictions which are not indispensable to the attainment of these objectives;
(b) afford such undertakings the possibility of eliminating competition in respect of a substantial part of the products in question.'

As Article 85 applies to vertical as well as horizontal arrangements, many distribution agreements have had to be exempted under 85(1). In fact, by the beginning of the 1980s, the Commission had been inundated with so many applications for exemption that it introduced a system of block exemptions for certain kinds of agreements. The exemptions cover such things as vehicle distribution and servicing agreements, franchising agreements, research and development agreements, patent licensing agreements, exclusive distribution agreements and exclusive purchasing agreements. Broadly speaking, the block exemptions identify those restrictions which are permitted and those which are prohibited.

The Commission's 23rd Competition Report explains how the exemption system can be used to promote sectoral restructuring. In certain sectors, overcapacity is exacerbated by the combined effects of recession and increased global competition. This may mean that firms wish to undertake restructuring to reduce capacity, but they need to have the assurance that their competitors share the same goals. This can be achieved by multilateral agreements which will satisfy 85(3) if, amongst other things:

(i) There are binding and detailed commitments to reduce and dismantle capacity, likely in the long term to increase competitiveness.
(ii) Consumers are likely to benefit from the enhanced competition in the market leading to greater choice.
(iii) There is not the long-term potential for the parties to find other ways of eliminating competition, so there must remain the likelihood of completion between those remaining in the market after restructuring or the potential for external competition.

Article 86

Article 86 aims to control the abuse by an undertaking of its dominant position. As with Article 85, infringement of Article 86 will only take place where the abuse has the potential to affect trade between Member States. Article 86 lists examples of the kinds of activity which could amount to an infringement of its provisions. These include:

(a) Directly or indirectly imposing unfair purchase or selling prices or other unfair trading conditions.
(b) Limiting production, markets or technical development to the prejudice of consumers.
(c) Applying dissimilar conditions to equivalent transactions with other trading parties, thereby placing them at a competitive disadvantage.
(d) Making the conclusion of contracts subject to acceptance by the other parties of supplementary obligations which, by their nature or according to commercial usage, have no connection with the subject of the contracts.

54

(a), (c) and (d) have been termed exploitative abuses as they arise from an undertaking's desire to take advantage of a dominant position by dealing with trading partners unfairly. (c) has been described as anti-competitive abuses as they tend to undermine competition in a market, but do not necessarily arise from the desire of a dominant firm to act unfairly. In fact, the absence of the intention to act anti-competitively can be irrelevant to deciding whether Article 86 has been breached. Abuse can occur independently of fault, as is illustrated by the recent ECJ decision in **Plasterboards** (BPB and British Gypsum)[14]. Here, the dominant producers in the British and Irish plasterboard markets had used tying and exclusive purchase agreements in contracting with their customers. It was acknowledged by the Court that such vertical agreements were common in many markets. However, the ECJ distinguished between competitive markets (where such arrangements may be acceptable) and the plasterboard market, where competition was already restricted. The Court stressed that dominant firms have a special duty not to distort competition and that, in the case of BPB and British Gypsum, Article 86 could be breached by the adoption of commercial practices common in other more competitive markets.

The interpretation and application of Article 86

Identifying a dominant position

The dominant position referred to in Article 86 is identified by assessing a firm's impact on its market. Unlike UK legislation, which identifies a monopoly as having a 25 per cent share (or more) of its relevant market, Article 86 does not use a formal – in legal terms – test to identify whether an undertaking has market dominance. Rather, dominance is decided by an economic analysis of the extent to which a firm is constrained by economic forces within its market, or, alternatively, the extent to which a firm may itself influence a market. At least three criteria for establishing market dominance can be discerned from the decisions of the Commission and the ECJ.

1   *An undertaking's independence from its competitors.*   In 1972, the Commission formulated a test of dominance which focuses on a firm's ability to act independently of competitive market constraints:

> Undertakings are in a dominant position where they have the power to behave independently, which puts them in a position to act without taking into account their competitors, purchasers or suppliers. That is the position when, because of their share of the market,

or of their share of the market combined with the availability of technical knowledge, raw materials or capital, they have the power to determine prices or to control production or distribution for a significant part of the products in question. This power does not necessarily have to arise from an absolute domination permitting the undertakings which hold it to eliminate all will on the part of their economic partners, but it is enough that they be strong enough as a whole to ensure to those undertakings an overall independence of behaviour, even if there are differences in intensity in their influence on the different partial markets. (OJ [1972] L7/25 'Continental Can')

This approach was affirmed by the ECJ in **United Brands v Commission**[15], where the Court decided that there could be dominance when an undertaking was in a position to 'behave to an appreciable extent independently of its competitors, customers and ultimately of its consumers.' **United Brands** illustrates the point that Article 86 does not require complete dominance. In that case, there was a breach of Article 86 even though the European operation of the undertaking concerned experienced strong competition in Denmark, Germany and the Netherlands.

2   *The ability to eliminate competition.*   In **AKZO**[16], it was alleged that a firm involved in the production of peroxide had cut its prices to its customers to below the cost of production in order to eliminate its competitors. The Commission here looked beyond the issue of independence from competitors to stress that dominance could be evidenced by a firm's capacity to use pricing to see off, or at least seriously weaken, its competitors or to prevent new competitors from entering the market.

3   *Dominant relationships with customers and suppliers.*   An undertaking's dominance can be rooted in the way that it deals with its customers, particularly in its ability to starve customers of supplies or restrict their availability. In **RTE v Commission**[17], this aspect of dominance was shown by television companies refusing to allow outside firms to publish their programme schedules. On the demand side, being the sole or principal customer for a product or service may place an undertaking in the position to impose unfair conditions on its suppliers.

Identifying the relevant market

In the context of Article 86, dominance is not an abstract notion. Rather, it is a factual state of affairs identifiable by a firm's status in, and relationship with, a particular market. This status and relationship will help to determine the market's structure. Accordingly, whether a firm is dominant depends on how a market is defined. For example, are shoes and bedroom slippers in the same market (i.e. footwear) or are they in separate markets? Clearly, it is in the interests of a slipper producer accused of abusing a dominant position to argue that they operate in the footwear market as their market share is thus reduced. The **United Brands** decision illustrates how the ECJ and the Commission go about deciding the relevant market. In that case, a number of distributors had complained of unfair practices on the part of UB, an undertaking which was a major supplier of bananas to the European market. The ECJ explicitly analysed the relevant product market and geographic market and, by implication, considered the temporal market.

As far as the relevant *product market* is concerned, the key criterion is the extent to which the market for the product in question is differentiated from other markets. In **United Brands**, UB put forward an argument based on the alleged high degree of cross-elasticity of demand between bananas and other forms of fresh fruit to support its contention that the relevant product market was fresh fruit, not simply bananas. Consumers, UB maintained, considered bananas reasonably interchangeable with other fresh fruit such as apples, oranges, grapes, strawberries, peaches, etc. The Court rejected this argument. It found that there were special qualities which distinguished bananas from other fruit which reduced the degree of interchangeability. In particular, 'the banana has certain characteristics . . . which enable it to satisfy the constant needs of an important section of the population consisting of the very young, the old and the sick.'

With regard to the relevant *geographic market*, this comprises an area where the conditions of competition are homogeneous. In **United Brands**, the relevant geographic market excluded the UK, France and Italy as these states, through national intervention, gave considerable preference to certain producers (of whom UB was not one). On the other hand, the markets in Germany, Denmark, Ireland, the Netherlands, Belgium and Luxembourg were without the same level of state protectionism. Therefore, from the standpoint from being able to engage in free competition, 'these six States form an area which is sufficiently homogeneous.'

The duration for which a market exists – its *temporal scope* – is also relevant in determining dominance. In **United Brands**, the Court discussed the fact that bananas were in constant production throughout the year, their production being unaffected by the changes in seasons. The ECJ found that there was no significant seasonal substitutability between bananas and other fruit.

Article 86 and collective dominance

Until recently, there was some doubt about whether Article 86 applied to the conduct of two or more undertakings which, although as individual firms have limited power, collectively have market dominance. This issue now appears to have been settled in **Italian Flat Glass**[18].

In that case, the Commission decided in 1988 that three Italian glass wholesalers had infringed both Articles 85 and 86 by operating restrictive agreements. As far as Article 86 was concerned, the Commission estimated that the parties had a combined market share of 80 per cent of the relevant market and that by exchanging commercial information they had abused their market dominance. The Italian firms challenged the Commission's decision in the Court of First Instance.

In a long judgement, the CFI was extremely critical of the way the Commission had made its decision on the basis of insufficient evidence and inadequate analysis. The Court, however, despite the intervening arguments to the contrary by the UK Government, was clear that Article 86 might apply to the situation involving the glass wholesalers: '. . . there is no legal and economic reason to suppose that the term "undertaking" in Article 86 has a different meaning to the one given to it in the context of Article 85. There is nothing in principle to prevent two or more independent economic entities from being, on a specific market, united by such economic links that, by virtue of that fact, together they hold a dominant position *vis-à-vis* the other operators on the same market.' **Italian Flat Glass** is an important decision, particularly when considered in the context on **Woodpulp** and **Nestlé/Perrier** (see Chapter 4 on mergers). Together, these decisions indicate how the Commission and the Courts have developed regulatory principles to deal with oligopoly where none are specifically provided by the Treaty.

References

1 Com (93) 700 final, 5 December 1995.
2 OJ 1992 L134/1.
3 Re Quinine Cartel, ACF Chemiefarma and Others v Commission [1970] *ECR* 661.
4 BMW Belgium SA and Others v Commission [1980] 1 *CMLR* 370.
5 AEG Telefunken AG v Commission [1984] 3 *CMLR* 325.
6 Korah, V., *Selective Distribution* [1994] 2 *ECLR* 101.
7 [1992] 4 *CMLR* 331.
8 [1993] 4 *CMLR* 120.
9 ICI v Commission [1972] *CMLR* 557.
10 Re Woodpulp Cartel: A. Ahlstrom Oy and Others v Commission [1993] 4 *CMLR* 407.
11 [1966] 1 *CMLR* 357.
12 [1973] *CMLR* 7.
13 [1966] *CMLR* 418.
14 XXIIIrd Competition Report from the Commission. Com (9) 161 final. 5 May 1994, p. 217

15 [1978] 1 *CMLR* 429.
16 [1987] 1 *CMLR* 321.
17 [1991] 4 *CMLR* 586.
18 [1992] 5 *CMLR* 301.

Questions

1 To what extent are considerations of collective dominance relevant to determining liability under both Article 85 and 86?
2 'The interpretation of Articles 85 and 86 have involved the ECJ and the CFI more in economic rather than legal analysis of the way firms behave.' Discuss this statement.
3 'Rigorous and uniform application – mitigated by appropriate exemption – is the only way to assure the place of competition law in the attainment of a single market.' Do you agree?

4 Brussels and the control of merger activity in the European Union

Leigh Davison and Edmund Fitzpatrick

Introduction to the Merger Control Regulation 4064/89

In December 1989, the European Community introduced the Merger Control Regulation. The Regulation – which came into full legal effect in September 1990 – had been under discussion in one form or another since at least 1973.

The Treaty of Rome in both its original and amended forms makes no particular provision for regulating merger (or concentration) activity within the EU. Prior to 1990, the only legal measures for dealing with concentration activity were Articles 85 and 86 (see Chapter 3). Neither of these two Articles was designed specifically with concentration activity in mind. Article 85 regulates restrictive practices and has as its target cooperative market behaviour between undertakings – such as price fixing or market sharing agreements. Article 86 is concerned with the potential abuse by dominant firms of their market positions.

Given the clear lack of specific provision for merger regulation in the Treaty, the Commission had no choice but to rely on the above articles in their efforts to regulate merger activity which might have the potential to distort or restrict competition in the common market. In this, the Commission received support from the European Court of Justice (ECJ) in two key decisions: **Continental Can** and **BAT**. In **Continental Can**, the ECJ accepted the Commission's argument that the acquisition of a competitor by a dominant firm could prejudice the competitive structure of a market and thereby have the potential to infringe Article 86. In **BAT**, the ECJ considered that the Community had the power to intervene under Article 85 in regard to an agreement between two firms under which it was undertaken that one of them would transfer a substantial shareholding in a third firm to the other if such a transfer had the potential to impede competition.

Despite the reliance by the Community on Articles 85 and 86 as means of concentration control, the Articles were generally regarded as inadequate legal tools for regulating mergers with a Community dimension. Because neither Article 85 nor 86 requires firms involved in merger activity to notify the Commission of their intentions, the Articles could only be invoked against an undertaking after a concentration had occurred. One unsatisfactory result of this approach to merger regulation was that it became difficult for firms to know with any degree of certainty – in advance of a merger – whether their actions would comply with Community law.

Over and above these legal problems, the requirement to complete the single european market (SEM) by January 1993 led to a greater urgency for the establishment of a uniform, EU-wide concentration control procedure. The SEM initiative, in seeking to achieve a single or common market within the EU as a whole by the removal of non-tariff barriers, has created the opportunity for firms to engage in cross-border takeovers in a way which had not previously existed. On the positive side, such activity enables a firm to exploit potential economies of scale; however, there is a real fear that the motive for much merger activity is not efficiency driven but aimed at strengthening market power and the reduction of competition. For this reason, the control of concentrations at Community level, as a flanking measure to the SEM, was a necessity. Moreover, if such regulation were left to each member state – with their differing perspectives on merger control – then a uniform EU-wide approach would be very unlikely to emerge and this would be prejudicial to the SEM initiative.

The scope of the Regulation

The Merger Control Regulation authorises the Commission to declare a 'concentration with a Community Dimension' (CCD) incompatible with the common market. Incompatibility arises where the CCD creates or strengthens a dominant market position so as to impede effective competition in the common market, or a substantial part of it.

The Regulation identifies the circumstances when concentration occurs for the purposes of Community control. Article 3(1) of the Regulation states:

A concentration should be deemed to arise where:
(a) two or more previously independent undertakings merge, or
(b) one or more persons already controlling at least one undertaking – or one or more undertakings – acquire, whether by purchase of securities or assets, by contract or by any other means direct or indirect control of the whole or part of one or more other undertakings.

A concentration is said to have a community dimension when:

(a) the combined aggregate worldwide turnover of all the undertakings concerned exceeds ECU 5 billion, and

61

(b) the aggregate community wide turnover of each of at least two of the undertakings involved exceeds ECU 250 million, *unless*

(c) each of the undertakings concerned derives more than two-thirds of their Community-wide turnover within one and the same member state.

The thresholds for determining whether a concentration has a Community dimension are cumulative. Where a concentration fails to satisfy any one of the three thresholds, it will escape Community control. The threshold relating to turnover derived in the same member state is sometimes referred to as the transnationality threshold and allows mergers which are essentially of a national character to be dealt with by national competition authorities rather than at the Community level.

If a concentration satisfies the definition of a CCD, then it falls under the sole jurisdiction of the Commission on competition grounds. If a concentration does not satisfy the definition it remains the concern of the competition policy of the relevant Member State. The result of the Regulation is that the concentration is either vetted by the Commission or the authorities of the Member State, but not by both. This is known as the 'one-stop shop' approach. The advantage of this approach lies in its apparent simplicity; businesses considering merger activity will be able to clearly identify whether they will have to deal with Brussels or national authorities.

This one-stop approach entails a substantial surrender of competence to Brussels by national competition authorities. However, under the *distinct market* provisions of the Regulation, Brussels has the discretion to return certain proposed concentrations to national authorities for consideration. This can only happen if a Member State formally requests that the case is returned to the jurisdiction of its national authorities. At this stage the Commission has the exclusive right to determine whether a distinct market exists by analysing the products or services in question and the relevant geographical reference market. In an explanatory memorandum the Commission stated that the provision 'would normally cover small "local" markets in, for example, the retailing or the hotel sector and exceptionally might be applicable to a national market which is somehow isolated from the rest of the Community, for example because of high transport cost'[1]. An illustration of the application of the distinct market test is the **Steetly/Tarmac** decision, where the Commission allowed the UK authorities to consider a merger in the brick and clay tile industry where significant barriers to entry meant that the merger would have little impact on the rest of the Community. In making this decision, the Commission gave particular weight to the fact that, because bricks are heavy and bulky, transport costs represent a significant proportion of their total price.

However, there is one clear inroad into the one-stop approach; that is the *legitimate interests* provision under Article 21 of the Regulation. While the article asserts the Community's sole competence to deal with CCDs on competition grounds, it allows member states to take measures (including the ability to block a proposed concentration) to protect legitimate interests. The article specifically identifies public security, plurality of the media and prudential rules as legitimate interests. In respect of other forms of public interest, a Member State does not have the automatic right to act unilaterally. The matter must be communicated by the member state to the Commission. The Commission, taking into account Community law, will decide whether the alleged public interest justifies allowing the merger to be dealt with by the Member State concerned.

Despite the Merger Regulation having the legitimate interests provision, a member state may nonetheless be reluctant to submit certain mergers to the Commission's scrutiny and this may cause it to seek ways of circumventing the requirements of the Regulation altogether. For example, at the time of writing, the UK's President of the Board of Trade, Michael Heseltine, has instructed the parties to BAe's bid for VSEL (the builders of nuclear submarines) not to notify the proposed concentration to Brussels[2]. Rather than relying on the legitimate interests provision of the Regulation, the Department of Trade and Industry (DTI) has asserted that the UK, under Article 223 of the Treaty of Rome, has the right to determine the matter nationally.

Article 223 lays down a limited derogation from the provisions of the Treaty of Rome on certain security grounds. The Article allows a Member State to refuse to supply information the disclosure of which would be 'contrary to the essential interests of its security'[3]. The Article also allows a Member State to take measures which it considers necessary 'for the protection of the essential interests of its security which are connected with the production of or trade in arms, munitions and war material . . .'[4].

There is a precedent for the use of Article 223 to avoid the investigation of a sensitive merger under the Regulation. In March 1993, France informed the Commission that the parties to a CCD involving the manufacturers of missile engines had been asked not to notify the merger. The Commission requested France to provide additional information to establish, among other things, that the merger would be limited to military applications and that there would be no spillover effects for non-military products. Moreover, the Commission had to be satisfied that, as far as other member states were concerned, there would not be any military – as well as non-military – spillovers. Once this information was supplied, the Commission took no further action.

In instructing the parties to the VSEL bid not to notify the Commission, the DTI is asserting the UK's rights under Article 223. However, the Commission has a different view of the merger and has responded to Mr Heseltine's ban on notification by stating that it will investigate the non-military aspects of the planned takeover[5].

It may be commented that the DTI's approach, if frequently adopted by other Member States, has the potential to undermine the Commission's authority to vet CCDs on competition grounds as national security related mergers may never reach Brussels. On the other hand, if the legitimate interest approach of the Regulation were to be used, this would require pre-notification. This, in turn, would entail the parties providing Brussels with a considerable amount of sensitive information on such matters as the state of their financial position, the structure of markets as well as research and development. In the VSEL bid this is deemed by the DTI not to be in the national interest.

Procedure under the Regulation

Under the Regulation, the vetting of concentrations by the Commission on competition grounds involves two stages – although the majority of notifications are disposed of during the first stage.

Stage One

This stage involves prior notification and the initial examination of the CCD by the Commission. The parties to the proposed concentration have one week under Article 4 to notify the Commission of their intentions. The one-week time limit is calculated from either the conclusion of the agreement between the parties, or the announcement of the public bid or the acquisition of a controlling interest. Failure by the parties to comply with the prior notification requirement is punishable by a fine of between ECU 1000 and ECU 50,000. However, the Commission has the power to impose a higher fine of up to ten per cent of the total turnover of the undertakings concerned. Once the prior notification requirement has been complied with, the Commission has a further three weeks to make one of the following three decisions:

1 The notified concentration does not fall within the scope of the Regulation.
2 The concentration does fall within the scope of the Regulation, but there are not serious doubts about its compatibility with the common market.
3 There are serious doubts about the concentration's compatibility with the common market and further consideration of the concentration will be required.

During Stage One, the proposed concentration cannot be put into effect. Where the outcome of Stage One is either (1) or (2), the concentration is cleared and can go ahead. However, where the outcome is (3), then Stage Two is triggered.

Apart from starting the legal process of ensuring compliance with the Regulation, Stage One plays an important role in establishing a vehicle for dialogue between the parties involved and the Commission. This is reflected in the fact that the parties can have pre-notification meetings with the Commission in which they can confidentially discuss their plans for merger activity. Extensive use has been made of this practice[6] which, from the point of view of the Commission, compels firms to evaluate the competition implications as part of their overall business strategy.

Stage Two

Stage One operates as the filter whereby, to date, the vast majority of concentrations have been cleared. By 25 October 1994, the Commission had received 265 notifications, of which 207 were cleared within one month. A further 21 were judged to be outside the scope of the Regulation, while five notifications were withdrawn by the parties during Stage One. As of the 25 October 1994, another 15 Stage One decisions were pending.

Once Stage Two has commenced, the Commission has four months to undertake a detailed review of the proposed concentration. The review process gives the parties the right to a hearing by the Commission and provides them with the opportunity to modify their concentration plans so as to avoid the possibility of the concentration being blocked by the Commission. So far, 17 cases have gone on to the Second Stage, only one of which has been blocked. Ten have received conditional clearance, four have received unconditional clearance, one has been withdrawn, leaving one decision pending (25 October 1994).

Application of the Regulation

Defining the reference market

In order to be in a position to determine whether or not a proposed concentration creates or strengthens a dominant position it is first necessary to identify the market(s) in which the merged entity will operate. Regarding the reference market, it is clear that the Commission will at least consider the relevant product and geographical markets.

1 Product market

The Commission's decisions show two criteria on the basis of which the distinct product markets can be identified. One of the two criteria is the degree of substitutability between the products in question. On this matter, the Commission takes into consideration the degree of both demand and supply substitutability. Demand side substitutability refers to the degree to which consumers are able to purchase alternative products of a similar quality and price. Supply substitutability concerns the capability of producers of similar products to enter the product market in question. By taking the latter into account, the Commission is seeking to assess the contestability of a particular product market.

The **de Havilland** decision illustrates how both demand and supply aspects of substitutability were employed by the Commission in defining the relevant product market. The case concerned the proposed acquisition of de Havilland – the Canadian commuter aircraft subsidiary of Boeing – by Aerospatiale of France and Alenia of Italy. In assessing the concentration, the Commission defined the product market as regional turbo-prop commuter aircraft. The parties to the concentration maintained that the relevant product market was the overall market for commuter aircraft with 20 to 70 seats. The Commission, however, on this issue of demand substitutability, subdivided the market into three distinct non-substitutable segments: 20 to 39 seaters, 40 to 49 seaters and 60 and over seaters. This division reflected the experience and practice of customers and competitors[7]. On the supply side, the Commission considered the following factors relevant. First, the proposed concentration, if allowed, would remove de Havilland as a competitor. Secondly, the new entity would be the only commuter manufacturer offering the full range of commuter aircraft. Thirdly, the Commission, after considering market demands and the high costs of entry into the market, concluded that it could not foresee potential competitors entering the market.

2 Geographical scope

The geographical scope of the Regulation is established by Article 2(3) which provides that the assessment of a concentration will consider the extent to which it impedes effective competition in the common market or in a substantial part of the common market. In deciding the geographical market in which any particular concentration will take place, the Commission has defined the relevant geographical market as 'the area where the undertakings concerned are involved in the supply and demand of products or services, in which the conditions of competition are sufficiently homogeneous and which can be distinguished from neighbouring areas because conditions of competition are appreciably different in those areas'[8]. In seeking to assess the homogeneity of competition within a geographical area the Commission's decisions have taken into account, among other things, the following:

1 Geographical distribution of market shares and relative prices.
2 Geographical location of major supplier.
3 Transport costs and shipping patterns.
4 Consumer preferences and product differentiation.
5 Barriers to entry and distribution systems.
6 Cross-border imports and exports.
7 'The impact of forthcoming changes, e.g. in the technical and regulatory environment'[9].

The above criteria help to establish whether a geographical market exists, and at the same time will assist the Commission in deciding whether the scope of that market is the common market or a substantial part of the common market, or a national market or a distinct market. Decisions about the geographical classification of a market are fundamental to deciding the Commission's jurisdiction and role in vetting the merger.

The importance of deciding the classification of a geographical market can be seen in relation to national markets. As already stated, a concentration will not have a community dimension – and thus the Commission does not have jurisdiction on competition grounds – if each of the undertakings concerned achieves more than two-thirds of its aggregate Community-wide turnover within one and the same member state. In such circumstances, the national authority assesses the concentration. However, when a proposed concentration taking place in a national market satisfies the definition of a CCD, it is still possible for the national authorities to invoke the distinct market provisions; and to this extent, national markets and distinct markets may be coterminous.

Defining geographical scope is particularly relevant to deciding whether a CCD may impede competition in a substantial part of the Community. A problem here is that the Regulation offers no definition of the term 'substantial part' and, accordingly, its interpretation has been largely left to the Commission. It is now the Commission's practice, according to Mr Alonso Briones[10] of DG IV, to interpret 'substantial part' – by analogy with Articles 85 and 86 – in terms of a merger's ability to affect trade between Member States. Therefore, in the Commission's view, a national market will usually constitute a substantial part of the Community, whereas regional and local markets normally will not. However, there have been situations where a merger affecting a national market has not been regarded as threatening competition in a substantial part of the Community. This reasoning was adopted in **Holdersim-Cedest** (Case M.460), where the Commission referred a merger in the French cement market back to the national authorities because the high barriers to entry in the cement market meant that the merger was unlikely to affect trade between Member States. This seems difficult to reconcile with decisions such as **Accor/Wagons-Lits** and **Nestlé/Perrier** (discussed in more detail below). Here there were also significant barriers to entering the French national market and yet the Commission treated the planned mergers as having the potential to impede competition in a substantial part of the Community.

Dominant position

After defining the reference market, both with regard to product and geographical scope, the Commission is in a position to assess whether the proposed concentration will create or strengthen a dominant position. The ECJ, in relation to Article 86, has interpreted a dominant position to be one where a firm is in a position to act independently of its customers, consumers and ultimately of its competitors. Where the Regulation differs from Article 86 is that liability under Article 86 arises where a dominant position is already in existence, whereas the Regulation considers the potential the concentration has to create a dominant position. To this extent, the Regulation requires an assessment of the probable consequences of the proposed concentration if it were to be allowed. In this regard, Picat and Zachmann state, 'The Commission's role is in fact to analyse the foreseeable strength of the entity resulting from the merger and its impact on the competition structure of the market in question'[11].

The process of analysing the competitive structure of a particular market has involved the Commission in examining a number of factors. Its approach has been similar to that of strategic analysts when assessing the nature and extent of competition within an industry, so as to determine the attractiveness of that industry. One model which is frequently used by strategists is Porter's 'Five Forces'. The five forces are: threat of entry into the industry, the power of buyers, the power of suppliers, the intensity of rivalry between existing firms and the threat of substitutes. In turn, in order to accurately gauge the extent of competition within the industry, each force is broken down into a series of components. For example, Porter's model, when assessing the intensity of rivalry between competitors, takes into account the following: industry growth, fixed costs, intermittent overcapacity, switching costs for customers, number of firms and their relative size, the extent and scale of exit barriers, differentiation of products and corporate culture [see appendix 4.1].

Picat and Zachmann's analysis of the Commission's decisions on competition structure confirms that there are some similarities with the Five Forces model. Picat and Zachmann identify four elements in the Commission's approach. These are:

1   The market position of the new concentration.

2   Rivalry from remaining competitors.
3   The power of buyers (demand side) and the power of suppliers (supply side).
4   The threat of entry and substitutes (supply substitutability).

The use of these elements can be seen in the following two cases. In **Du Pont/ICI**, the proposed concentration involved the acquisition of ICI's nylon production activities by Du Pont, the world's nylon industry leader. ICI at the time was the leading European manufacturer of nylon fibre used in carpet production and was Du Pont's closest competitor. The new concentration would have had an EU market share exceeding 40 per cent, which was double that of its nearest rival, Rhone-Poulenc/SNIA. The Commission concluded that the merger would lead to a considerable reduction in competition, especially in the area of product development. Moreover, it was noted that the rivals to the new concentration did not cover the full range of fibres produced by Du Pont/ICI and the Commission thought that it would be a long time before competitors could produce substitutes. In addition, the Commission thought it unlikely that there would be new entrants into the market as the industry suffered from overcapacity. Taking these considerations into account, the Commission was only prepared to sanction the concentration in return for undertakings as it believed that the merger would significantly reduce competition.

In **Accor/Wagons-Lits**, there was a bid by Accor, a French hotel and catering group, for all the shares of Wagons-Lits, a Belgian group in the same industry. The effect of the acquisition – as assessed by the Commission – on French motorway catering services would be to give Accor an 80 per cent share of the market for full catering services and a 60 per cent share of the market for light catering services. It was also noted that the competition in this market was small and very dispersed, with no one competitor having a market share exceeding 5 per cent. This meant that the new entity would have considerably greater financial power than any of the residual competition. In addition, the Commission determined that there were considerable barriers to entry which included the limited number of motorways, difficulty for non-French firms to enter the French market, legal barriers for establishment, long duration of licences and heavy administrative costs for small enterprises. On the basis of this analysis, Accor was only allowed to proceed with the merger on the undertaking that it divested all Wagons-Lits catering services on French motorways.

Oligopolistic dominance

The foregoing considers the application of the Regulation in terms of single or monopolistic dominance. The **Nestlé/Perrier** decision saw the Commission extending the scope of the Regulation to oligopolistic dominance.

The facts were as follows. On 25 February 1992, Nestlé notified the Commission of a public bid of £1.58 billion for 100 per cent of the shares of Source Perrier. A month before the bid, Nestlé had reached an understanding with BSN – the largest food group in France – that in return for BSN's tactical support in acquiring Perrier, Nestlé would transfer Volvic, Perrier's second largest brand, to BSN. The whole transaction, including both the bid and the proposed sale of Volvic, involved France's three leading producers of bottled mineral water. Nestlé already controlled well-known brands such as Vittel and Hpar while Perrier's bottling activities included Contrex, Volvic, Perrier, Saint-Yorre and Vichy. BSN's principal brand was Evian.

In assessing the impact upon the competitive structure of the French bottled water market, the Commission's focus was not so much on the position of the new entity but on the resulting market power of Nestlé and BSN; in other words, the market structure was assessed in terms of duopolistic dominance. The Commission recognized, even before the merger was planned, that the market was oligopolistic in nature, being dominated by the three companies. Therefore, to approve the new entity and the transfer of Volvic, the Commission realized that this would lead to only two dominant players – Nestlé and BSN – controlling 82 per cent of the market by value and approximately 75 per cent of the market by volume.

However, it may be debatable whether the Commission has the legal authority to interpret the Regulation in this way. The regulation makes no specific reference to joint or oligopolistic dominance and this leaves the Commission's approach in **Nestlé/Perrier** open to the suggestion that it cannot be justified on strict legal grounds. This is a point acknowledged by Juan F Briones Alonso of the Commission's General Competition Merger Task Force. Mr Alonso has commented, 'Whether the Merger Regulation could be applied to collective or oligopolistic dominance has been the subject of some debate and controversy in the past . . . Both the "for" and "against" sides have developed reasonable legal arguments on the issue of whether the Merger Regulation covers oligopolies'[12]. Mr Alonso goes on to welcome the Commission's approach while making the point that there will remain legal uncertainty until such time as the matter is finally resolved by the ECJ and this will not take place until there is an actual appeal by a party who is aggrieved by the Commission's use of the **Nestlé/Perrier** approach. Legal uncertainty notwithstanding, the Commission has used the oligopolistic dominance approach in other decisions.

Joint ventures

The Regulation, in addition to dealing with straightforward mergers, applies to certain joint ventures. It is only concerned with the concentrative joint venture and this is defined by Article 3(2) as follows: 'a joint venture performing on a lasting basis all the functions of an autonomous economic entity [the 'positive condition'], which does not give rise to coordination of the competitive behaviour of the parties amongst themselves or between them and the joint venture [the 'negative condition'] . . .' The Regulation specifically excludes from its scope what have been termed cooperative joint ventures. A cooperative joint venture is one where the undertakings involved – including the joint venture – coordinate their competitive behaviour. Even though cooperative joint ventures are excluded from the scope of the Regulation they may nonetheless fall within the terms of Article 85 of the Treaty of Rome.

Although the Regulation defined concentrative and cooperative joint ventures, there remained some uncertainty about the language it used. This led the Commission to issue additional guidance in the form of an explanatory Notice[13]. The Notice reiterated that the hallmarks of the concentrative joint venture were its independence from its parents and absence of coordination of behaviour between the undertakings.

With respect to autonomy (the 'positive condition') the notice identified certain characteristics. These were, first, that the joint venture must act as an independent supplier and buyer on the market. A concentration will not arise where the joint venture remains an auxiliary to the commercial activities of its parents or is substantially reliant on its parents for the maintenance and development of its business.

Secondly, the joint venture must be established to carry on its business indefinitely or at least for a substantial period of time. Here, the Commission will look at the resources that the parents make available for the joint venture. The endowment of the joint venture with human, technical and financial resources must be sufficient to ensure the long-term existence and independence of the joint venture.

Thirdly, a crucial question for determining autonomy is whether the joint venture is in a position to exercise independently its own commercial policy. However, the Notice states that parental involvement in certain decisions, such as the alteration of the objects clause or of the capital of the joint venture, are not necessarily incompatible with economic independence. This approach recognizes that in many circumstances parent companies, being the only or principal shareholders in the joint venture, will inevitably be required to make decisions relating to the corporate governance of the joint venture. A concern, however, is that the Notice does not directly address the question of shareholder appointment of directors even though it does make the point that common membership of the parents' boards and the joint venture's board might suggest coordination. It is clearly possible for the parents, as the main shareholders, to appoint biddable individuals to the board of the joint venture who are not on the boards of the parent companies.

In assessing the likelihood of coordination of competitive behaviour (the 'negative' condition) the notice identifies two situations where there is the clear possibility of coordination. The first is where one or more of the parent companies remain in the same market as the joint venture. In this case cooperation is presumed by the Commission and it is for the undertakings involved to rebut this presumption.

The second relates to where the joint venture is either upstream or downstream of the parent companies' business operations. In this situation, the Commission believes that cooperation in the area of sales (upstream) or supply (downstream) between the parents becomes likely. In the Commission's view, it becomes more difficult to assess the likelihood of coordination of competitive behaviour where the parent companies and the joint venture are in neighbouring markets. The outcome of the Commission's assessment 'will depend in particular on whether the JV's and the parent companies' products are technically or economically linked, whether they are both components of another product or are otherwise mutually complementary, and whether the parent companies could realistically enter the JV's market'[13].

The Commission's decision in **Pasteur-Merieux/Merck** illustrates the application of the 'positive condition', i.e. the requirement that the new JV should be autonomous of its parent companies. The two parents in this case were major producers of human vaccines who ranked second and third in the world market. They agreed that they would pool their Western European undertakings and Pasteur-Merieux transferred all its distribution systems to the new JV. However, the parents, because the geographical scope of the new JV was restricted to Western Europe, chose not to transfer their research and development activities to the new undertaking. In addition, they retained certain production activities and intellectual property rights.

In the vaccine industry, research and development is of fundamental importance. Under the JV agreement, the new undertaking could only make recommendations to the parent companies about R&D for products already in existence and could have access to the parents' new R&D activities only through the intermediary of a development committee. In the light of the JV's very limited opportunities for initiative in the area of R&D, the Commission decided that the requisite degree of autonomy from the parent companies was absent and that, accordingly, the matter would have to be considered under Article 85 rather than the Merger Regulation.

As far as the 'negative condition' (the absence of coordination of competitive behaviour) is concerned, this test was applied in the **Philips/Thompson/ Sagem** decision. Here, the parents were in neighbouring product markets and between them the parents and the joint venture would be involved in the markets for screens. In the light of the interdependence of the markets for plasma, liquid crystals and cathode ray tubes and the complementary nature of these products, the Commission concluded that it was extremely likely that there would be the coordination of competitive behaviour between the parents themselves and between the parents and the new JV.

Conclusion: The Merger Regulation and the principle of subsidiarity

Much discussion of the Merger Regulation has involved the idea of subsidiarity. The fact that it took the Member States nearly two decades to agree to the Regulation in its final form indicates their cautious approach to surrendering certain decision making powers to the Commission in such an important area of competition policy. At present, certain Member States are reluctant to see the CCD thresholds reduced and this leaves them considerable scope to formulate and apply their own competition policy and rules for non-CCD mergers. Although in recent times there has been a marked convergence in the Member States' thinking on competition policy, the fact that only a relatively small number of mergers are dealt with each year at the Community level means that there is still a clear possibility that fragmentation of merger policy at the level of the Member States will make the goals of the single European market more difficult to achieve.

It is tempting to justify this fragmentation on the basis of subsidiarity and to argue that the accretion of decision making powers in Brussels offends against the principle – expressed in Article A of the Maastricht Treaty – that in the Union 'decisions are taken as closely as possible to the citizen.' However, there is more than one definition of subsidiarity; Article 3b of the amended EU Treaty provides procedural criteria, based on the idea that decision making should be efficient as well as democratic, for determining where decisions are made. Article 3b states:

> . . . In areas which do not fall within its exclusive competence, the Community shall take action, in accordance with the principle of subsidiarity, only in so far as the objectives of the proposed action cannot be *sufficiently* achieved by the Member States and can therefore, by reason of the *scale* or *effects* of the proposed action, be *better* achieved by the Community. (Emphasis added)

Clearly, Article 3b seems to be creating a presumption that the Community will hold back from decision making in many areas. Nevertheless, in the area of competition regulation aimed at supporting the SEM there is a need for Europe-wide coordination which cannot be sufficiently achieved by Member States acting individually. Moreover, in terms of their scale and effects, CCDs – particularly because they frequently involve cross-border economic activity – are by their nature better suited to control by Brussels. It is, therefore, at least arguable that operation of the Merger Regulation is entirely consistent with the principle of subsidiarity and that a further reduction of the thresholds would enhance rather than undermine that principle.

Appendix One: Porter's Five Forces approach to competitive structure

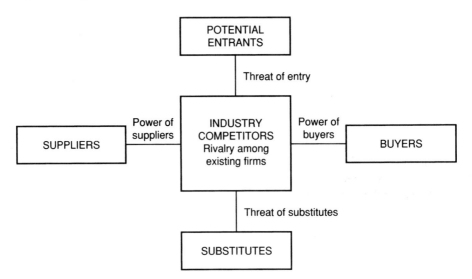

Source: Reprinted with the permission of The Free Press, a division of Simon & Schuster Inc. from *Competitive Strategy: Techniques for Analysing Industries and Competitors* by Michael E. Porter. Copyright © 1980 by The Free Press.

Each of the Five forces is determined by a number of factors. Namely:

1   *Rivalry Determinants*
Industry growth
Fixed and storage costs
Intermittent over-capacity
Product differences, brand identity and switching costs
Number of firms and their size
Corporate cultures
Scale of exit barriers

2   *Threat of Entry*
Economies of scale
Product differentiation and brand loyalty
Switching costs for buyers
Access to distribution channels
Absolute cost advantages
Government policy
Expected retaliation
3   *Determinants-supplier power*
Differentiation of inputs
Switching costs of firms to other suppliers
Availability of substitute inputs
Supplier concentration
Importance of volume to supplier
Costs relative to total purchases in the industry
Impact of inputs on costs or differentiation
Threat of forward vertical integration
4   *Determinants-Buyer Power*
Price sensitivity of purchase decisions
Price relative to total purchases
Product/service differences
Brand loyalty
Buyers' profitability
Decision makers' incentives
Bargaining leverage
Buyer concentration and volume
Buyer switching costs
Buyer information: quantity/quality
Availability of substitutes
Threat of backward vertical integration
5   *Determinants-threat of Substitution*
Relative price and performance of substitutes
Switching costs
Buyers' propensity to substitute

References

1 Commission memorandum 22.12.1989 See Elland, W. (1990) The Mergers Control Regulation (EEC) No 4064/89 3 *European Competition Law Review (ECLR)*, 111.
2 *Financial Times* 20 October 1994, p. 28.
3 Article 223, Treaty of Rome.

4 *Ibid.*
5 *The Times*, 5 November 1994, p. 23
6 Picat, M. and Zachmann, J. (1993) Community Monitoring of Concentration Operations: Evaluation after over Two Years. Application of Regulation 4064/89, 6 *ECLR*, 242.
7 Hawkes, L. (1992) The EC Merger Control Regulation. Not an Industry Policy Instrument: the De Havilland Decision. Analysis Section, 1 *ECLR*, 35.
8 22nd Report on Competition Policy. Commission of the European Communities 1992, p. 134.
9 Ibid, p. 135.
10 Telephone conversation with Mr Juan F Briones Alonso 15 December 1994.
11 Picat and Zachmann *op. cit.*, p. 243.
12 Alonso, J.F.B. (1993) Economic Assessment of Oligopolies under the Community Merger Control Regulation. Analysis Section, 3 *ECLR*, 118.
13 Explanatory Notice OJ 1990 C203/10.

Questions

1 The Single European Market requires Brussels to vet all concentrations within the Community but this is clearly at odds with the current trend towards subsidiarity.
Appraise this contention.
2 The Commission when assessing whether a CCD impedes effective competition in the Common market, or a substantial part of it, has the task of defining and appraising the relevant market(s).
Examine the way in which the Commission undertakes this task.
3 Assess the claim that the distinction between cooperative and concentrative joint venture is largely unnecessary given that they are already dealt with under Article 8.5 of the Treaty of Rome.

5 Competition policy in the Member States: a case of convergence?

Colin Turner

Introduction

Ultimately the function of competition policy, within any system, is to ensure that the structures and conduct of the industries and firms within it are in the broader interest of the economy as a whole. How you define 'interest' is naturally the key issue. However, if the competition policy system, within an economy, is to be effective in achieving its declared objectives then it has to meet certain criteria. These are:

1 Clarity: the rules must be easily understood by all economic actors affected by them.
2 Consistency: the rules must be applied in a uniform fashion across the economy.
3 Predictability: the outcome of the application of these rules must be known with a degree of certainty by those that are affected by them.
4 Credibility: the rules and the authorities that apply them have to be believable in the eyes of those undertakings to which they apply.

In simple terms, the rules affecting competition can be form-based or effects-based. The form-based system judges an action by its legal form, often expressed in terms of the proportion of the market a company, agreement or merger affects. The rationale for such a form-based policy is that a concentration of market share is an agglomeration of economic power and this may not be in the broader interest of the economy. Thus, for example, a competition authority could examine a merger purely on the basis of its potential ability to have excessive control over a market, regardless of its actions. The effects-based system concentrates on the actual actions of an undertaking and its economic consequences. Thus, for example, a monopoly is only detrimental in those instances where it acts to distort competition in its favour. The monopoly is not assumed injurious just because it has a large share of the market.

EU policy has altered domestic competition in a number of ways as it has forced governments to offer fewer favours to its domestic industry over its EU competitors. However, while companies and governments are subject to EU law, insofar as their actions create trade distortions, there has been little said upon how domestic competition law has responded to the changing economic environment. Therefore the key theme of this chapter is to examine the extent to which the advent of the single market has altered domestic competition law.

The advent of the single European market (SEM) and competition policy

Perhaps one of the most important watersheds in the evolution of the European economy in the twentieth century was the move of the EU towards a SEM. Such a move spelt fundamental changes in the relationships between economic operators in the EU and for the management of competition. Competition is basically managed in a two-tier system, with most firms being subject to the rules of competition at both a national and supranational level. Increasingly, in a single market, there has to be a perceptible desire for a single set of rules to govern the activities of firms within that area. Differences in rules are, over the longer term, likely to frustrate the attempts to integrate the economy of the EU. One of the major aspects of the SEM is the more vigorous enforcement of EU competition policy to ensure the so-called 'level playing field'. The notion of the 'level playing field' has been implemented by the challenges to domestic policy from EU regulation upon state aids, liberalization and public procurement to name a few. It is clear that if there is to be truly single market then national competition law should not be allowed to fragment the market.

Competition policy in the EU towards undertakings (both public and private), as opposed to government activity, is largely based upon Articles 85 and 86. In short, Article 85 seeks to prohibit those agreements between undertakings that add to the market power of firms and as a result lead to a distortion of trade between member states. Article 86 outlaws those market situations where an abuse of a dominant position by an economic operator inhibits trade between member states. There are a number of similarities between these rules that should be considered.

First, these articles only apply to an agreement or dominant position insofar as it impedes trade between member states. Therefore where an agreement has no perceptible effects on trade flows there is scope for a domestic competition policy. Secondly, these articles are a form of conduct-based regulation where it is the economic effects of an agreement, or a dominant position, that are assessed not the structure of the industry *per se*. This is important for it says, implicitly, that monopolies or cartels, for example, are not necessarily to the detriment of the effective and satisfactory functioning of the market. Thirdly, another important facet of EU competition policy is that it is largely based upon a rule of reason approach to the management of competition. In this instance each case is examined in the light of its own merits and there is no *per se* illegality of any action. However, in a number of instances, *per se* exemptions are made, most notably from Article 85.

These two Articles for many years were the basis of EU action. In more recent times they have been complemented by the EC Merger Regulation. The function of this Regulation was to give the EU a role in vetting mergers with a clear 'community dimension'. Such power over mergers was only scantily covered by Articles 85 and 86.

The operation of a two-tier policy relies upon the authorities being able to effectively distinguish between the economic effects of an operator's actions at the supranational and national level. The key issue is that, as result of the internal market programme, such a system, especially if it is based upon two differing sets of rules, becomes increasingly difficult to manage effectively. This is perhaps natural, as the spillover effects of a firm's activities grow, and its actions become inherently multinational. Over the medium to longer term it is likely that, as a result of the SEM, national competition policy becomes ever more irrelevant on a domestic level and starts to merely examine competition in a very narrowly defined relevant market. Thus differing spheres of activity for national and supranational institutions become increasingly blurred.

Therefore one of the major aspects of the SEM, for national competition policy authorities, is that it has effectively limited the scope for their activity by redefining the relevant market more broadly. That is, the market in which firms now operate is no longer purely national but European. There has also been another area of change in that the growing interdependence between the constituent economies of the EU has led many member states to examine the domestic rules governing competition. This has tended to result in either an adjustment of policy in the light of the changing economic environment (by introducing new laws to take account of these economic and institutional changes) or, at the time of writing, the proposing of such action. However, as we shall see, such action is by no means uniform across the EU. Overall the result of this, albeit limited, action has been a move by member states to, at least partially, realign domestic competition law alongside that of the EU.

Rationale for convergence

The convergence of competition policies can come in a number of forms:

1 Institutional: the assessors of competition have similar agendas and powers.
2 Technical: the rules via which firms are assessed are similar.
3 Procedural: the method of assessment, in terms of process, is harmonized.

The remainder of this chapter will concentrate upon technical convergence, that is a remodelling of the domestic laws of competition as an indication of the existence of a harmonization process.

Convergence, in this instance, is a process where competition policy at the lower (national) level, and the preferences expressed therein, starts to reflect the rules applied at the supranational level. Thus national policy starts to reflect the effects-based approach, where each assessment of market power is carried out by an apolitical institution judging the activity on a rule of reason approach. Consequently, as a result of convergence, national policy mirrors the preferences formed at the supranational level.

One of the major reasons for this move towards convergence is a recognition that competition is no longer contained to a purely national or even european theatre but to one which is increasingly global. However, since all firms, in the case of the EU, operate in a 'single market' it is therefore perhaps only rational that all firms operating in this area should be subject to the same set of rules and regulations governing their activity. For a company to be subject to two different rules and judged upon differing criteria within a single market is rather anomalous. As such, convergence enables a firm to act with a degree of certainty and predictability throughout the market.

Of course, one of the other major reasons behind the international harmonization of competition rules is that economic activities increasingly fail to respect political borders. The legacy of this is that it becomes increasingly difficult to come to a satisfactory definition of a relevant market. This is essential if competition policy is to be effectively implemented. Evidently the move towards a European, and even global, operation means the nature of the market, in which the undertaking's activities and their effects are to judged, becomes ever broader.

Such moves towards a converged set of competition polices should, on the face of it, be unsurprising as one economy effectively necessitates a single set of rules governing the operation and conduct of undertakings. Uniform, or even harmonized, rules are essential as the management of competition in terms of achieving the 'level playing field' for undertakings. This realignment of policy can occur via one of two means:

1 member states harmonizing competition policy, a process which is more in line with the current obsession with subsidiarity;

2   a single competition policy, where national policy is not harmonized but replaced with a single set of rules developed, and implemented, by a single supranational institution.

To an extent, both of these imply that the objectives of competition and industrial policy have to be the same. Implicit in the harmonization process is a recognition that no set of regulations applied at the national level will influence all the forces of competition acting within the borders of the member state. Thus for domestic competition policy to have a greater influence it may be necessary to coordinate policies between member states. To be successful this policy coordination has to overcome the following problems. First, asymmetric information; each member state has to be clear on every other state's objectives. Probably the best way to overcome this is to devise a single set of rules applicable to all states that effectively prohibits any member state indulging in self-seeking discretionary action. Secondly, incentives to compete and cheat: if the conditions above are not in place other member states have both the incentive and means to cheat and partake in an effective beggar thy neighbour policy.

However, in practice, the move towards competition harmonization is formed out of the desire for consistency on behalf of business and economic operators. In addition, the move towards harmonization is formed around an established benchmark: Articles 85 and 86. In this instance policy is not being formed in the dark and the motives of other national competition authorities should, therefore, be fairly transparent. It is perhaps justified to argue that the move towards regulatory harmonization in the EU is a market-led process, born out of a passive form of regulatory competition where, given a free market, the differences in regulation between member states converge upon those which are most favourable to business. In a multinational market, as the SEM clearly is, firms want to invest with certainty. This necessitates the establishment of a market where the rules discourage any discretionary action by the authorities which could undermine an undertakings strategy. Thus a policy of harmonization is a passive way of attracting investment into an economic space. Harmonization should, by reducing the risk of discretionary action and giving greater uniformity of rules over the entire market, ensure that the entire EU is able to benefit from the SEM. This factor is compounded by the fact that the advent of the SEM has led to some member states introducing competition laws for the first time. Therefore, it is, perhaps, only sensible that they should model their new rules upon those that have already been tried and tested at the supranational level.

Competition policy in the member states: a case of convergence?

The function of this section is to examine developments within competition policy in the member states of the EU to see if there is clear evidence of a convergence of policy.

Eire

The Irish Competition Act (1991), replaced the old Abuse of Competition Act. The reform of Irish competition law gives a clear example of where a member state has reformed national competition rules alongside those of the EU. The new rules governing competition in Eire are explicitly designed on the provisions of Articles 85 and 86. Such a move represents a fundamental shift to an effects-based competition policy moving away from its traditional assessment based upon legal form. In terms of anti-competitive agreements, the new law automatically declares null and void all those which are deemed to be a restraint upon trade. Additionally, like EU policy, the new law offers the competition authorities limited power to offer exemptions. The provision of the Competition Act upon dominant position mirrors, almost word for word, Article 86 of the Rome Treaty. In terms of mergers, there was a partial move by the competition authorities to mirror to provisions of the EC Merger Regulation, but such action was very limited. Another aspect of convergence, which has also been introduced within the Competition Act, was a reform of the procedures and methods of enforcement which are now similar to those which are undertaken within DG IV.

Belgium

Belgium is an example of another small member state that has re-modelled its domestic competition policy upon EU law with the Law on Protection of Economic Competition (1991). One of the features of this is that the new policy will use EU case law as a basis for action. In terms of collusive agreements, the meaning of undertakings is similar to the EU definition, and the context within which it is applied corresponds to its use within Article 85. In addition, Article 2 of the law contains the same non-exhaustive list of concerted practices as Article 85(1) of the Rome Treaty. This article applies to practices that restrict competition to an 'appreciable extent' according to the criteria laid out in the law. Similarly to the Rome Treaty's Article 85(3), there are exemptions allowed to the provisions of the law. The position taken by the Belgian authorities upon dominant positions (Article 3) is reformed along the lines of Article 86, and like EU law, it also gives a list of those practices that are deemed to be abusive. However, there was an intense debate as to whether predatory pricing could be seen as anti-competitive in all instances. Unlike the Irish, the Belgians have gone further in the convergence of competition law by offering a more radical reform of their competition law in terms of mergers. The reform of Belgian merger law (Article 9) is more explicitly modelled upon EU law. For example, concentration is defined along the lines of the EC regulation (4064/89) and appropriate thresholds have been set before a merger qualifies for examination. In other dimensions, there is convergence in procedural and institutional terms, where the investigative power of the competition authority is similar to that of the European commission.

Italy

The impact of the single market upon Italian Competition policy is perhaps more pronounced than in any other member state. As a direct result of the SEM, Italy, for the first time in its history, introduced a competition policy. In October 1990, the Italian authorities introduced the Law in Defence of Competition and the Market. The structure of this law deliberately reflected Articles 85 and 86. Evidently the process of convergence is inappropriate in Italy's case. Within this context convergence has been supplanted by a more explicit 'borrowing' of EU law by the Italian authorities. Thus from its introduction Italian and EU law are harmonized. Title 1 of the law explicitly mirrors EU law upon collusive practices by directly shadowing all parts of Article 85. In turn, policy on dominance, and its abuse, and those upon concentrations also mirror the respective EC law. In addition, the new Italian law has management features and procedures that are very similar to those used at the supranational level. It is sensible for the Italians, in setting up an entirely new competition policy system, to base it upon a set of rules that have been tried and tested and have a degree of familiarity and credibility with Italian business. It is also an important indicator that Italy will be a lot less tolerant of the traditional industrial structures which have tended to restrict competition within the economy. However, there has to be clarity in the jurisdiction of the policy. Thus the Italian authorities are on a very steep learning curve.

Spain

Since the original 1963 Competition law, industrial structures have changed markedly. One major factor causing this has been Spanish membership of the EU. To reflect these changes in the economic environment, the competition laws of Spain were changed in 1989 with the Protection of Competition Act. One of the major functions of the change in Spanish competition policy was to remove any possible inconsistencies between EU and Spanish law. The new law's provisions on anti-competitive practice run parallel to the provisions of the Rome treaty upon competition. Indeed, the list of prohibited practices and exemptions mirrors those which are stated in Article 85. The Spanish authorities have attempted this realignment whilst trying to ensure that its legal and economic obligations are not threatened or impeded. The realignment of competition law in Spain can only be said to have been partial as there has, as yet, been no real attempt to make policy on dominant positions more akin to Article 86 of the Rome Treaty. However there have been attempts to partially harmonize the legal framework along-side that of the EU. Overall the Spanish approach to the reform of competition law has been slow. The reforms which have, to an extent, been forced upon them reflect the changing nature of competition and the economy. However, such reformist tendencies are tempered by political and economic commit-ments to intervene, even if in a passive fashion, in the economy.

Greece

The Greek competition law of 1977 promoted a limited harmonization with the EU. It formulated a set of rules to govern competitive forces within Greece based loosely upon the relevant articles of the Rome Treaty. Articles 85 and 86 provided a template for these reforms by providing the models and guidelines for greater competition within the Greek economy. Such moves towards convergence were intensified by the reform of Greek merger regulation in 1991. However, the Greeks do not seem to possess the same zeal and enthusiasm for competition that is encapsulated in the relevant articles of the Rome Treaty. Indeed, the Greek competition authorities have, in their time, come in for a lot of criticism from the supranational authorities for their somewhat inconsistent decisions. Such policy restraints upon competition are furthered by the protection that is often afforded, by execu-tive power, to local oligopolies and monopolies. Often schemes of patronage and nepotism seem to be offered priority over freeing up the forces of competition. However, the move towards the harmonization of EU competi-tion law is in part a positive response by the Greeks to the advent of EU membership, but one cannot say that this has led the Greeks to consider the benefits of competition in the same agreeable light.

Denmark

The 1989 Competition Act was an attempt to reform Danish law in the light of the perceived internationalization of the economy. In some aspects the law has broad similarities to the EC law in that it is an effects-based policy founded upon the idea of undertakings partaking in concerted prac-tices to undermine fair competition. Similarly the overall thrust of the system is to ensure that abuses are controlled where they exist. However, there is, to a limited degree, a measure of divergence with the EU law. Perhaps the major difference is that under EU law once an agreement has been found to be against the objectives of the Treaty it is declared null and void. Such a general prohibition does not exist under Danish law as firms have the right to appeal and, in many instances, these agreements can be negotiated away with the assistance of the Competition authorities. In the case of dominant positions, like EU law, it is not about dominance *per se* but about its abuse, and then such anti-competitive action has to be proved by the competition authorities.

Netherlands

Competition policy in the Netherlands is based upon the Economic Competition Act of 1956. This act has resulted in a competition law that tends to be tolerant of restrictive practices and other forms of market distortion. The justification for this approach was based upon the relative openness of the Dutch economy to foreign competition. However, such a stance in policy led to distortions, and consequent welfare losses, especially in those sectors that were not exposed to foreign competition. Hence from the late 1980s, the Dutch set about reforming their competition policy along the lines of the EU approach. Due to the nature of the reform, and the time that it will take, the Dutch authorities have taken a twin-track approach to reform. Over the short term the plan is to reform existing policy to clamp down on restrictive practices. By 1997 this will have been replaced by an entirely new competition policy based upon the EU articles. However, due to the decision-making mechanisms being slow, the process of convergence is likely to be a gradual and evolutionary process.

Portugal

Being one of the newer member states, and having an economy that has traditionally been tightly regulated, has meant that Portugal has had to respond perhaps more sharply to the changing economic environment than other member states. The first competition law in Portugal was introduced in 1983. It was primarily an effects-based policy seeking, typically, to curtail unfavourable agreements and expressions of market power. However, due to the nature of the Portuguese economy, large sectors of the economy tended to be exempt from the full brunt of this law. In 1993, there was a revision of competition law which, largely in response to the changes in the EU, led to the number of exemptions to the laws on competition being reduced. This was further enhanced by the 1994 reforms which further shifted the policy towards an effects-based system. However, to a large extent the large state-owned monopolies are still exempt. Such similarities were enhanced by the changes to the merger regulation which stressed the broad themes with the EU Regulation. Indeed, the procedures are very similar to these which are laid out within the EU Merger Regulation. Despite this lurch towards freer market forces within the economy, it is fair to say that competition policy has not been embraced as warmly as perhaps Portugal's EU partners would have liked. Suspect exemptions remain: most notably restrictive trade practices are not deemed anti-competitive if they increase the competitiveness of the participants. In the case of Portugal, it is a bit misleading to talk about convergence as such because policy has tended to be formed in the light of EU experience and has not been remodelled upon supranational policy.

France

The French, with their traditional interventionist stance, have often been in conflict with the supranational competition authorities, for example in the case of state aids. Nevertheless, in response to the internal market, its stance has been softened somewhat as the nature of French economy has changed. In some instances, the French have fought to keep market distortions in place, most notably in the case of the car market. However, there has been a gradual softening of their interventionist stance which has led to a convergence with the laws of the EU. In part the laws of competition in France are modelled upon Germany, by, for example, the existence of an independent competition authority. Where reform has occurred, French law has been made more compatible with EU law but has not really converged as such. Its traditional attitudes expressed in modern conventions have really prevented that. One area where the French have acted is in those areas where state intervention has explicitly tempered the forces of competition. To a large extent French competition law has changed as EU directives have been brought within it. Overall, the policy is an effects-based regime in that the remit of the Competition Council is to examine the abuses of market power. This it does by examining it in terms of a familiar EU term: the relevant market. The big change in French competition law came since the mid-1980s, as at least a partial response to the SEM, where there have been moves to deregulate the economy. These moves were aided by a shift to a more effects-based system away from the usual proscription based regime. Overall, the response of French competition law to the advent of the SEM has resulted in a shift of emphasis in its overarching objectives. Competition policy is now less of a complement to a broader industrial policy and emphasises more of a market-based approach to economic management.

Germany

Policy in Germany, like any other member state, reflects the economic tradition of the state. One of the most notable features of the German competition law is that it is much more tolerant of cartels than would be expected in those instances where there was a more forceful application of market-based rules established along the lines developed by the EU. The German competition rules, especially where market dominance is concerned, are much more form-based than those established at the supranational level. In this case, dominance is based upon actual and potential competition. Abuse does not have to be seen to make the firm subject to the rules of the system. However, strong links and power over other enterprises is a factor that will influence the authorities so the effects-based regime is not totally ruled out. Generally, if a firm has one-third of the market it comes under the scrutiny of the competition authorities. Therefore policy is about stopping excessive concentration and not merely controlling the abuse of dominance. In the late 1980s there were minor amendments to German competition law to bring it more in line with the EU provisions. The Act against Restraints upon Competition (1990: fifth amendment) responded to EU law by extending competition to previously excluded industries, most notably the utility sectors. There was also a shift from the form-based system, as merger control could be extended to mergers/concentrations below the 25 per cent threshold, in those instances where clear evidence of the restrictive influence of the activity can be proven.

United Kingdom

By and large, the UK has a form-based competition policy system. That is to say, undertakings become subject to UK law when they reach a certain size or market share. Generally a figure of 25 per cent is used as the benchmark where there is assumed to be enough power to exert an influence over the market. When these firms are referred to the Monopolies and Merger Commission they tend to be assessed on competition concerns only; other industrial policy concerns are often only incidental to the decision. In terms of anti-competitive practices, there has been some general convergence with EU policy with the 1980 Competition Act. However this was relatively minor to the overall functioning of the policy. There have been attempts to reform the competition law of the UK in the late 1980s/early 1990s with the aim of bringing the system more in line with Articles 85 and 86. The first of these was the 1988 proposal to reform restrictive trade practices policy so that the system would be similar to Article 85. Despite a White Paper being published there has been little action by the UK government to put these proposals into legislation. In 1992 there was a Green Paper on Abuse of Market Power, where one of the three options was to move explicitly to a policy modelled on Article 86. After a period of consultation the decision was taken to reform existing law and not move towards the EU model. Thus despite two White papers there has been no real overhaul of UK competition law. The law, at the moment, offers no real set of sanctions for non-compliance. As a consequence of the UK's government policy to only consider, and not implement, reform along the EU lines many firms are subject to differing sets of rules. There is a great concern that the UK competition policy is too discretionary and allows politicians too great a say in the outcome of the case; the final say is with the President of the Board of Trade. In this instance the development of an apolitical institution, developed along the lines of DG IV, can be justified. Evidently over the last decade the UK has missed a good opportunity to overhaul its system.

Competition law and the new Member States

To an extent, the members of Efta should already be accustomed to the Competition laws of the EU as these were the basis for the respective rules laid out in the EEA treaty; Articles 53 to 60. Article 53 of the EEA treaty is a direct mirror of Article 85 with each of the relevant sections directly mirroring its counterpart in the Rome Treaty. That is, for Article 53(1) read Article 85(1) and so on. Article 60 of the EEA treaty deals with the same kind of exemptions that are allowed under EU law. Article 56 concentrates upon the abuse of dominant position and is a replicate of Article 86. Annex XIV of the Treaty applies the EC merger regulation to the EEA agreement with minor modifications to reflect the broader market that it covers. Consequently, competition law within the EEA runs parallel to the policy of the EFTA states and the EC. However, the purpose of this section is to examine the extent to which the development of the EEA rules, and the possibility of impending membership of the EU, has led to a reform in competition policies of the new EC states.

Austria

The Austrian economy has traditionally been tightly regulated with cartels generally being tolerated, high tariffs walls being erected and large subsidies given to producers. The desire to be part of the broader process of European integration has created the political momentum to reform competition policy. Thus far, policy has been slow to respond to these challenges. There have been cuts in subsidies and there is a gradual opening up of the markets as the number of legalized cartels is reduced. Clearly more needs to be done.

Finland

Finland has largely an effects-based system, with there being a great deal of flexibility in the rules and only a limited *per se* prohibition of certain practices. There has been a limited amount of harmonization as a result of the EEA agreement. Most notably, it has led to an extension and partial re-modelling of competition policy. However, within the Finnish economy as a whole, a significant number of artificial barriers to entry remain, due to excessive regulation. The EEA has changed the law upon foreign ownership and there has been an extension of the number of illegal horizontal cartels but this is only a small part of the general overhaul that is required. There has been an explicit attempt at harmonization; however, it remains incomplete, especially in the case of mergers.

Sweden

Within the Swedish economy, there has been a greater shift towards the freeing of competitive forces than in the other Efta states. In part this was a reflection of the belief that it was the regulation of market forces that was leading to the uncompetitiveness of the Swedish economy. Traditionally, competition policy is judged on broad 'public interest' grounds not upon the desirability of increasing competition in its own right. The Swedish system is generally an effects-based system established on the rule of reason approach, though there are limited *per se* prohibitions. The OECD claims that the abuse-based and public interest system has tended to encourage the formation of cartels. The signing of the EEA agreement has proved a very powerful force in the evolution of Swedish competition law. To this extent, in 1992, the Swedish authorities introduced a new competition law that is almost identical to the EU laws. The shift is towards encouraging competition *per se* and less emphasis on public interest concerns. Also there is a move to prohibit all collusive agreements that distort competition. Such moves have been mirrored by the development of procedures for the implementation and enforcement of competition law based on EU practices. The new Swedish merger regulation is also based on the EU equivalent. However, the Swedish regulation is less strict; to stop a merger the authorities must show that competition will suffer.

Across the Efta member states there has been a limited degree of convergence with the EU policies with the Swedes going the furthest. Clearly, in many of these states, there is generally a greater tolerance of competitive distortion than there is among EU member states. It is apparent that there is a shift in the rules of competition as these states respond to the Europeanisation of their economies and to the challenges of membership. Clearly if they are to become members of the EU trade block, based upon the 'level playing field', then domestic industries and their treatment will have to adjust as many of the favours they receive are inconsistent with such a shift.

Conclusions: a move towards a single competition policy for Europe

Across the EU a trend can be seen in the development of competition policy. As a result of member states accepting the stricter enforcement of EU competition law and more intense competition *per se* there is a process of convergence or remodelling which is, by and large, based upon the rules which are applied at the supranational level. At first sight such a move should not be surprising as the nature of markets and industrial sectors change as they become increasingly globalized. However, the pattern of convergence across the member states is not uniform as the greatest leaps towards convergence is among the smallest member states. The larger member states, most notably the UK and Germany, seem to have done very little to seek to realign their competition laws. In the UK, the advent of the single market seems to have prompted little more than a discussion and nothing, in terms of concrete action, has really occurred. In Germany there seems to have been little more than a tinkering with the existing rules. In an evolving single market the attitude of not fixing something which does not seem to be broken is inappropriate. National competition laws were designed to meet a certain set of conditions and must prove malleable as these conditions change. In short, if laws are inappropriate change them.

Over time there can be a clear justification for believing the national policies will become increasingly obsolescent. As markets become increasingly European then it will become more and more difficult to isolate those activities which have a purely national effect. If these effects are difficult to isolate there seems to be little point in there being any national policy. Maintaining national competition policy in such instances may indeed lead to coordination problems and an ignoring of spillover effects. Such scenarios are likely to inhibit the proper allocation of resources which lies at the heart of the move towards the internal market. Of course on a broader scale, as globalization takes hold, there may evolve a stronger global policy to manage these changes. As such, national policy may become largely irrelevant as EU policy converges on the global norm. Naturally such a situation is merely conjecture at this point in time but the changing nature of competition and business inevitably creates the need to respond with vision.

Selected references

European Competition Law Review
Hay, D. (1993) Competition Policy. *Oxford Review of Economic Policy*, Vol. 9, No. 2.

Organization for Economic Cooperation and Development (1993/94) Economic Surveys (various).
Smith, A., *et.al. Competition Policy Research: Where do we stand?* Centre for Economic Policy Research.

Questions

1 Examine, within the context of this chapter, what you understand by the process of convergence.
2 'A single market requires a single competition policy.' Critically examine this statement.
3 Explain why some member states of the EU have decided to copy the rules of competition applied at the supranational level.

6   Social policy and competition

Campbell McPherson and Sue Stacey

Introduction

In December 1993, the European Commission presented its long-awaited White Paper, *Growth, Competitiveness, Employment – the Challenges and Ways Forward into the 21st Century*[1] which sought to tackle Europe's growing unemployment problem. The document, some of whose conclusions and recommendations are considered later, constitutes a further stage in the evolution of European policy towards a balance between social and market forces within the European Union.

This chapter concentrates on the relationship between competitiveness and the requirements of the 'Social Charter' (and the Social Protocol of the Maastricht Treaty which later gave legally binding status to the Charter) in the light of arguments put forward by the UK government and business. This is not, therefore, an exhaustive analysis of all of the issues involved in the competitiveness–social market trade-off. In the UK, arguments about the balance between improved social provision and competitiveness have focused almost exclusively on the assumed negative impact of the former on the latter.

There is, in fact, considerable controversy among economists as to which factor(s) are most significant in producing an environment in which goods are produced 'competitively' – the concept of 'competitive advantage'. In particular, issues such as the impact of exchange rate changes on competitiveness should not be neglected. The upgrading of skills, production processes and attempts to reposition industry through the production of higher value-added products also play a key role in competitiveness but, because they have not figured prominently in the UK arguments, have not been given the consideration in this chapter which they might otherwise deserve.

The Social Charter and the SEM

The signing of the Single European Act (SEA) in 1986, and the consequent creation of the single European market (SEM), was intended to complete the Common Market as envisaged by the Treaty of Rome in 1957. Central to this, and to the theory underlying economic integration, was the principle that individual companies and nations should compete on the basis of a 'level playing field' (LPF). Gone would be advantages resulting from national protectionism and different technical standards. The Europe of the SEM would be one in which successful sales resulted from superior quality and/ or design or lower costs for comparable products. This was to be the basis for the much vaunted:

> ... large market without frontiers (which) because of its size and because of the possibilities it offers for scientific, technical and commercial cooperation, gives a unique opportunity to our industry to improve its competitiveness.[2].

At this level the SEM seemed to be concerned only with a Europe based upon free movement of factors of production – a market of market forces in fact. It was this vision of Europe which appealed to, and which was seized upon by the administrations of, Margaret Thatcher and John Major.

However, both Socialist and Christian Democratic parties in Europe were generally committed to the concept of social welfare and accepted the role of the state in attempting to achieve this objective. There was thus substantial demand on mainland Europe for measures which would ensure that the completed SEM would balance increased competition and the protection of living and working conditions. Hence, when the President of the European Commission, Jacques Delors, talked of the need for the SEM to have '... a social as well as an economic dimension (which) must lead to a more unified Community'[3], he was reflecting the majority view of the mainland members of the European Community. In the UK, however, the government and hostile sections of the media portrayed the Social Charter as an attempt to reintroduce socialism into the UK through the back door.

Central to the above concerns of mainland Europe was the possibility that the SEM could become a 'hunting ground' for companies roaming Europe in search of the lowest wages and social costs, such as sick pay, that they could find; a phenomenon which rapidly became known as 'social dumping'. This would put unacceptable pressure on countries which afforded higher standards of protection for their workforce to reduce their standards.

Because of these concerns over the prospect of social dumping, the Commission responded by proposing the Social Charter which enshrined minimum social rights for Europe's workforce. This document was adopted by 11 member states in Strasbourg in December 1989. Included in the original proposals[4], were measures to establish:

- Improved living and working conditions which '...will be brought about by an upward approximation of those conditions and which will concern the organization and flexibility of working hours, in particular by establishing a maximum working week ...'

- The concept of fair remuneration.
- The 'Right to Social Protection' including the right to social assistance and 'adequate means of subsistence' for those excluded from the labour market and, in particular, the elderly.
- The right to freedom of association and collective bargaining. This included not only the right to belong to a union and the right to strike but also placed a central emphasis on the concept of 'social dialogue'.

Central to this concept of social dialogue was inclusion in the proposal of:

- The right to information, consultation and worker participation.

These proposals met considerable opposition from the UK government. Other member states were equally insistent that they be given legally binding status through incorporation into the Maastricht Treaty – the stage of political, legal, economic and social integration which followed from the Single European Act. But, in order to obtain UK assent to Maastricht, the UK was allowed to 'opt out' from the Protocol attached to the Treaty which was concerned with social issues. So it was that, when the heads of state signed the European Union Treaty on 7 February 1992, it contained an 'Agreement on Social Policy Concluded Between the Member States of the European Community with the exception of the United Kingdom of Great Britain and Northern Ireland'.

The Social Charter and the UK

The intentions of the Charter are clearly summarized in Article 1 of the Social Protocol which states:

> The Community and Member States shall have as their objectives the promotion of employment, improved living and working conditions, proper social protection, dialogue between management and labour, the development of human resources with a view to lasting high employment and the combating of exclusion. To this end the Community and the Member States shall implement measures which take account of the diverse forms of national practices, in particular in the field of contractual relations, and the need to maintain the competitiveness of the Community economy.

On the face of it there appears little radical content here, given that the UK government also recognizes the importance of lasting employment and the problem of exclusion. 'Exclusion' is the term used by the Commission to describe groups such as the unemployed, ethnic minorities, the disabled, etc. who have difficulties fully participating in economic life.

The Article continues in an uncontroversial manner by committing the Community and member states to the implementation of measures in a manner which takes account of the diversity of national practices, especially in the field of contractual relations, and which specifically recognizes the need to maintain the Community's economic competitiveness.

Also in line with UK policy is Article 6 of the Treaty Protocol which reconfirms the EU's commitment to equal pay for men and women, thereby reinforcing the legal status quo in Britain. Article 2.2, which commits the Council of Ministers to the adoption of directives which avoid imposing administrative, financial and legal conditions which would hold back the creation and development of small and medium size undertakings, is also fully in harmony with current British thinking.

Despite these assurances and policy similarities, the UK government feared that the policies to achieve these objectives would impose additional costs on companies thus rendering them uncompetitive on world markets. Of particular concern was the emphasis on improved living and working conditions and proper social protection. It was feared that, although not specifically articulated in the Charter, this would result in the development of European-wide policies with regard to minimum wages, pensions and the like. This would not only increase the direct cost of labour but also the indirect cost to employers (indirect costs are those costs associated with the hiring of labour which do not constitute the direct wage payment received by the employee).

Social protection is normally funded via direct taxes and social security contributions. Any increase in such protection resulting from the social policy of the European Union will therefore result in higher direct taxes and contributions. The UK government believes that the resulting reduction in take-home pay will reduce incentives to work. Increased unemployment benefits and other related social assistance will serve to exacerbate this problem as those out of work may find themselves worse off if they accept a job offer. This is due to the 'implicit marginal rate of tax' which consists of all the taxes and contributions that a previously unemployed person will have to pay on accepting a job, plus all of the social benefits that will consequently be lost. Thus many unemployed people could find themselves caught in the, so-called 'poverty trap', becoming permanently reliant on social assistance.

But perhaps of greater significance are the foreseen increases in employer social security contributions. High employer contributions increase indirect labour cost which it is argued would severely weaken the ability of British companies to compete with international firms not facing such costs. Ultimately, it is argued, this would result in high domestic unemployment and a worsening of the balance of payments, due to an increasing dependence on imported goods and services.

Further worries centred around elements of the Charter which legalized employee involvement in decision making through the creation of Works Councils which exist to inform and consult employees and trade unions. This, it was feared, would put further upward pressure on direct labour costs, again reducing competitiveness. Other disadvantages anticipated from strong unions were interference with the 'management's right to manage', and reduced efficiency through demands for better working conditions and 'interference with the decision making of management'.

This contrasts strongly with the situation in mainland Europe where Works Councils and strong trade unions are comparatively common, either by virtue of legislation or by the belief that trade union involvement in the overall management process improves industrial relations and increases the commitment of the workforce. It is not unusual for the workforce to have a legally guaranteed role in economic affairs in the rest of Europe and there is frequently the concept that trade unions are 'social partners'. In France, Italy and Germany, such rights are enshrined in the constitution and are therefore extremely difficult to change. For example, Article 9(3) of the German Federal Constitution guarantees the right of association of workers to improve working conditions, while labour laws such as the Co-determination Act (Mitbestimmungsgesetz) guarantee considerable powers for trade unions in company policy development.

The Charter also gave the European Parliament and the Economic and Social Committee a role in the formulation of policy affecting working conditions. This was considered politically unacceptable to the UK government due to the Socialist majority of the European Parliament and the 'interventionist' inclinations of the Economic and Social Committee.

Thus the Charter was seen as being both economically and politically unacceptable to the UK government. It appeared to pose the threat of undoing policies which had reduced trade union protection since 1979.

The economic basis for and impact of social protection

The fundamental reasons for social protection are to enable members of a community to achieve at least a minimum standard of living, to have access to health care when necessary and to be assured of a reasonable standard of living should they suffer the loss of their usual income stream. Such a loss of income may result from unemployment, old age, having children or illness. Social protection therefore removes many of the social risks of the market place.

A further argument for social protection is the existence of externalities. Examples of external diseconomies arising from inadequate social protection include the increased crime associated with poverty and unemployment and the spread of contagious dizeases due to a lack of availability of health care for the impoverished. Thus social protection not only benefits those in receipt of such protection but also spreads advantages to the rest of the community.

It can be argued that the benefits from social protection can be achieved equally well by a system of self-protection, whereby individuals save part of their income to provide economic security for themselves. However, there are numerous problems with this. First, it can only apply to individuals who earn sufficient income in order to save. Secondly, it is difficult for individuals to access accurately how much protection they are likely to need and thirdly, some people may not think long-term and therefore fail to make any sort of provision for future risks whatsoever.

Due to these problems, managing risk collectively may be the only effective way of making sure everyone is adequately protected. This is achieved by forcing individuals to make sufficient provision through a system of income tax. It also enables those that cannot afford individual protection, by either having insufficient income or through being a high risk, to be subsidized by others who are more fortunate.

Economies of scale are also an economic argument for collective risk management as information costs for those covered can be substantially reduced. Additionally, far fewer institutions will be involved with a collective social scheme thus allowing administrative and marketing costs to diminish.

By opting out of the Social Charter, it is clear that the UK government foresee any advantages to be achieved through increased social protection being by far outweighed by the perceived disadvantages. That is to say, as social protection tends to be financed through the taxation of labour any increase in such protection will, most likely, lead to an increase in the relative cost of labour. This, *ceteris paribus*, will lead to a reduction in the competitiveness of firms now facing higher costs and a consequent reduction in the use of labour, hence increasing unemployment.

Although it is difficult to provide an analytical framework in which to test these assertions, some comparisons can be made between countries. Thus, the next section attempts to assess whether there is a direct linkage between high social costs and competitiveness as measured by the economic success of individual countries.

Direct and indirect wage costs and economic success

The UK government and business argument on this aspect of the Charter is crystal clear – the Charter is portrayed as an overt threat to business because of its potential for creating additional costs. This might occur because of the potential inherent in the Charter to address issues such as minimum wages, thereby increasing direct wage costs, or issues such as minimum pensions, maternity/paternity rights etc. which would raise indirect wage costs. As indicated above, the UK government and employers' organizations such as the Confederation of British Industry (CBI) and the Institute of Directors (IOD) believe that the near-automatic result of this is an increase in unit labour costs resulting in increased unemployment, a worsening balance of payments and a decline in the growth of GDP as economies stagger under additional costs and bureaucracy.

If this argument is correct, we would expect to find a clear correlation between social costs and competitiveness, as reflected by unemployment levels, balance of payments and growth of real GDP. Table 6.1 illustrates the considerable variations in direct and indirect labour costs which existed in key OECD economies in 1992.

Table 6.1 *Direct and indirect manufacturing labour costs 1992 in DM per hour*

	Direct costs	Indirect costs	Total	Indirect as % direct
W. Germany	22.5	19.5	42.0	45.2
Italy	15.9	17.0	32.9	51.7
France	14.6	13.2	27.8	47.5
Spain	14.1	8.8	22.9	38.4
UK	15.9	6.9	22.8	30.3
US	17.9	6.9	24.8	27.8
Japan	22.8	7.2	30.0	24.0

Source: CBI evidence given to the House of Lords Select Committee on the European Communities on 7 December 1993
Figures for indirect labour costs includes holiday payments

Accepting the UK premise that higher wage costs lead to higher unemployment, the figures would obviously suggest that, on the basis of total wage costs, the UK should be in a position to beat European and international competition and that Germany should be in severe economic difficulties with high levels of unemployment.

Table 6.2 sets out levels of total unemployment and average percentage wage increases in selected countries. From this, it is apparent that there is no direct correlation between total labour costs and unemployment, or between wage increases and unemployment. The UK, for example, had the lowest total labour costs in the sample, but it had one of the highest rates of unemployment over the period 1988–1992. However, looking at the average yearly wage increases over the same period it appears that the UK experienced the greatest rise of the sample, with an average increase of 8.5 per cent. This, it might be argued, could be responsible for the high unemployment and may justify the opposition to the Social Charter. However, average annual wage increases in France over the period were considerably lower at 3.7 per cent, yet they too suffered relatively high rates of unemployment (9.6 per cent). There must therefore be other factors that influence the level of employment.

Table 6.2 *Average unemployment in selected countries compared with average annual manufacturing wage increase 1988–1992*

	USA	Japan	Germany*	France	Italy	UK
Unemployment (%)	6.0	2.2	5.1	9.6	10.5	8.2
Annual % wage increase	2.6	3.7	4.2	3.7	6.1	8.5

Source: Unemployment data – *Economic Outlook*, OECD, December 1993, Table A19
Wage data – *Economic Survey of France*, OECD, 1994, Appendix
* Excludes the former GDR

Ceteris paribus higher wage costs should result in a loss of competitiveness which, given the limited ability of exchange rates to restore such competitiveness, will be reflected by a worsening of a country's balance of trade. A comparison of the data from Table 6.1 and 6.2 with the data from Table 6.3, which summarizes averages trade balances for 1983–1987 and 1988–1992, reveals once again that there is little sign of a direct relationship between total wage costs, wage increases and competitiveness.

Table 6.3 *Average trade balances (US$ billions) – 1983–1992*

	USA	Japan	German	France	Italy	UK
1983–87	– 121.3	+ 64.2	+ 40.2	– 5.9	– 2.1	– 9.3
1988–92	– 104.22	+ 94.14	+ 57.5	– 7.5	– 0.2	– 30.7

Source: *Economic Outlook*, December 1993, OECD, Table ABBE

This analysis can be taken further. Table 6.4 shows the average percentage growth of real GDP over the periods 1983–1987 and 1988–1992. Japan and Germany clearly stand out as having experienced the greatest growth of real GDP over the periods shown yet neither had the lowest total labour costs of the sample. In fact, as can be seen from Table 6.1, Germany

99

actually had the highest total labour costs and a large share of these costs (45.2%) were indirect. Again it becomes apparent that there is no simple correlation between total wage costs and economic success.

Table 6.4 *Growth of real GDP 1983–1992 (annual % change)*

	USA	Japan	Germany	France	Italy	UK
1983–1987	3.86	3.74	2.08	1.74	2.46	3.72
1988–1992	1.9	4.2	3.92	2.68	2.26	0.84

Source: *Economic Outlook*, December 1993, OECD, Table A1

In summary, total wage costs in the UK in 1992 were lower than those to be found in any other country of the sample. If the UK government is correct, the UK should have experienced greater economic success than its main competitors. However, average UK unemployment of 8.2 per cent between 1988 and 1992 was among the highest in the sample. Over the same period, the UK's average trade balance was one of the worst with an average deficit of $30.7 billion and the UK's growth rate was the lowest in the sample at 0.84 per cent. The higher growth experienced by the UK between 1983 and 1987 does not necessarily add credence to the UK's position: a large element of this growth can be explained by both the growth in North Sea oil production and by recovery from the substantial negative growth experienced in the early 1980s.

By contrast, high wage Germany has had considerably more success – as indicated in the figures above – when measured, for example, by levels of economic growth and employment. This clearly illustrates that the issue is more complex than a mere 'wage cost/competitiveness' correlation.

Minimum wages

The issue of minimum wages, an area in which the UK has gradually been removing the statutory regulation which once existed in the form of industry-specific Wages Councils, has stirred controversy. The UK government and employers were fearful that the Social Charter would result in the introduction of a European minimum – sometimes described as a 'social' wage, which would establish a minimum hourly rate at a certain percentage of the national average. Such a policy runs counter to British insistence on labour market flexibility and the belief that:

> Employees should be rewarded for their individual contribution to the success of the enterprise. Their pay should reflect performance and the commitment and

Social policy and competition

skills which they bring to their job. Rates of pay should recognize the value of their skills within the labour market.[5].

A number of member states of the Union have legal minimum wages. If the British position is correct, it should be substantiated by a degree of correlation between national economic performance and the level of minimum and 'typical' wages. Taking white collar minimum wages, the situation shown in Table 6.5 existed in 1991.

Table 6.5

	Minimum wage (French Francs per month)	Year of legislation
Holland	6330	1968
Belgium	6280	1975
Luxembourg	5920	1986
France	5400	1950
Spain	2890	1963
Greece	2160	1982
Portugal	1580	1975

Source: TEF 93/94, French Government Statistical Service, 1994

If one then compares the minimum salary in these countries with levels of unemployment, the situation shown in Table 6.6 existed.

Table 6.6

	Ranking by minimum wage	Unemployment (%)
Netherlands	1	7.0
Belgium	2	7.5
Luxembourg	3	1.6
France	4	9.5
Spain	5	16.3
Greece	6	7.7
Portugal	7	4.1

1 = highest, 7 = lowest minimum wage in French Francs. All figures refer to 1991
Source: TEF 93/94, French Government Statistical Service

The above figures again appear to suggest that there is no clear, direct correlation between direct wage costs and unemployment. It is also interesting, in the light of UK arguments, that UK unemployment was 9.1 per cent in 1991 – that is, higher than in the above countries (bar Spain and France) which all, unlike the UK, have legal minimum wages.

Indirect costs

Clearly, direct labour costs are but one element in total employment costs and any consideration of the role of labour in decreasing or increasing competitiveness within the Union must also consider the issue of indirect costs. These include not only employers' payments in terms of pensions, sickness benefits, etc., but also holiday entitlement. This is an area in which the Social Charter has a potential impact as it offers, *inter alia*, the prospect of minimum entitlement in terms of holidays and pensions and a maximum in terms of hours of work. An analysis of these issues again suggests a far from clear link between the burden of indirect costs and national competitiveness.

An examination of the current situation regarding the working year (see Table 6.7 below) reveals once more that there is no evidence to suggest that a more generous attitude towards workers' employment conditions automatically results in an economy becoming more successful. Once again, one can identify the apparent paradox that countries such as Germany have been economically successful with 42 days holidays per annum.

Table 6.7 Average entitlement to holidays and public holidays

	Annual leave	*Public holidays*	*Total*
Germany	30	12	42
France	25	11	36
Italy	31	9	40
UK	27	8	35
Spain	22	14	38
Holland	36	7	43
Belgium	20	11	31
Denmark	26	8	34
Greece	22	9	31
Portugal	22	14	36
Ireland	20	8	28
USA	12	11	23
Japan	11	14	25

Indeed, the figures for Germany tend to underestimate the actual levels of leisure in that certain social rights are virtually unique to Germany and do not therefore generally appear in international comparisons of working conditions. Specific examples of this can be seen in both the 'kuur' system and in the length of working life of many Germans. With reference to the former, consideration might be given to the DM 2.5 billion paid for additional 'health holidays', and which are additional to the normal holiday entitlement as indicated above. The average German's working life is also shorter than that prevailing in the UK. The average German university graduate does not start work until his/her late 20s or early 30s and retires before the age of 60. Germany has the shortest working life in Europe, but a 30 year or so working life is not uncommon in many mainland European societies. It appears, until now, to have made little difference to economic competitiveness.

Competitiveness and growth

So far it has been shown that there is no clear direct relationship between the level of total labour costs (both direct and indirect) and economic success, as measured by growth of GDP, unemployment levels and trade balances. This is not to say, however, that labour costs are an unimportant consideration for business. There can be no doubt that labour costs consti-tute an important element of European competitiveness, but it is clear from the evidence shown that there must also be other factors that have to be taken into account.

Unit labour costs (i.e. labour cost per unit of production) are a far better indication of competitiveness than average labour cost per worker. In other words, productivity levels per worker are of paramount importance. High productivity levels can compensate for high labour costs and can therefore play a vital role in maintaining competitive advantage. Therefore, the emphasis of the European Union must be on increasing productivity levels in order to be able to sustain higher levels of social protection without jeopardising the competitiveness of its members.

Productivity growth

There are many factors that contribute to productivity growth, including:

- Levels of investment.
- Technological advances.
- The use of resources such as energy and raw materials.
- Size and skills of the labour force.
- Management skills.

103

In order to achieve the objectives laid out in the Social Charter (i.e. improved living and working conditions, proper social protection and the promotion of employment), it is essential that there are complementary policies to influence overall levels of productivity growth throughout the Union. The White Paper on Growth, Competitiveness and Employment made some recommendations to the European Council with regard to this. Of particular relevance was the recommendation to promote non-physical, knowledge-based investment: training, research and general know-how, therefore, would become the top priority of any general investment policy. A further recommendation was for a redistribution of the taxation burden so as to reduce the tax on the use of labour and to increase the cost of the use of natural resources. The aim of this is to enable the Union to achieve sustainable growth in the future without disastrous consequences for the environment or any increases in unemployment.

These measures may well help to reduce unit labour costs overall throughout the Community. However, it may be considerably easier for some firms to achieve productivity improvements than others. In particular, small and medium sized enterprises (SMEs) may find this more difficult. The next section will explore this problem in more depth.

The Social Charter and SMES

SMEs (firms with fewer than 500 employees) employ more than two-thirds of the Community workforce and generate approximately two-thirds of Community turnover. Thus they are considered to have the greatest potential for creating employment. In view of this, it is important that the European Union creates an environment in which SMEs can flourish. Otherwise a valuable source of potential growth will be lost.

The Social Charter will undoubtedly increase the cost of labour to some firms. As has been argued above, increases in productivity are necessary to compensate for any such cost increases if a competitive advantage is to be maintained. As it is generally large companies that can most easily afford to undertake additional investment and R&D it will, therefore, be these larger firms that which will be most readily able to meet the challenge of improving productivity levels. Therefore, any increase in costs of production may severely reduce the ability of SMEs to compete and hence survive.

So, despite the lack of clear linkage between wage costs and successful competitiveness outlined earlier, many individual businesses – particularly small and medium ones – live in a short-term environment in which the smallest difference in unit costs may make the difference between success or bankruptcy.

While the completion of the SEM was clearly intended to increase competition through, for example, the removal of trade barriers, the Social Charter implies the creation of a base line below which increased competition would not be permitted to drive wages nor negate workers' employment conditions. However, the Commission has recognized the sensitivity of SMEs to additional costs and the White Paper commits the Union to:

> Identifying and alleviating the constraints of a tax, social security, administrative, financial or other nature that hamper the establishment or continued operation of SMEs[6].

Opting out of the Social Charter

Although the UK has secured an opt-out from the Social Charter, this has not meant that it has escaped all of the legislation in this area. One reason for this is that some social measures can be introduced via directives under the Treaty of Rome rather than through the Social Protocol of the Maastricht Treaty. This requires only a majority vote to pass legislation, as opposed to the unanimous vote required under the Maastricht Treaty.

A clear example of the reach of EU social policy was demonstrated when the UK opposed the introduction of the Working Time Directive which was intended – in its simplest form – to establish a 48 hour maximum working week throughout the Union. The UK argued that this would impose extra rigidities for business, would reduce employers' willingness to take on labour, and possibly result in upwards pressure on wages as a compensation for lost overtime.

Despite its opt-out, the UK was forced to face this issue when it was introduced as health and safety legislation under the Single European Act rather than under Maastricht. After negotiations, the UK secured a compromize by which it was obliged to introduce the legislation after 10 years rather than the 3 year period which applied to other Union members. However, the compromize also permitted UK workers who wished to work more than 48 hours to do so: those who did not would theoretically have the protection of the law. Workers in the UK would also have the right to a minimum of 3 weeks paid holiday for the first 6 years after the formal adoption of the directive and 4 weeks thereafter, bringing the UK into line with other EU countries. The legality of this directive is being challenged by the UK government in the meantime, as it claims that the Commission is abusing its power by introducing the directive as a health and safety measure.

The UK's 'opt-out' is also being undermined by the actions of some major companies. Around 100 such companies are now likely to introduce Works Councils in the UK. This is because the specific provision of the Works

Council directive legally enforces companies to set up these Councils if they have at least 1000 workers outside the UK and more than 150 in two or more member countries. Thus, the UK's opt-out is already losing credibility. However, the opt-out clause will still be used regarding areas such as the right to three months paternity leave and giving equal employment rights to both full- and part-time employees.

But, Britain may face a greater threat as Brussels has warned that it is seeking to end the opt-out and press ahead with European Employment laws. Padraig Flynn (the Social Affairs Commissioner) highlighted the importance of a single legal framework for all members of the Union when he said: 'The way forward is to have everybody playing with the same football[7]. The UK responded by threatening a legal challenge.

Conclusion

The impact of social protection and the Social Charter on competitiveness and employment has been the source of much debate and disagreement. While it is difficult to provide an analytical framework to examine the exact impact, it is possible to make some comparisons between countries.

The evidence shown in this study establishes that there is no clear link between high levels of social protection (leading to higher wage costs) and loss of competitiveness and employment. Countries that have achieved the most economic success have often been those with the highest levels of social protection. Germany is a clear example of this.

However, it is not possible to dismiss the impact of high wage costs on competitiveness on the basis of such an analysis. There are a number of aspects that affect firms' abilities to compete and wage costs are certainly one of them. But there are many other factors to take into account, such as productivity and quality and employee/management relations. Undoubtedly a social protection scheme which is partly or totally funded through employer contributions will increase the indirect cost of labour. This could, in theory, weaken a firm's ability to compete. However, it may also have the effect of increasing productivity levels by improving employer/employee relations. Greater employee consultation through Works Councils could also boost productivity.

Given the enormous differences in wage costs between developed countries and LDCs, it is unrealistic to believe that the European Union can compete internationally on the basis of wage costs. Therefore it is imperative that competitiveness is maintained via increased productivity and quality levels. Thus the White Paper on Growth, Competitiveness and Employment stresses the need to compete on the basis of quality and technology innovation:

Differences in worker wages alone can be misleading. It is true that modern technology spreads much faster and more easily than in the past to different areas of the world. But poorer education, lower skill levels, lower levels of capital investment overall and inadequate infrastructure can offset the possible advantage to be derived from low wages.[8].

Particularly emphasized is the importance of training and the upgrading of skills to raise the stock of human capital. If this can be achieved, then the higher wage costs anticipated as a result of the Social Charter can be fully offset by higher productivity levels.

The arguments about the Social Charter are important therefore. But, at one level, they are more convincingly important for politico-social rather than for economic reasons. The Social Charter poses a threat to the economic and social model which the UK government has developed since 1979. In this model, there is no role for 'social partnership', the right to training or the right to consultation. In this Anglo-Saxon model, workers are units which have to adapt to market forces. By contrast, it is generally accepted that traditional German policy – upon which the Social Charter is largely based – is more heavily dependent upon the concept of 'social partnership'.

Many non-UK companies fear the development of a Union in which individual members, such as the UK, can opt out from specific policies – an à la carte Europe. This not only may give a perceived advantage to the country which has opted out, but also creates uncertainties and instabilities because it destroys the concept of a level playing field – which is central to the SEM – and which may encourage the development of special pleading by national governments. What is at stake, therefore, in the Social Charter issue, is not an argument which has a clear economic answer but represents a choice for Europe between different models of economic development. The model which underpins the Social Charter has, so far, proved the more successful in yielding economic growth and prosperity than the UK alternative.

Bibliography

Commission of the European Communities (1993) *Social Protection in Europe.* Green Paper (1993) *European Social Policy. Options for the Union.*

References

1   Com (93) 700 December 1993. (Our pagination refers to the final public version, *Growth, Competitiveness and Employment – the Challenges and Ways Forward into the 21st Century'.*

2   Delors, J. in Cecchini, P. (1988) *1992 – The Struggle for Europe*, Wildwood House. p. XI.

3 Delors, J. *op. cit.*
4 Commission of the European Communities Background Report ISEC/25/89.
5 The Future of European Social Policy. Submission to the European Commission by the Institute of Directors, September 1993.
6 Com (93) *op. cit.*
7 *The Times,* 8 November 1994.
8 Com (93) *op. cit.*

Questions

1 What are the advantages and disadvantages of social protection?
2 What are the likely effects on competition of the UK's opt-out from the Social Protocol on (a) the UK and (b) the rest of the European Union?
3 What factors affect competitiveness? Assess their relative importance. Where do social costs figure in your ranking? Justify your choices.
4 Describe different measures of productivity and evaluate the role of productivity in the competitiveness debate.

7 The external dimension of EU competition policy

Lee Miles

Introduction

The external impact of EU competition policy upon non-member states has remained an important, yet mostly ignored aspect of European Union (EU) competition policy. The purpose of this chapter will be to evaluate the existence of an external dimension to the EU's competition policy and will argue that EU competition rules have had increasingly profound implications for non-member states. Moreover, as the Union has widened and deepened its level of integration, this external dimension has become more prominent. In particular, the chapter will divide the impact of EU competition policy into two areas. First, its repercussions for European non-member states and the potential for a pan-European, EU-based competition policy. Secondly, the broader international scene and compatibility with global competition rules. By taking this structured approach, the central themes of the chapter will become evident – that there will be a tendency to harmonize or at least approximate competition rules across Europe, using EU competition principles as the central core and provoking strong reactions from non-member states internationally.

The growing importance of EU competition policy for non-member states

The first point to make is that the original Treaty of Rome only incorporated an internal focus and was to be primarily directed at dealing with competition within the member states. Under the original Treaty of Rome and according to Articles 85 and 86, competition policy was only to ensure that competition was not distorted within the Common Market (Article 3(f) of the Treaty of Rome). It did not require that EC companies operate in particular ways abroad, except where their conduct might affect trade between member states. Hence, the main objective of EU competition policy, like other competition policies, was the protection of domestic competition and European consumer welfare.

Nevertheless, due to a number of influences within the European Union, the impact of EU competition policy on non-member states has substantially grown since the late 1980s.

The 'Europeanization' of business activity

Business activity in Europe has become increasingly internationalized and 'Europeanized'. In particular, the number of international mergers has increased significantly, for instance more than doubling between 1983 and 1988. Furthermore, the number of cross-border mergers involving European partners has increased from 29 in 1983 to 111 in 1988, representing just under a third of all mergers (see Table 7.1). More generally, there has been a wave of mostly horizontal mergers and acquisitions involving the EU's top 1000 firms (from 303 in 1986 to 622 in 1989–90. In practice, the growth in number of cross-border mergers and European multinationals has meant that large companies from non-member states become extensively involved in acquisitions, mergers and economic activity within EU markets.

Table 7.1 *National, EU and international mergers in the European Union (including acquisition of majority holdings)*

	1983/84	1984/85	1985/86	1986/87	1987/88
National	101	146	145	211	214
European Union	29	44	52	75	111
International	25	18	30	17	58
Total	155	208	227	303	383

Source: Commission of the European Communities, *Annual Reports on Competition.*

Thus, the strategies of companies based outside the EU, but with subsidiaries and branches within the Union, have been affected by EU competition policy[1]. The Commission has for example has been forced to rule on the suitability of mergers, which include parent companies based outside the EU member states. For example, the Commission in 1988 had to decide upon the right of European concerns to acquire companies in third countries. The 1988 bid by Nestlé of Switzerland for Rowntree, one of the main UK confectioners, provoked an outcry that it should be disallowed because the Swiss market structure prevented British companies from acquiring Swiss firms and overall reciprocity. The acquisition was eventually approved.

The evolving influence of the European Court of Justice in competition cases and the principle of 'extra-territoriality'

The European Court of Justice (ECJ) has found it necessary to rule on the conduct of firms who operate within EU markets, but do not necessarily have their headquarters located within them. Thus, the influence of EU competition policy has been felt upon firms based in non-member states but operating within the single European market through the principle of 'extra-territoriality'.

The principle of 'extra-territoriality' was established by the ECJ during the Dyestuffs case of 1972 (ICI v Commission, Case 48/69, (1972) CMLR 557), when the Court judged that the British firm ICI was involved in concerted practices within the Common Market and fined the company (despite its defence that it was headquartered in the UK, which was at this time a non-member state). 'Extra-territoriality' dictates that the EU cannot be denied the right, on the basis of public international law, to take the necessary steps to safeguard its measures against conduct distorting competition within the EU's market, even if those responsible for the conduct reside in non-member states[2].

Thus, according to 'extra-territoriality', the jurisdiction of the Commission in proceedings under EU competition law against an undertaking established in a non-member state is based not solely on the effects of actions committed outside the EU, but also on activities attributable to undertakings within the territory of the EU. Hence, although territoriality and nationality remain the primary basis of jurisdiction, it has been recognized by the ECJ that these rigid concepts have to be interpreted more flexibly to take account of the economic interdependence among the EU and non-member states.

In the Woodpulp case (OJ 1985 L26), the Commission also decided to apply Article 85(1) to foreign companies selling into the Union's SEM without any presence in its territory whatsoever. In 1985, the Commission found that restrictive practices and agreements were operational between Finnish, US and Canadian pulp producers in the bleached sulphate pulp market and imposed 36 fines between ECU 50,000 and ECU 500,000 on these firms[3]. In 1988, the ECJ upheld this extraterritorial application of EU competition rules to the non-EU undertakings (Woodpulp, 1988, CMLR 901). Thus, the impact of EU competition rules upon firms based in non-members and greater interdependence between markets has been facilitated by the concept of 'extra-territoriality'.

The successive enlargements of the European Union

The various enlargements of the European Union to include Denmark, Ireland and the UK in 1973, Greece in 1981 and Spain and Portugal in 1986 also had fundamental implications for the rest of Europe. Not only did successive enlargement firmly establish the EU as Europe's and the world's largest trading bloc, but it also meant the transfer of key trading nations from the European Free Trade Association (EFTA) to the (then) EC. The defection of the UK to the EC especially had repercussions for the trading patterns of European non-member states. Germany and the UK, which formed the backbone of trading links with most areas of Europe, were now inside the EC and obliged to adopt its competition policy. In addition, increasingly the EU's trading balance has shifted from a reliance on extra-EU trade with third countries to intra-EU trade between member states[4]. This process will, of course, be continued with the 1995 enlargement of the Union to include Austria, Finland and Sweden. Thus, enlargement has raized both the profile and competence of EU competition policy as well as the stakes of isolation for non-member states.

The dynamism of the single European market (SEM) programme and the revitalization of the European Union

In practice, the development (and external dimension) of an EU competition policy is also intrinsically related to the internal dynamics of the European Union. A workable competition policy is an essential component for an effective common market between the member states. The European Commission's decision in its 1985 White Paper to embark on completing the single European market was instrumental in raising the profile of EU competition policy in the eyes of member states.

The fear of an ever enlarging, whilst simultaneously integrating, European Union has increased non-member states' preoccupations with the development of a 'Fortress Europe' and the future raising of trading barriers to third countries. Large firms based outside the EU have seen the SEM as both a threat and an opportunity and lobbied their own governments to ensure that they are not disadvantaged. For example, Sweden was 'shadowing' the development of the SEM from 1987 and in 1991 embarked on wholesale revision of its own competition policy, which eventually led to the creation of an EU modelled competition regime in 1993 (see Case Study 4).

These culminative influences eventually brought a more formal response from the European Union and an open awareness that EU competition policy did have an external dimension and had substantial repercussions for non-member states.

A formal external dimension to EU competition policy

The European dimension

In general, then, the external dimension of the EU's competition policy had two contrasting influences. On the one hand – and in a positive way – the competition policy could be used to regulate the foreign activities of firms. A more liberalized market, increased investments and exports as part of intra-European trade and improved market access for firms will be of net benefit to companies based outside the EU. However, on the other hand, the overarching dominance of EU competition policy could be perceived by external non-member states and their firms as formal EU protection for its own firms and discriminating against non-member state competitors. Nevertheless, there have been two major formal responses at the European level, namely the 1989 Merger Regulation and the extension of EU competition policy rules through third country agreements.

The 1989 Merger Regulation

Indeed, the EU when formulating the 1989 Merger Regulation recognized the external implications of its fledgling policy towards mergers and marks a movement towards rejecting strict territoriality:

- The Regulation can be applied to concentrations between firms headquartered outside the EU where they meet the criteria defining concentrations with a Community dimension (a worldwide aggregate turnover greater than ECU 5 billion and sales in the Community above ECU 250 million). Yet, notification is required and it must be established that the merger will create or strengthen a dominant position as a result of which effective competition would be significantly impeded in the SEM or, indeed, part of it.
- Article 24 of the Merger Regulation also explicitly accommodates the external dimension. However, this Article is focused on dealing with the rights of Union companies in non-member states and pays no attention to the rights of non-member state companies in the EU (see Figure 7.1) The Article especially deals with concentrations in non-member states and requires information and action in order to give EU operations participating in such operations comparable treatment to that granted to foreign corporations acting within the EU. In fact, the Regulation states that effective competition is the only reference for accepting or prohibiting a merger within the EU and Article 24 implies that the use of alternative criteria by a foreign country for blocking an acquisition by an EU firm would lead to international negotiations.

As Jacquemin argues[5], these changes suggest that there is a growing overlap between internal and external competition and this will ironically lead to a multiplication of international conflicts and competing jurisdictions in which companies will be caught in the middle.

The extension of EU competition policy rules through third country agreements

Rising demands for a trading accommodation with the European Union from European non-member states have been met by the EU usually through

Relations with non-member countries

1   The member states shall inform the Commission of any general difficulties encountered by their undertakings with concentrations as defined in Article 3 in a non-member country.
2   Initially not more than one year after entry into force of this regulation and thereafter periodically the Commission shall draw up a report examining the treatment accorded to Community undertakings, in the terms referred to in paragraphs 3 and 4, as regards concentrations in non-member countries. The Commission shall submit those reports to the Council, together with any recommendations.
3   Whenever it appears to the Commission, either on the basis of the reports referred to in paragraph 2 or on the basis of other information, that a non-member country does not grant Community undertakings treatment comparable to that granted by the Community, the Commission may submit proposals to the Council for the appropriate mandate for negotiation with a view to obtaining comparable treatment for Community undertakings.

Figure 7.1   1989 Merger Regulation: Article 24

the formulation of specialist and advanced agreements. The main aim of these agreements is to establish preferential trading arrangements between the EU and groups of countries or individual nations, such as the multilateral European Economic Area (EEA) or trading and cooperation agreement between the EU and individual non-member states, for instance the 'Europe' Agreements between the EU and the individual nations of Hungary, Poland, Czech Republic, Slovakia, Romania and Bulgaria. These have for the most part been seen by the non-member states as providing the first step towards EU full membership.

It is within these agreements that rights of non-member states' firms within the EU seem to have partially clarified. However, it is noticeable that these agreements, in their most advanced form, such as the EEA or Association Agreements, usually include either the harmonization with or complete acceptance of EU competition rules (see below). The net outcome has been the extension and influence of EU competition rules upon non-member states (see Case Study 3 on Hungary).

The European Economic Area (EEA) and EEA competition rules   In particular, the economic grouping with the greatest concern arising from the development of the EU's SEM and competition policy were the European nations of the European Free Trade Association (EFTA). The EFTAns (namely Sweden, Finland, Norway, Iceland, Switzerland, Austria and Liechtenstein) were the largest trading partner of the EC and vice versa. Therefore, the development

114

of stronger competition policy would have direct repercussions for these non-member states.

Indeed, in order to secure EFTAn access to the SEM and its four freedoms, and at the same time hopefully avoid the possibility of future membership applications, the Commission President, Jacques Delors, offered to create 'a new more structured partnership' between the EU and the EFTA states. The net result was the signing of the European Economic Area (EEA) agreement in May 1992 between the EU and the EFTA states, which became operational in 1994[6]. The EEA in practice has extended access of the SEM to the EFTA states and established an advanced free trade area, that also includes 'flanking policies' such as cooperation in research and development, the environment, energy and transport matters.

However, although the EEA did not avert full EU membership applications from several of the EFTA states and did not prevent Austria, Sweden and Finland from joining the EU in 1995, the EEA did provide for a new EEA competition policy to govern the enlarged SEM to cover the remaining EFTA states (excluding Switzerland). One of the objectives of the EEA agreement was and is:

> to establish a dynamic and homogeneous integrated system based on common rules and equal conditions of competition[7].

In reality though, these equal conditions of competition were to be achieved by virtually the complete absorption of EU competition rules to cover the EFTA territories. Indeed, Article 1 of the EEA Agreement provides for the setting up of a system ensuring that competition is not distorted and that the corresponding rules are similarly respected. The substantive rules applicable in the EEA are those, as adapted for EEA purposes, of the corresponding provisions of the EEC and ECSC Treaty and the Acts adopted in application of those provisions (see Table 7.2). Not surprisingly, then, the EEA competition rules are based on Article 53 prohibiting agreements which restrain competition between enterprises (Article 85 EC) and Article 54 which prohibits the abuse of a dominant position (Article 86 EC). According to Article 6 of the EEA Treaty, their implementation and application shall also be interpreted in conformity with the previous and present relevant rulings of the EC Court of Justice, even when given prior to the date of the signature of the EEA Agreement.

However, the EEA competition rules are enforced by the EU Commission and a new EFTA Surveillance Authority (ESA) on their respective territories, establishing a 'two-pillar system'[8]. The creation of the EFTA Surveillance Authority marked a new stage for the EFTA nations as this required an explicit acceptance by these nations of creating supranational institutions – something that since the creation of EFTA in 1960 they had been mostly

115

Table 7.2 *Correspondence between the main competition provisions in the EEA agreement and in EC legislation*

	EEA*	EEC
GENERAL		
Agreements, decisions and concerted practices	Article 53	Article 85
Abuse of a dominant position	Article 54	Article 86
Mergers	Article 57(1)	Article 2 (3) of Regulation (EEC 4064/89)
Specific procedural rules	Article 55	Article 89
COAL AND STEEL		
Agreements, decisions and concerted practices	Article 1 of Protocol 25	Article 65 (1), (2) and (4)
Abuse of a dominant position and concentrations	Article 2 of Protocol 25	Article 66 (1), (2) and (7)
Definition of the term 'undertaking'	Article 3 of Protocol 25	Article 80

* This correspondence is given only for indicative purposes and is without prejudice to the interpretations which might be given by the EC Court of Justice or the EFTA Court. Furthermore, the more procedural provisions have sometimes, for obvious reasons, been slightly reworded to better suit the EEA context
Source: Commission of the ECs

averse to. In practice, the EFTA Surveillance Authority has comparatively similar powers and functions regarding competition policy as the EU Commission; for instance, the granting of exemptions and negative clearances.

Yet, in accordance with the one-stop shop principle, cases are examined either by the Commission or by the ESA. Nonetheless, regarding the control of concentrations in the EEA, the EU Commission is the senior partner. Assessments shall be carried out by the EU Commission in cases where the criteria of the EU Merger Regulation are fulfilled or in 'mixed cases' between the two territories. A corresponding competence is established on the EFTA only within the territories of the EFTA states, but even then the EU Merger thresholds will still apply.

Thus, in practice, the EFTA states have more or less fully accepted the remits of EU competition policy and, from 1994, EU-based competition rules have become a unifying link between the EU and EFTA states, covering almost 370 million citizens in 17 European countries. In its first decision in the field of competition policy in January 1994, the ESA adopted ten notices and guidelines, corresponding to existing Commission acts[9] and adopted state aid rules dealing with regional aid to specific industrial sectors, such as textiles and clothing, synthetic fibres, automobiles and steel[10]. Indeed, the ESA has acted as a kind of surrogate EU Commission in its first year, even to the point of jointly investigating state aids to airlines with the Commission in March 1994[11].

Moreover, with the accessions of Austria, Sweden and Finland into the European Union in 1995, the hegemony of the European Commission in determining a pan-European competition policy has been further strengthened. Even the Norwegian negative vote (by 52.3 per cent) on EU membership will not require changes to competition policy as Norway still remains an EEA member. Thus, the net outcome is that EU competition policy is increasingly becoming the norm across Western Europe, as non-member states either transform their own competition policies in line with EU competition policy principles or are influenced by these competition rules regardless through the rising profile of the EU.

Association agreements: extending the influence of EU competition policy

In addition, the influence of EU competition policy has been further extended to parts of Eastern Europe through the EU stipulation that any advanced third country agreement (which includes the establishment of an advanced free trade area) must also include a degree of approximation of competition rules. In particular, the signing of association agreements with Hungary, Poland, the Czech Republic, Slovakia, Romania and Bulgaria has also facilitated the rising influence of EU competition policy.

Within each 'Europe' Agreement, there includes an extensive programme and timetable for trade liberalization, mostly over a ten-year period. Nevertheless, the Agreements also include other areas of future economic cooperation of which competition policy is a constituent and integral part.

In order to reinforce the liberalization process and to govern free trade between the two parties, the 'Europe' Agreements also envisage the development of a European-wide competition policy, which would bridge the gap between East, Central and Western Europe. The Agreements note that if trade is to be fair then an agreed framework to prevent distortion of competition by traders in the market is a prerequisite for the success of the Agreements[12] especially if integration on competition policy allows for anti-dumping and safeguard measures to be discarded.

However, like the EEA Agreement, the Europe Agreements envisage these competition measures to be based almost entirely on existing EU competition policy, including the removal of restrictive practices, controls on abuse of a dominant position and 'any public aid which distorts or threatens to distort competition.'[13] However, although competition practices shall be assessed based on the criteria of Articles 85, 86 and 92 of the Treaty of Rome, these areas are less contentious as they are usually a condition for close economic integration with the EU. At the practical level, the new regimes in Eastern Europe need such regulatory systems and the EU framework is the obvious one to adopt.

More ambitiously, the Eastern European states are to start to apply EU anti-trust laws within three years of the signing of the agreements. Considering the state control of the Eastern European command economies and the fragility of many of their emerging market economies, this seems somewhat optimistic. However, these new anti-trust laws must not be too rigid. According to EU rules, development orientated loans can be authorized and specific rules will be applied to the large coal and steel sectors within Eastern Europe. Indeed, the Europe Agreements contain a common provision (Article 63(4a)) that allows any grants to be awarded by the Eastern European governments to be assessed on identical terms to those operating in the EU (under Article 92.3 (EC)) and will be permitted for backward, less industrialized regions. Thus, the impact of EU competition policy will become increasingly evident within the Eastern European states, especially considering EU state aid codes. Indeed, the ability of the Association Councils to grant exemptions for these states on economic grounds will be the most important aspect regarding competition in the Agreements.

Therefore, there seem to be several factors affecting EU competition policy regarding the external European dimension:

- The growing influence of EU competition policy upon European non-member states due to rising profile and enlargement of the Union to become Europe's undisputed trading bloc and the ECJ's principle of 'extra-territoriality'.
- The geographical extension of EU-based competition policy through third country agreements.
- The transformation of domestic competition policies in line with EU competition rules (see Case Study 4 on Sweden).

In effect, a de facto formation of a pan-European competition policy seems to be emerging based on EU competition rules. Yet, owing to the increased role of EU competition policy, this has also led to implications for the wider global level. In practice, there has been a growing overlap between EU competition policy and the wider international environment.

The international dimension

The rising global influences upon EU competition policy

The effects of EU competition policy are not simply restricted to multi-nationals or exports based in European non-member states and the EU Commission has increasingly had to accommodate the fact that markets are now becoming 'globalized'.

In many ways, the 1989 Merger Regulation already incorporates this effect regarding the control of mergers. Among the criteria for determining if the merger will lead to the creation of a dominant position are two important considerations regarding the size of the wider international market. First, one of the thresholds for mergers includes that the merger will fall under the Commission's remit if the aggregate worldwide turnover of all the undertakings concerned is over ECU 5 billion. Secondly, the Commission must take account of the 'actual and potential competition from firms located within and outside the Community' under the Regulation.

The problems associated with dealing with the international dimension of competition policy is not new though. Since the mid-1960s, the European Commission has participated in the Organization for Economic Cooperation and Development's (OECD) Committee on competition law and policy. However, the growth of economic interdependence, international trade and, more importantly, new markets in, for instance, information technology have meant that the global perspective has become more relevant. In particular, since the ECJ's decision to uphold the 'qualified effect' and 'extra-territoriality' doctrines in the 1988 Wood Pulp case and the adoption of the 1989 Merger Regulation, the EU has been conscious that the effects on non-member states has increased and therefore so has the potential for conflict. In effect, EU competition policy has wider implications for international firms as well as for European non-member states.

As Jacquemin argues, the Commission has found it increasingly necessary to consider the global market as being the relevant one. For example, in the de Havilland case, it was decided that the world market was also the relevant geographical market. In this case, Aérospatiale of France and Alenia of Italy had decided to acquire de Havilland, the Canadian subsidiary of Boeing. The Commission argued that the acquisition would have given de Havilland and ATR (the Franco-Italian joint venture) fifty per cent of the world market and sixty-seven per cent of the EU market for 20–70 seater commuter aircraft. This would have created a dominant position, affecting even the largest producers, such as British Aerospace and Fokker as there was no competition from the United States or Japan.

The use of bilateral agreements between the EU and non-member states

In order to provide some rules regarding the reaction of competition policies to the role of international firms, the EU has signed bilateral Agreements. The 1988 Woodpulp decision, which involved North American firms, and the 1989 Merger Regulation were especially important in changing EU–US relations on competition matters and in promoting an agreement to avoid the possibility of concentrations with a Community dimension being scrutinized twice[14].

Sir Leon Brittan (as then Competition Commissioner) in a speech at Cambridge in February 1990 and later to the New York Chamber of Commerce officially stated that there was a political willingness in the European Commission to conclude an administrative agreement to provide a more detailed framework for cooperation. This resulted in the September 1991 EU–US bilateral agreement whose main aim was 'to promote cooperation and coordination and lessen the possibility or impact of difference between the Parties in the application of their competition laws.' The European Commission and US competition authorities have committed themselves to exchanging information and taking into account the important interests of the other parties at all stages of their enforcement procedures and activities, subject to the conditions defined in the agreement.

Thus, recognition of the growing international trends in business activity and the consequent necessity of reducing the potential for trade friction have been the two influential factors in determining the international dimension of EU competition policy. For the European Union, avoiding the imposition of trade sanctions by the United States under Section 301 of the 1988 US Trade Act was especially significant.

The lack of a comprehensive multilateral competition policy framework

Moreover, despite the attempts at the Uruguay Round of GATT (General Agreement on Tariffs and Trade), a global competition policy has failed to really appear. GATT was originally intended to cope with competition rules (and the Havana Charter included a chapter dealing with restrictive practices) and, in effect, has become the main forum for multilateral discussion on questions of international trade. Nevertheless, although the Uruguay Agreement will transform the GATT into an eventual World Trade Organisation (WTO), it marks only a limited improvement in creating new 'codes of conduct' for anti-dumping subsidies and public procurement procedures and made little headway in developing common competition rules. Indeed, the concept of regional trade blocs governing world trade has been reinforced by developments, such as the NAFTA (North American Free Trade Area). Thus, as long as there remains a deficiency of global competition rules, EU competition policy will remain important in providing the most supranationally advanced international framework, especially as EU competition policy covers the majority of the OECD and most of the advanced industrial nations in the world today.

Conclusions

Overall, given growing international economic interdependence in European and world trade, EU competition rules have become increasingly important to and influential upon non-member states. Over time, the geographical remit of EU competition policy has come to include European states who are not full EU members, primarily through third party agreements. As the EU has established preferential trading zones and arrangements with European non-member states so has the demand for extending competition rules to ensure the functioning of competitive conditions as part of these arrangements. In this respect, competition policy remains one of the few EU policies that is coordinated and can even apply to non-member states' territories. In practice, extending the geographical remits of EU competition rules has meant that it now represents a de facto pan-European wide competition policy covering most of Western Europe and parts of Eastern Europe.

Nevertheless, the emergence of a pan-European competition policy has been accompanied by an active international dimension. Since EU competition rules are fast becoming a European norm, this also increases the likelihood of friction with non-European multinationals and in particular, the United States and Japan. Moreover, the lack of complex WTO global competition rules may ensure that EU competition policy is not threatened, but it also means that a comprehensive assessment of the external dimension of EU competition rules is essential. This perhaps remains one of the largest challenges for EU competition policy in the future.

References

1 Mortagnon, P. (1990) *European Competition Policy.* London, RIIA/Pinter. p. 85.
2 See *Common Market Law Reports* (1972), Part 60, p. 561.
3 See Jones, A. (1993) Woodpulp: concerted practice and/or conscious parallelism. *European Competition Law Review,* 6 ECLR, p. 273. These fines were subsequently reduced, although the ECJ upheld the Commission's position on 'extra-territoriality' and concerted practices.

4 For a more detailed analysis see Miles, L. (1994). The European Community and external relations. In Barnes, I. and Davison, L. *European Business – Text and Cases,* Butterworth-Heinemann. p. 70.

5 Jacquemin, A. (1993) The international dimension of European competition policy. *Journal of Common Market Studies,* Vol. 31, No. 1, March 1993, p. 95.

6 The EEA Agreement does not however apply to Switzerland, even though she is a full member of EFTA. In a referendum in December 1992, the Swiss electorate voted against joining the EAA.

7 Commission of the ECs (1994) *Brochure Concerning the Competition Rules Applicable to Undertakings As Contained in the EEA Agreement and their Implementation by the EC Commission and the EFTA Surveillance Authority,* Brussels, Commission of the ECs. p. 3.

8 See Stagier, J. (1993) The competition rules of the EEA agreement and their implementation. *European Competition Law Review,* 1 *ECLR,* p. 30.

9 EFTA (1994) *Surveillance Authority Adopts Competition Notices and Guidelines,* Brussels, EFTA. p. 1.

10 EFTA (1994) *Surveillance Authority Decision on State Aid Guidelines,* Brussels, EFTA. p. 1.

11 EFTA (1994) *Surveillance Authority Requests Information From Commission on State Aid to Airlines,* Brussels, EFTA. p. 1.

12 Horovitz, D. (1991) Second generation agreements between the European Community and Eastern Europe – some practical considerations. *Journal of World Trade,* Vol. 25, No. 2, April 1991.

13 Commission of the ECs (1991) *EC–Hungary Association Agreement,* Article 63(3), p. 26.

14 Riley, A. (1992) Mailing the jellyfish: the illegality of the EC/US government competition agreement. *European Competition Law Review,* 5, *ECLR,* p. 101.

Questions

1 To what extent is the principle of 'extra-territoriality' important in enabling the European Commission to adopt a uniform approach towards non-member states in competition matters?

2 Is it realistic to assume that the European Union's competition policy has become the governing competition regime throughout Europe?

3 To what extent has the 1988 'Woodpulp' case and the adoption of the 1989 Merger Regulation by the EU been influential in accelerating the need for accommodating the views of non-member states?

Part 2   The Case Studies

Case 1 Open skies over the European Union?

Leigh Davison

Introduction

This case focuses upon the drive to liberalize the scheduled air transport market of the European Union (EU), which can be rightly seen as an integral part of completing the single market programme. It discusses the various factors that, individually or acting in concert, could undermine, slow down or distort this process. Such factors include: the over-common giving of state aid by member states to prop up their respective inefficient, loss-making national airline or flag carrier; the existing barriers to entry which have the capability, unless quickly addressed, to render open competition unattainable in the near future; the negative impact the recent recession has had on the financial position of European airlines, limiting their ability to fully exploit the new opportunities made possible by the partial liberalization of the airways that has already taken effect – though 1994 has turned into a boom year for the airlines, with traffic growth (in terms of passenger-kilometres flown) being predicted at 8.5 to 9 per cent

Liberalization of the EU Airways – the role of the EU Commission

In line with the single market initiative, the European Commission has actively sought the liberalization of all air routes between and within member states for domestic-based airlines – an 'open skies' policy for the European Union. The task the Commission has set itself is considerable, given that the intra-Community air transport market has been shaped by a series of bilateral agreements between member states. These agreements were highly protectionist in nature, controlling rigidly such matters as route entry, capacity and pricing. Many international routes within the Community were single destination, which, under the terms of the ruling bilateral, meant that entry was restricted to one airline from each partner. The response from Brussels has been the 'first', 'second' and 'third' aviation packages which, if the Commission does not lose its nerve, will by 1997 bring about open and fair competition to an industry notorious for the high degree of protectionism that has prevailed. The three packages represent a gradualist approach to liberalising the intra EU air transport market, allowing Community-based airlines time to adjust to the prospect of open competition by 1997.

The First Aviation Package, adopted in December 1987, can be seen as the initial tentative step down the road to full-blown market liberalization, though, for the most part, it left the existing bilateral framework untouched. The Second Aviation Package followed in July 1990 but it made no substantial progress toward further liberalization; that came with the Third Aviation Package. The Third Package represents the culmination of the process establishing the single market in air transport, which will be fully implemented by April 1997. For EU-based airlines, the Third Package gives three important 'freedoms':

1 The right to set their own fares, subject to tightly drawn safeguards against unfair or predatory pricing. The EU Commission will have the power to arbitrate when such a dispute arises.
2 Any airline satisfying common safety, nationality and financial fitness criteria is entitled to an EU operating licence. Once granted a licence, an airline has the right to operate *anywhere* in the EU. Member states, however, do retain some powers to limit access where congestion or environmental problems can be demonstrated, but only on a non-discriminatory basis. (In other words, such powers cannot be used by a member state to protect their own domestic airlines against competition from other EU airlines.)
3 The introduction of 'consecutive cabotage', thereby guaranteeing an airline from one member state the right to operate limited capacity on onward domestic route sectors in other member states, such as British Airways flying from Heathrow to Orly (Paris) and then on to Marseilles or Toulouse. Full cabotage – the right, subject to acquiring the necessary slots, of any EU-based airline to operate anywhere in the Community – has to wait until 1 April 1997.

The EU-based airlines

The EU airline industry, which is witnessing the gradual liberalization of the industry under the single market initiative, as discussed above, is both complex and heterogeneous with regard to its structure. One important characteristic is that the industry can to some extent still be seen as twelve fragmented markets, with each member state having a dominant national airline. In a number of cases this dominance has been allowed by the state:

Air France has a monopoly of internal domestic scheduled flights; Lufthansa retains a similar position concerning Germany. Even in the UK, British Airways was responsible for 83 per cent of the total scheduled revenue passenger kilometres in 1992. In terms of size – number of passengers carried by an airline per annum, for example – there are enormous differences between these national airlines. By any indicator chosen, it is clear that Lufthansa, Air France and British Airways (BA), are the big three in terms of size (though they remain smaller than their US counterparts). At the other extreme are the likes of Aer Lingus of Eire and Sabena, Belgium's flag-carrier. Not surprisingly, given that these airlines are flag-carriers, the majority are state owned (see Appendix C1.1). The exception is BA, which is a listed public company; it should also be noted that Lufthansa is in the process of being privatized. The Dutch flag-carrier, KLM, is publicly listed, although the state still holds an important 38.2 per cent stake in the company.

Financial performance

Concerning the last few years, what is most apparent is the negative correlation between state ownership of an airline and its financial performance. As table C1.1 reveals, the combined loss of the EU's flag-carriers was

Table C1.1 *Financial performance of EU airlines*

Airline	Net profit [1]	Net margin [2] (%)
BA	298	+ 3.2
Sabena	12	+ 0.7
Luxair	1	+ 0.2
Alitalia	− 12	− 0.2
SAS	− 127	− 2.2
Lufthansa	− 250	− 2.3
Air France	− 617	− 5.7
Iberia	− 340	− 8.2
Aer Lingus	− 196	− 14.2
TAP	− 200	− 18.0
Olympic	− 225	− 24.4

Source: Airline Business, September 1993. As quoted in the Civil Aviation Authority report, Airline Competition in the Single European Market, November 1993, p. 103
[1] Operating profit is often calculated as profit before tax but after interest has been deducted; net profit is after tax and other extraordinary items
[2] Net margin is simply net profits expressed as a percentage of group sales

not far short of $2 billion in 1992. The only real jewel in the crown was the privatized BA, making a net profit of $289 million. 1993 witnessed the fourth successive year of losses: Aitalia of Italy saw its deficit grow massively, Iberia of Spain recorded a near doubling of its net loss to $550 million, and TAP of Portugal lost $224 million. Similarly Greece's Olympic airline notched up an increased deficit, estimated at $589 million, with interest payments on its huge debts being a major contributor. But the mother of all losses went to Air France, with a deficit estimated at $1.28 billion and its debt burden reaching FFr 38 billion. It is little wonder that a number of these airlines duly brought out their begging bowls and sought financial assistance from their respective governments. (The issue of state aid is examined in depth later in this Case Study). Poor financial performance has not prevented Air France from making strategic acquisitions, swallowing up two smaller French airlines, Air Inter and UTA, and taking a large minority equity interest (35.6%) in Sabena. In July 1994 Air France completed the fourth and final payment for its stake in Sabena.

Not all is financial doom and gloom, however. At least this is true for KLM, Lufthansa and BA. They have benefited from the upturn in both passenger and freight traffic in 1994, and the measures to improve productivity taken independently by KLM and Lufthansa seem to have had the desired result. KLM, whose productivity gains and strict cost controls enabled it to reduce unit costs by 5 per cent, saw a near doubling in its first-half net profit to $280 million from $144 million. Lufthansa, after undergoing a major restructuring, which it claims has improved productivity by 31 per cent in the two years to June 1994, revealed for the first time in five years that it had made a profit in the first half of the financial year; pre-tax profits came in at DM 105 million, against a DM 221 million loss in the same period in the previous financial year. These good tidings at KLM and Lufthansa are not the result of state aid; in fact, the opposite is true.

Poor productivity and other concerns

Comments have already been made about Lufthansa and KLM actively implementing measures to improve their productivity. Low productivity is endemic to European operators. *Expanding Horizons*, a report by the Comité des Sages for Air Transport to the European Commission, concluded that European airline labour costs per employee are slightly higher than in the USA, 'but due to much lower labour productivity in Europe the total labour costs in Europe per available tonne kilometre (ATK) are nearly 37 per cent higher'[1]. Likewise, the recent Civil Aviation Authority (CAA) report entitled *Airline Competition in the Single Market* found that 'US carriers have a higher labour productivity than Community carriers with similar stage lengths, with Olympic, Sabena and TAP appearing to have particularly low productivity'[2]. It found the most productive airlines to be BA, Alitalia and British Midland. In 1993 a comparison between TAP and BA noted that, although BA had nearly five times as many staff as TAP, it flew about eight times as many passengers.

On this matter, the European Commission in a Commission communication titled *The way forward for civil aviation in Europe* declares: 'The Civil aviation industry presents the same symptoms as other sectors in Europe, as identified in the White Paper on "Growth, Competitiveness, Employment". This significant lack of productivity leads to a major cost disadvantage, applying both to the internal costs of the airlines and the costs beyond direct management control, such as user charges'[3]. The communication stresses that the control of airlines' internal costs, when attempting to improve efficiency, is the concern of management. This is not always true, however, as the Commission requires, among other things, a restructuring plan from an airline if it is to get approval from Brussels for one last dose of state aid. User charges refer to items such as airport charges and air traffic control (ATC) costs. The Comité des Sages found that the EU carriers suffered from exceptionally high user costs, putting them at a competitive disadvantage. It revealed that airport charges for scheduled EU-based airlines accounted for 4 to 6 per cent of the operating costs, compared with under 2 per cent in the USA. The Comité further noted a differential in ATC charges that favoured US carriers. In the short term, at least, these problems will remain.

To get into a position to be able to take advantage of the opportunities – and meet successfully the increased likelihood of competition – resulting from full cabotage in 1997, EU airlines must improve their competitive performance and they must also rid themselves of their excess capacity in terms of planes. Again, the Commission views this as a management task. The next section of this Case Study reveals that, even for airlines that have undergone the necessary restructuring, a number of barriers still exist which collectively could have the capability to undermine the goal of attaining a single European aviation market.

Reducing barriers to entry – increasing contestability

Overall, the extents to which airlines will be able to exploit the opportunities offered by the Third Package are constrained by a relatively small number of powerful barriers to entry. These are now discussed.

Congestion – infrastructure problems in general

Two recent reports – *Airline Competition and the Single European Market* by the Civil Aviation Authority and *Expanding Horizons* by the Comité des Sages for European Air Transport to the European Commission – point out

129

that airport congestion, which is becoming more widespread across the EU, can be viewed as a considerable and growing barrier to entry. Within this umbrella term, potential barriers to entry include: too few landing and take-off slots; shortages of terminal capacity, runway capacity and aircraft stands; as well as problems of surface access. Heathrow to a varying degree suffers from all of these.

As stated, Heathrow is not alone in facing these difficulties; according to IATA, for example, the following major airports in the summer of 1992 were, for most of the day, at or close to saturation point regarding runway usage: Athens, Berlin, Dusseldorf, Frankfurt, Heraklion, Madrid and Milan (Linate). Another fourteen airports – including Barcelona, Brussels, Copenhagen, Paris (Charles de Gaulle and Orly), Lisbon and Manchester – were listed as suffering from the same constraint in peak periods. Concerning terminal capacity, Berlin, Madrid, Milan (Linate) and Rome have had major problems; for Lisbon a further headache was the shortage of apron capacity. Among the ten busiest airports in Europe, only Amsterdam proved to be 'relatively unconstrained'. A similar picture is given by a study entitled *A European Planning Strategy for Air Traffic to the Year 2010* by Stanford Research Institute. It predicts serious capacity difficulties for approximately half of all European airports, even after allowing for planned increases in capacity.

This capacity crisis has led the Comité des Sages to argue that it is not sufficient to allow local authorities, acting independently, to deal with the matter; instead it suggests that an effective solution requires action to be taken at the EU level. The Comité advocates that the EU should take the lead and assume political responsibility in three areas. Namely:

1   Further develop guidelines for an EU airport network system so as to move toward a European Airport capacity improvement scheme.
2   Provide funds to ensure that an ongoing assessment of the said infrastructure problems is made possible.
3   Vigorously pursue infrastructure improvements so as to ensure that these programmes reflect European rather than purely national needs.

Of course, providing additional capacity does not come cheap – the projected Terminal Five at Heathrow has been costed at around $1232–1386 million; a new terminal and associated facilities at Frankfurt airport will generate a bill of nearly $924 million.

My kingdom for a slot

Given the major infrastructure and capacity problems faced by many of the major EU airports, especially at Heathrow, and the fact that the problem is likely to get worse in the immediate future, the resultant shortage of take-off and landing slots will act as a serious barrier to entry. The same conclusion was reached by the Comite des Sages: 'The Comité fears that with future growth in air travel, the situation at certain Community airports will deteriorate further. Slots will again become the crucial issue for achieving real liberalization of the market[4]. One possibility, though not a long-term solution to the slot shortage, is to reallocate the current available slots in such a way as to enable new entrants to compete on existing routes and to offer new services. This raises the issues of how to compensate airlines which have lost slots to new entrants and to what extent will the reallocation actually increase competition overall? It is possible to envisage, for example, a situation where an airline, on account of a reduction/loss of slots, is forced to cut back the number of routes offered and/or the frequency of flights on some of its existing services.

Brussels' response to this matter took effect in February 1993: Council Regulation (No. 95/93) on Common Rules for the Allocation of Slots at Community Airports. The Regulation can be seen as an attempt to provide a framework of rules so as to facilitate neutral, transparent and non-discriminatory decisions on the allocation of slots. To be effective, the Regulation must be uniformly applied across the whole of the EU. Its main provisions are:

1   Acceptance of the principle of Grandfather rights.
2   The establishment of a slot pool, giving new entrants up to 50 per cent of the newly created, unused and returned slots.
3   The right to a slot would be lost by an airline if it were not used for a minimum of 80 per cent of the time for which it was available.
4   Airlines can freely exchange slots as well as transfer them between routes and types of service.
5   Slots for domestic services may, under special circumstances, be protected by government.

It can be seen that the Regulation does not force incumbent airlines to give up a proportion of the slots they currently hold; in fact the reverse is true, for it actually guarantees their Grandfather rights. Grandfather rights mean that an airline that had control of a slot in one season has first call on the slot in the following season. At Heathrow the result has been that almost all slots have been held on to, with British Airways in 1992/93 retaining a massive 38.5 per cent of total available slots; next in line came British Midland with a mere 13.4 per cent. No other airline held more than 5 per cent.

To further encourage competition, the UK Civil Aviation Authority argues that the best way forward is to build upon the new EU slot Regulation. The Authority rightly fears that allocating up to 50 per cent of the slots in the newly created slot pool to new entrants may not lead to the desired injection of competition:

Article 10 of that Regulation requires that all newly created slots, unused slots, slots which have been given up by a carrier during or at the end of the season or which otherwise become available should be placed in a pool and that up to 50% of the slots in the pool should be allocated to new entrants. There is no requirement that these slots should be used to promote competition on particular routes, and to the extent that they are given to genuine new entrants they are unlikely to be deployed on routes where two powerful airlines already operate[5].

Given the above concerns, the CAA recommended that all the slots in the slot pool should be focused upon adding new services to existing busy long and short haul routes, thereby increasing competition. Moreover, where possible, these slots should be given to airlines which have a confirmed track record of pro-competitive behaviour. Obviously for this proposal to be successfully implemented, the new entrant must be given an appropriate block of slots otherwise effective competition with incumbent airlines is made impossible. If, after a specified period of time, this proposal failed to bring about the desired goal because insufficient slots were made available, the CAA advocates, reluctantly, that a scheme whereby incumbent airlines are compulsorily made to release slots must again be considered.

Ensuring market access – dog fight over Orly

Without all member states fully complying with the Third Aviation Package, especially in relation to consecutive cabotage and from 1997 full cabotage, and if the EU Commission does not act to vigorously enforce these, then the denial of market access by one member state to an airline from another member state is made easy. This would effectively destroy the single market in air transport. The recent debacle over Orly gets to the very heart of this concern.

Paris is served by two airports: Charles de Gaulle and Orly. To get a valuable foothold into the French domestic airline network, access to Orly is essential for it serves an estimated 80 per cent of the network. However, the Air France group, including its subsidiary Air Inter, has a near-monopoly of the French domestic market, having a market share of around 85 per cent. At Orly, for example, they control about 55 per cent of runway slots. As noted earlier, in 1992 BA acquired a 49.9 per cent stake in the Orly-based private French airline TAT. Presumably BA, anticipating the Third Aviation Package, saw its stake in TAT as a way of gaining access to the French domestic market. Accordingly, both BA and TAT sought to expand their services out of Orly. TAT, in particular, wanted slots for the Orly–Heathrow service, thereby competing against Air France, and to operate services on southern routes between Orly and Toulouse and Marseilles, currently Europe's third and fourth busiest routes, where Air Inter is the dominant player. TAT's inability to get slots for the above routes led it to complain to the Commission, arguing that it was the victim of a monopoly at Orly.

In late April of 1994, after a wait of seven months, the Commission's report upheld TAT's complaint, although when the Commissioners actually voted on whether to adopt the report, Jacques Delors (the President of the Commission) abstained and the other French Commissioner, Mrs Christiane Scrivener, opposed it[6]. The report ordered the French authorities to immediately open up the Orly–London route. Concerning the Toulouse and Marseilles routes, the French were given a six month breathing space before these too, had to be opened up. Bernard Bosson, the French Transport Minister, said that France would appeal against the ruling to the European Court of Justice (ECJ). It did and duly lost – though the French Transport Ministry announced that competing services on the Toulouse and Marseilles routes could not start until January 1995.

The battle for access to Orly itself flared up again on 11 May when the French government unilaterally decided that both BA and Air UK, who were each planning to start flights from London to Orly on Monday 16 May, would not be granted immediate access to Orly despite the Commission's ruling. BA responded determinedly, arguing: 'The French authorities have no right to prevent us from going there. We have the landing rights and we are preparing to operate to and from Orly from Monday[7]. The grounds for denying improved market access at Orly were spelt out by Bosson. He stated that greater access was dependent upon a number of problems being tackled: the present congestion at Orly; the need to adapt airline schedules had to be addressed; and the need to guarantee access to Heathrow for airlines (Air France?) wishing to compete on the Orly–Heathrow route. BA claimed that it did not recognize these as problems, it and Air UK already having gained the required slots at Orly. The next player on the scene was none other than the UK Transport Minister, John MacGregor, representing the UK government interest in the Orly affair. Obviously matters were now at a crucial juncture. The outcome of two days of telephone calls between London and Paris was an accord reached by the two governments, which opened flights to Orly from London by the end of June. The UK also agreed to consider improving access for French airlines to Heathrow.

Open access to Orly is not yet guaranteed, however, as the recent friction with Lauda Air and KLM proves. The French government, in September 1994, refused Lauda Air, in which Lufthansa has a 39 per cent equity holding, the right to land at Orly even though the airline had acquired the necessary landing slots. In November, and after much wrangling, Lauda Air was allowed into Charles deGaulle but not Orly, the latter being more convenient for internal French connections. In the same month, the French government thwarted KLM's plans to start services between Amsterdam and Orly by refusing the airline landing rights; KLM responded by asking the Commission to intervene. A month earlier, in a related development, the French Transport Ministry, on environmental grounds, limited the number of slots available at Orly to the current level of two hundred thousand flights per year; critics have argued that this is one way of preventing expansion at Orly and keeping foreign competition at bay.

Ensuring fair competition: the issue of state aids

The recent, and possibly continuing, practice of some member states propping-up their financially ailing, inefficient state-controlled flag-carrier by the use of discriminatory state aid, can only be viewed as being contrary to the specified goal of an open, single, competitive market for air transport within the EU. This form of subsidy has led Sir Michael Bishop, chairperson of British Midland, to argue: 'Fair competition cannot exist in Europe's airlines whilst direct state subsidies and indirect government actions continue to distort the market, allowing national airlines to escape the commercial pressures faced in the real world[8]. Of course, the pressures of open competition forcing an airline toward maximum efficiency are considerably diluted if it knows that it can always turn to the state for a financial handout, if and when needed. The result is a culture within the airline that goes along with or readily accepts perpetual inefficiency. This in turn can lead to a noticeable lack of urgency or willingness to face important issues such as overmanning, poor productivity, overcapacity and so on. Table C1.2 details the huge amounts of EU-approved state aid that has been poured into the airlines listed.

When a member state seeks to provide financial support for its flag-carrier, the proposals are reviewed at Brussels by the Transport Directorate DG7, and not the Competition Directorate DG4. DG4 has only a consultative role in air transport cases. DG7 is split into four Directorates: A, B, C, D. Directorate C deals with air transport issues. Having both DG7 and DG4 responsible for the very same issue, albeit concerning different sectors of industry, gives rise to possible differences in interpretation of the rules governing state aid. One critic has asserted that 'this means that the decisions on applications for airline state aid are strongly influenced by political and social concerns, while aspects relating to market forces often take a back seat. Significantly, while DG4 opposed the recent aid cases involving Air France, Sabena and Iberia [see Table C1.2], its decisions were overruled by DG7[9]. The words of Heinz Hilbrecht, a Head of Unit in Directorate C, when the said cases were assessed, seems to give tacit support for the above assertion. He declared: 'From a starting point we in DG7 were perhaps more inclined to see that the airlines had special problems, especially

Table C1.2 *EU-approved state financing for domestic airlines, 1991–94*

Airline	State financing approved ($ million)	Brussels assessment
AIR FRANCE (1991)	942	SATISFIES MEIP, NOT AID
AIR FRANCE (1993)	262	STATE AID, NOT APPROVED
IBERIA (1992)	1027	STATE AID, APPROVED
SABENA (1991)	1040	STATE AID, APPROVED
AER LINGUS (1993)	250	STATE AID, APPROVED
TAP (1993)	200	STATE AID, APPROVED
TAP (1994)	1100*	STATE AID, APPROVED
AIR FRANCE (1994)	3800	STATE AID, APPROVED
OLYMPIC (1994)	2273*	STATE AID, APPROVED

Source: European Commission
* As well as aid both TAP and Olympic received loan guarantees of $1088 million and $363 million, respectively

in recession, whereas DG4 has responsibility for competition and so feels it has to look at the proposal from the competition point of view[10].

Seeking approval from Brussels

Based on the provisions of the Treaty of Rome, the Commission in its 'Memorandum 2' of March 1984 set out guidelines on state aids in the air transport industry. They have since been reiterated. In brief, some of the important points are:

1 State aid will be incompatible with the common market where it distorts or threatens to distort competition.
2 Exemptions to this principle may be allowed but only on the grounds of common interest considerations.
3 Member states must inform the Commission in advance of all intended new state aids, or changes to existing state aids.
4 The giving of aid to cover an airline's operating loss is viewed as not being compatible with the common market except in instances where real improvement, restoring the airlines financial position and competitiveness, is the objective.
5 The provision to an airline of capital or loans or guarantees by a member state and/or public institutions must be vetted to see if it is the equivalent of a normal commercial transaction or aid or a combination of both.

Point 5 above relates to what is termed the market economy investor principle (MEIP), which the Commission employs when determining to what extent a capital injection or loan or guarantee by a member state to an airline, or any other industry for that matter, constitutes state aid. An insight into how the MEIP is applied is explained in the following passage taken from a communication to member states by the Commission. It reads:

> Any requests for extra finance naturally call for public undertakings and public authorities, just as it does for private undertakings . . . to analyse the the risk and the likely outcome of the project. In turn, the Commission realizes that this analysis of risk requires public undertakings, like private undertakings, to exercise entrepreneurial skills, which by the very nature of the problem implies a wide margin of judgement on the part of the investor. Within that wide margin the exercise of judgement by the investor cannot be regarded as involving state aid . . . Only where there are no objective grounds to reasonably expect that an investment will give an adequate rate of return that would be acceptable to a private investor in a comparable private undertaking operating under normal market conditions, is state aid involved . . . (Quoted in *Airline Competition in the Single European Market* by the CAA, p. 115. *Source*: Official Journal of the European Communities No 91/c 273/02 paragraph 27.)

In particular, when applying the MEIP to state financing, the Commission will take into account a number of considerations, such as whether or not a loan or guarantee to an airline was made on terms equivalent to that of a normal commercial transaction, and would a commercial bank be prepared to offer a loan in the first place. If it is probable that a commercial bank would not, then it is highly likely that some degree of state aid is present, allowing the airline an improved borrowing position in terms of either amount or interest rate charged. Clearly, if proven, this is a form of anti-competitive behaviour. In fact the application of the MEIP can be far more complex than has so far been described, and the process itself may not escape the political/nationalistic dimension that seems endemic in these matters.

The Air France case, as shown in Table C1.2, provides us with an illustration of the application of the MEIP. In 1991 and 1992, it was the recipient of over $942 million of funding: $310 million capital injection from the State itself and $632 million in the form of two loans, involving the state-owned Banque Nationale de Paris. Brussels did not view these as representing state aid as they were deemed to satisfy the MEIP. A prominent Commission official from the Air Transport Directorate made the following comment about the decision: The big question was whether the capital increase should be considered aid. We evaluated Air France very carefully. It appeared quite a well run company, with efficiency indicators better than others in the EC and a programme of staff reductions and other cost-cutting measures. We thought it could be accepted as commercial[11]. Yet, despite the monetary support, the financial position of Air France became worse. This resulted, in March 1993, in the airline receiving a further capital injection of around $262 million; however, the Commission decided that the injection – financed by the airline issuing bonds which were underwritten by a subsidiary of Caisse de Depot et Consignations-Participation – did not satisfy the MEIP. It was deemed to be aid in the sense of Article 92.1 of the Treaty of Rome. As the aid was not linked to any restructuring plan, the Commission determined that it was incompatible with the common market, so the airline must repay the subsidy. The French government has appealed against this decision to the ECJ. Air France, as commented upon below, has again asked for a third dose of financial assistance, a massive $3.8 billion capital injection.

Even when the Commission found that a proposal, or part of a proposal, did constitute state aid, this did not necessarily mean that it would be deemed incompatible with the common market; for example, it could come under one of the specific derogations set out in Article 92 of the Treaty of Rome (see Chapter 2). The Commission, in accordance with Article 92, has in the recent past approved aid to several EU airlines (see Table C1.2), all suffering financial problems, so that they could, in a relatively short period of time, return to financial viability and have no further requirement for aid. At least that was the theory. Accordingly the aid was granted for a limited period only, with any proposed alteration requiring Brussels permission. The permitting of state aid to Sabena provides us with an illustration of the policy in action. The airline made huge losses in 1991 and the Belgian government gave aid, in the form of cash, debt transfer and bridging finance, to the tune of $1040 million. Brussels approved it, with the Commission claiming that it:

> could be considered as an example of the Commission's policy to give airlines supporting past financial burdens a chance for a fresh start within the framework of a reorganization programme aimed at regaining commercial viability[12].

State aids and the Comité des Sages

In its report, the Comité des Sages came out strongly in favour of terminating all forms of privileged treatment for flag-carriers and sees privatization as the way of achieving this goal. It declared that state financing of airlines should be banned unless it meets normal market conditions. However, and for a brief period only, the Comité reluctantly accepted the need for state aid on a genuine 'one time, last time' condition, so as to enable restructuring leading to commercial viability. In addition, the Comité is in favour of applying strict terms to those airlines requesting approval for a last dose of

137

state aid, such as: the submission of a restructuring plan leading to financial and competitive viability within a predetermined time period, given credence by access to capital markets; the plan as well as attracting considerable interest from the private sector must eventually lead to privatization; the efficacy of the restructuring plan to be attested by independent professionals and this is to form part of the Commission's assessment procedure of these cases; that the airline must not use the state aid to take over another airline or expand its own capacity beyond the overall market growth.

These recommendations are non-binding. Even before the report of the Comité des Sages was published in January 1994, the Comission advocated that, on account of the third aviation package coming into force on 1 January 1993, a more rigorous approach to vetting potential aid proposals to EU airlines will be necessary[13]. The Commission communication entitled 'the way forward for civil aviation in Europe', contains an assessment of the principal recommendations put forward by the Comité des Sage. On state aids the communication asserts that 'most of the recommendations made by the "Comité des Sages" are very close to the Commission's decisions in a number of recent aid cases[14]. As evidence of this the Commission can point to the conditions it set when approving state aid to both Iberia and Aer Lingus.

In July 1992, the Spanish government were permitted by the Commission to provide financial support for Iberia, but only on the understanding that the capital injection would be the last one involving state aid; and that the aid must be used to restructure the airline as envisaged, and the monies must not be used to acquire shares in other EU airlines. Nearly eighteen months later, in December 1993, the Irish government, in its desire to provide Aer Lingus with state aid, had to meet similar conditions as set by the Commission. They included: the cost reduction programme at Aer Lingus must go ahead as agreed; the Irish government are required periodically to report to the Commission on the financial and economic progress of Aer Lingus; the airline may not expand its operating fleet; the Irish government will not grant any further aid to the airline; and the aid must not be used to acquire shares in other EU airlines.

State aid approval after the Comite des Sages

The report of the Comite was published in January 1994, and with the passing of only six months the Commission had duly sanctioned state aid totalling $7.1 billion to three EU airlines: Air France, TAP and Olympic Airways. This staggering amount of aid is equal to around 45 per cent of the losses western airlines made on their international scheduled flights in the last four years. TAP, in June, was the first to see its request for aid – $1.1 billion in the form of a cash injection plus $1088 million worth of loan guarantees – permitted by the Commission, but conditions were attached. Such as the payment of the second, third and fourth tranches of aid could only take place if TAP meets its operational targets; the airline must not go above the capacity ceiling set on flights in the European Economic Area (EEA); the Portuguese government have to provide the Commission with a yearly report on the restructuring of the airline; aid is not used to buy shares in other EU airlines; the Portuguese government must refrain from giving any further aid to TAP. The Commision also noted that it was the expressed intention of the Portuguese authorities to begin a partial privatisation of the airline in 1997.

A month later, the Commission agreed to both Air France's request for $3.8 billion in aid and Olympic Airways' subsidy package. As in the case of TAP, the Commission attached conditions. Air France, for example, has to sell its stake in Meridien hotels; the government, acting only as ordinary shareholders, has to allow the airline to be ran on commercial lines, so no further aid will be allowed; the aid is to be exclusively used for restructuring purposes as detailed in the restructuring plan, and its subsidiary, Air Inter, is excluded from the monies. Air France was further instructed not to increase the size of its fleet. Bernard Bosson, the French transport minister, was satisfied with the decision and added that the privatization of Air France was not on his agenda. A very different view was expressed by Sir Colin Marshall, the chairperson of BA. He argued that there was 'no justification for a subsidy of this size and the conditions imposed are wholly inadequate. Air France is once again being protected from the forces of competition[15]. Others agreed, for seven airlines – BA, Maersk, KLM, SAS, Air UK, TAT and British Midland – as well as the UK government have mounted a legal challenge to the Commission's granting of aid to Air France.

A new twist to the state aid affair has now been provided by Iberia. It again is after another handout, with the value of the requested aid package being around $986 million. The problem is that Iberia has already received a 'one time, last time' aid injection. In 1992 the Commission approved aid to Iberia on the understanding that this would be the last dose of aid to the airline. This thorny issue, if not quickly decided, will fall into the lap of the incoming transport Commissioner, Neil Kinnock, who took up his position in January 1995. Obviously this will be the first serious test of the 'one time, last time' policy.

Conclusion

In February 1994 the *Guardian* newspaper[16] scathingly declared that 'more than 95 per cent of all European routes are monopolies or duopolies. A meagre 26 routes out of more than 600 boast more than two operators.'

In regard to international scheduled city-pair routes within the EU, the CAA report[17] reached similar figures – 65 per cent of the routes are operated by monopolies, 29 per cent are in the hands of duopolies, with a mere 6 per cent operated by more than two airlines. Both the Comité des Sages and the Commission recognize that the new freedoms of the third aviation package have so far been little used by airlines. The Commission argues that the recent recession in the industry, coupled with the fact that full cabotage will not happen until 1997, has contributed to the slow take-up of the new freedoms. But some progress, albeit very limited, has taken place. BA, for example, with its stake in TAT, can now challenge the French in their own domestic backyard.

Appendix C1.1 EU Flag-carriers: ownership structure

Flag-carriers	Home base	Ownership
Aer Lingus	Eire	100% state owned
Air France	France	98.6% state owned
Alitalia	Italy	86.4% state owned
British Airways	UK	Listed public limited company
Iberia	Spain	99.8% state owned holding company INI
KLM	Netherland	38.2% state owned; 61.8% publicly listed
Lufthansa	Germany*	* 51.42% state owned; 5.51% public sector institutions and 43.07% private sector
Luxair	Luxembourg	23.11% state owned; 13.41% state owned bank; 37.62% private companies; 13% Lufthansa; 12.86 Luxair Group and others
Olympic	Greece	100% state owned
Sabena	Belgium	61.8% state owned 37.5% Finacta (itself 66.7% owned by Air France)
SAS		42.9% SILA (Sweden); 28.6% DDL (Denmark); 28.6% DNL (Norway). All three have a minimum state ownership of 50%
TAP	Portugal	100% state owned

* As part of the privatization process, in late September 1994, Lufthansa had a rights issue; the design being that the German government would not take up its right to new shares thereby reducing its equity stake in the airline from 51.42 per cent to just over 40 per cent

Select readings

Civil Aviation Authority (1993) *Airline Competition in the Single European Market*, CAP 623, London, November 1993.

Comité des Sages (1994) *Expanding Horizons*, A report for Air Transport to the European Commission, January 1994.

Commission communication, *The way forward for civil aviation in Europe*, No. 6976/94 MAR 17 [Com(94) 218 Final].

References

1 Comite des Sages (1994) *Expanding Horizons*, A report for Air Transport to the European Commission January 1994. p. 14.

2 Civil Aviation Authority (1993) *Airline Competition in the Single European Market*, CAP 623, London, November 1993. p. 106.

3 Commission communication, *The way forward for civil aviation in Europe*, No. 6976/94 MAR 17 [Com(94) 218 Final]. p. 6.

4 *Expanding Horizons op. cit.*, p. 20.

5 CAA report *op. cit.*, p. 61.

6 *Financial Times*, 28 April 1994, p. 26.

7 *Financial Times*, 12 May 1994, p. 22.

8 *Management Today*, April 1993, p. 38.

9 Ibid., p. 43.

10 Heinz Hilbrecht quoted in *Management Today*, April 1993, p. 42.

11 Ibid., p. 43.

12 Ibid., p. 43.

13 *23rd Competition Report*, Commission of the European Communities, 1993, p. 327.

14 Commission communication, *The way forward for civil aviation in Europe op. cit.*, p. 15.

15 *Financial Times* 28 July 1994, p. 2.

16 *The Guardian* Outlook Section, 5 and 6 February 1994. p. 23.

17 CAA report *op. cit.*, p. 117.

Questions

1 'Both KLM and Lufthansa have restructured without recourse to a government handout, so the recent approval by Brussels of the granting

of aid to Air France and other EU airlines is plainly an anti-competitive act.'
Discuss.

2 Identify and assess the factors which could undermine the implementation of the single Market in Air Transport initiative.

Case 2 Competition in European financial services: the banking industry

Max E Good

Introduction

The single market programme was designed to remove barriers to the free movement of goods, services, persons and capital within the European Community. Despite much scepticism and many misgivings, by the end of 1992 the programme was virtually complete, with agreement on over five hundred measures. An important part of the programme relates to financial services. The aim of the single market in financial services is to remove regulatory barriers to EC firms operating outside their country of origin. Hence, authorization to conduct business in one country within the Community will also constitute authorization to conduct business in all member states. This creates the so-called EC 'passport' the basis of which is that EC member states will mutually recognize, i.e. accept as adequate, the regulatory standards of other member states.

Under the passport system an EC member country authorising a firm to operate in its own country, its home state, will give de facto authority to operate in other member countries, 'host states'. Such authorized firms will generally be able to choose whether to supply services through branch networks, in which case such firms will establish a physical presence in host states, or they may choose to supply services on a cross-border basis without having a permanent physical presence in the host country. Subsidiary companies, set up outside a home state, will be subject to local authorisation requirements on a non-discriminatory basis.

A major factor underpinning the philosophy of the single market is the need to improve the competitiveness of European companies. The EC passport system seeks to achieve this underlying theme by attempting to open up markets to a wider range of participants and by allowing firms to choose the most cost-effective means of supplying services to a particular market. For example, firms can now operate throughout the community using a single unified capital base. This removes the need to establish subsidiary companies with separate capital bases. Such capital is often difficult to transfer and may be under-utilized as business shifts from country to country. A single unified capital base gives firms greater flexibility in the organization of their management and internal systems and enables them to deal with fewer sets of regulations and hence regulators.

The detailed definition of a passport is given by Directives. Each type or area of financial services has a Directive or set of Directives defining the scope in terms of the type of institution and the activities which it carries out. This is extremely important for the working of the single market as the activities covered by an authorization within a single country in the community will vary between countries. For example, in the UK a banking licence is only required for institutions taking deposits. In other member countries a banking licence is required for many non-deposit taking activities. As such, a Directive which referred only to 'banks' without further qualification would apply to different activities in different countries.

The Directives relating to financial services require that firms in a particular area are authorized. The Directives then go on to set out the conditions that a firm has to satisfy to be and continue to be such an authorized institution. The conditions relate to such areas as the adequacy of management and control activities, capital requirements and the 'fitness and properness' of the owners and managers of the firm. Authorising home-state supervisors are required to vet large shareholders prior to initial authorisation and have a continuing responsibility in this area particularly if a firm is planning significant changes.

The Directives protect not only the direct trading partners of a firm but should also reduce the possibility of systemic risk, by the setting of standard requirements particularly in the area of capital adequacy. Systemic risk is risk to the whole financial system due to the existence of poorly managed and/or under-capitalized firms. The Directives also help prevent unfair competitive advantage accruing to firms based in countries with inadequate prudential requirements.

The performance of foreign firms operating in a host state will be of interest to the state in which they operate. The Directives also spell out the division of responsibility between home and host states. Home states tend to take responsibility for prudential supervision of a firm as well as fitness and properness. Host states largely concentrate on the conduct of business with customers. The Directives acknowledge the need for cooperation between home and host states and they provide mechanisms for such cooperation. For example, 'gateways' are defined for the passing of confidential information.

In an undertaking as complex as the single market the legislators have accepted the need for possible change at a later date. As such, provision for later adaptations has been made in the Directives which allow limited amendments to be made without the need for full EC legislative procedure. Similarly, Directives may also contain transitional provisions, usually concerned with differing timetables for implementation between states.

Single market legislation in banking

The key piece of legislation is the Second Banking Coordination Directive (2BCD) This is set within a network of enabling and complementary controls. Figure C2.1 sets out the framework and highlights the central role of 2BCD.

An important point to note is that without the implementation of allied or enabling legislation the concept of a single market would be effectively undermined. For example, the Capital Liberalization Directive allows nationals of member states to open bank accounts in other member states and to carry out many cross-border transactions. Directives in such areas as solvency and company accounting standards are also of crucial importance. Developments outside the EU have also to be taken into account. In the wake of the Third World debt crisis the Bank for International Settlements (BIS), the central banks' central bank, has introduced capital adequacy and liquidity requirements for all banks, known as the Basle Ratios. The work of the Cooke Committee, the working party of the BIS which undertook to

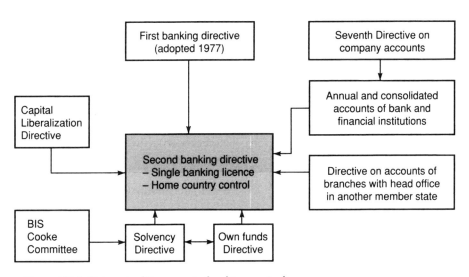

Figure C2.1 Network of Community banking controls

examine good practice and common standards, has as such been of critical importance to the Community in its deliberations with respect to the banking Directives. This underlines the close contact between the Community and the rest of the world.

The European Community is a huge bureaucratic entity with relationships between member states determined in detailed legal terms. The implementation of the single market in financial services in general and in banking in particular is based on a series of direct and related Directives. Some of the more important ones relating to banking are given in Table C2.1.

Work towards the creation of a single market in banking has been under

Table C2.1 *Directives: Financial services (banking)*

Directive	Purpose
First Banking Directive	Set up systems for authorising and supervising institutions' credit
Second Banking Directive	Provides authorization for cross-border business
Winding-up Directive	Provides for mutual recognition of insolvancy laws and reorganization winding-up procedures
Deposit Guarantee Directive	Harmonizes compensation schemes
Takeover Directive	Sets minimum standards for takers
Capital Adequacy Directive	Sets minimum capital requirements
Consolidated Supervision Directive	Provides for supervision of similar institutions on a common basis
Own funds	Set out a common definition and classification of capital
Solvency ratio	Lays down common risk asset ratios
Bank Accounts	Seeks to harmonize accounting rules
Bank Branches	Lays down reporting requirements for branches within a Member State
Large Exposures	Harmonizes rules concerning large deposits/loans to individual borrowers

way for a considerable time. The principle of free movement of capital was included in the Treaty of Rome which established the Community in 1958. The importance of banking is recognized by the member states. In recent years the financial services sector in Europe has experienced rapid change. Markets have become increasingly global, rather than national or even continental, in nature. Many firms have grasped the opportunities offered by deregulation and microchip technology. Many in the USA and Japan and to a lesser extent Europe have built up operations in centres outside their own countries. Over the next decade such progress is likely to continue. A single European market will give firms the scale required to compete with the biggest and best worldwide.

However, over the years all advanced economies have created restrictions and barriers on their domestic markets to cross-border activities. Such restrictions are not purely aimed at protecting domestic firms but are to protect investors or promote particular social, economic or other objectives. But all of these restrictions determine the organization and nature of a country's banking systems. The European Commission has established a programme of legislation intended to open up the single market in banking and, indeed, in financial services in general. Firms now have the right to trade financial services throughout the EU on the basis of single authorisation 'passport' from their home member state. The negotiations have resulted in a comprehensive home-country authorization regime for banking.

Notwithstanding the above, three major obstacles to a true single market in financial services remain. The first is taxation. Differences in the tax treatment of many financial products affects sales and what is sold. There are significant differences in the tax treatment of financial products throughout the community. Such differences may prove difficult to resolve, particularly as tax measures require the unanimous approval of member countries. Secondly, most directives give countries the right to apply local conduct-of-business rules to foreign firms, if a broad general good is involved. The concept of the general good could be used to justify protectionist measures in domestic markets. The third and possibly most pervasive of all barriers is culture. Customers and institutions tend to be extremely conservative and tend to naturally favour domestic financial institutions. Such cultural problems are often underpinned by institutional arrangements such as the state-ownership or cross-ownership of financial and industrial firms which entrench relationships and raise significant barriers to competition.

Banking and related Directives

The starting point to the creation of a single market in banking services was the First Banking Coordination Directive (1BCD) of 1977. This required member states to set up systems for authorising and supervising credit institutions – which in the UK largely referred to banks and building societies. The Directive was implemented by the Banking Act 1979 (now Banking Act 1987) and the Building Societies Act 1986. Under these acts authorization requires that a credit institution has to have capital separate from the resources of its proprietors, be able to meet an unspecified initial capital requirement test, be directed by at least two persons and be directed by persons of 'sufficient repute' and of 'sufficient experience'. It permits member states' credit institutions to set up elsewhere in the Community on a non-discriminatory basis. There is also provision for cooperation between supervisory authorities.

The second major building bloc of the single banking market was the Second Banking Co-ordination Directive (2BCD) of 1989 which came into force on 1 January 1993. This directive permits a credit institution to do cross-border business within the Community without the need for further authorization and together with the Own Funds and Solvency Ratio Directives gives the 'passport' for credit institutions throughout the community. 2BCD sets out the conditions on which a credit institution authorized in one member state has a right to establish a branch in, or provide banking services to, other member states on the strength of its home-country authorization.

The scope of the passport under the Directive includes deposit-taking, lending, money transmission services, leasing, participation in securities issues, issuing credit cards, traveller cheques and other means of payments, securities and foreign exchange trading, and portfolio management and advice. If a credit institution's authorization in its home state covers these activities, it can supply them throughout the Community.

Such an undertaking has not been lightly given and the two banking directives and their associated directives set detailed and wide-ranging criteria that have to be met in all areas of banking authorization, control and supervision for a credit institution to be and remain authorized. 2BCD requires credit institutions to have a capital base of at least ECU 5 million, it sets minimum requirements for information disclosure about major shareholders and it sets limits on the level of banks' shareholdings in non-financial institutions. Of particular importance among the related directives are the Own Funds and Solvency Ratio Directives which respectively define capital and lay down minimum capital requirements.

The Large Exposure Directive requires that loans or deposits of ten per cent or more of a credit institution's own funds be reported to the supervisory authority and it prohibits exposure of more than a quarter of its funds. Similarly, consolidated supervision provides that where credit institutions own directly or indirectly 25 per cent or more of the capital of another credit or financial institution, they will be supervized on a consolidated basis. Such supervision is exercized by the competent authorities in the country where the head office of the institution owning the share of capital is situated.

Competition in practice

The Second Banking Coordination Directive (2BCD) came into effect in the European Union on 1 January 1993 and for those EFTA countries who have chosen to participate in the European Economic Area (EEA)[1] on 1 January 1994. As a consequence a total of 99 branches of European banks in London are now designated as European Authorized Institutions (EAI) and are supervized solely by their home-country supervisor for all purposes except liquidity, which is a shared responsibility with the host country. The aim of the single market legislation, that any bank incorporated in an EEA country is free to branch out elsewhere in the EEA, has been achieved in theory. What of the 2BCD passport in practice?

Pressure for change in financial services has come from a variety of sources in recent years:

- Changes in market structure due to deregulation and the abolition of protectionist measures have occurred in Europe, the USA and Japan. Of such measures the widespread abolition of exchange controls allowing the free movement of capital between major economies was particularly important, as were the removal of legal barriers and administrative regulations concerning mergers, acquisitions and other alliances.
- Technological advances – such as telephone and screen-based banking – have improved the way in which financial services are provided as they lower entry costs.
- Widespread recession has led to large losses in domestic markets while at the same time the introduction of international supervisory agreements has forced banks to strengthen their capital bases. This has led to scaling down of activity and/or a selling-off of non-'core' activities.
- The single market programme within the European Union has removed restrictive regulations and sought to allow financial services companies to compete in previously closed markets. The aim has been to improve efficiency and lower costs to consumers.

Options for change

The above pressures have given rise to a need for a strategic response from firms engaged in the financial services sector. There are various possible strategies open to these firms. Mergers are one option. Cross-border mergers between major banks have not yet occurred and are thought unlikely. The larger banks tend to have very well defined identities which they would not wish to lose. Mergers between smaller institutions to improve their positions against larger rivals and to pool resources is much more likely as is the acquisition of smaller businesses by larger ones. Other likely options are loose alliances, share swaps and cooperation agreements among smaller institutions.

As a general point the single market was not expected to have much impact on banks' strategies for wholesale business. In London, for example, foreign banks have been active in the wholesale money markets (corporate banking, money and capital markets) far more than in the retail markets. The former do not require large costly branch networks and they are global in nature. Thus, such markets are highly contestable. Within Europe, the largest banks from each member country have been present in the major financial centres for some time.

The retail sector is seen as far less contestable. Generally, such markets are highly profitable, but the major institutions have expressed considerable scepticism concerning the development of a single market in this area. The major problem for potential entrants is the existence of significant sunk costs such as the need for very large distribution networks, a local reputation and a knowledge of the local customer base.

Responses to the single market – an overview

Recent work by the Bank of England has investigated a sample of 247 cross-border alliances between EU financial institutions during the period 1987–1993[2]. Although the study does not claim to be comprehensive it reaches some interesting conclusions. The data collected by the Bank of England refers to banking and other financial services. The Bank found that the most common form of cross-border alliance has been the purchase of stakes in small entities by larger institutions which have a dominant position in their domestic market. Outright acquisition or the purchase of a majority stake totalled 46 per cent of the sample. The purchase of minority interests were also popular accounting for 32 per cent of the deals. Joint ventures, often cited as an alternative route for entering new markets, took only 5 per cent of the total. There have been no cross-border mergers between institutions with a dominant position in their domestic markets. Differences in culture, management style and cost have been cited as the underlying reasons.

The evidence collected by the Bank shows that banks in the EC have been quite active in forging cross-border links in recent years. Their data indicates that French banks have been the most active in forging alliances and that Spain and the UK have been the most popular target countries. It is evident that many firms have been successful in identifying opportunities at an acceptable price. Opportunities have arisen where other institutions have withdrawn from particular markets either to concentrate on core businesses or because of poor performance. However, very few of the alliances have provided a foreign institution with a major share of a core national market.

The bulk of the alliances undertaken have been concerned with retail markets, despite the fact that barriers to cross-border alliances are much lower in wholesale markets. This undoubtedly reflects the fact that such markets have been international in character for a considerable period of time. In the retail banking sector the single market has yet to make a significant impact. Perceived barriers to entry remain high and areas most often quoted as problems are the cost and availability of branch networks, language, culture and customs, national regulations and continuing differences in taxation regimes.

Interestingly, the Bank finds it difficult to assess the extent to which cross-border activity has been prompted by the single market. Banks' decisions have for a number of years been driven by diverse factors of which 1992 is just one. 2BCD is undoubtedly responsible for some of the restructuring seen to date as it put pressure on authorities to deregulate to ensure both competitiveness and compliance prior to 1992.

It should also be noted that a number of developments which are in the pipeline will also affect banks' future strategy. Notable among these are further single market measures, the expected privatization of state-owned banks in countries such as France and Italy and perhaps most importantly further progress towards the integration of European economies and economic and monetary union (EMU). Few banks are currently prepared for EMU; indeed, in general they have not yet begun to take into account the profound effects EMU will have on their business.

Experiences with cross-border alliances

The various forms cross-border alliances can take have been outlined above. They include mergers, acquisitions, loose alliances based on cooperation, the setting-up of branches and subsidiaries and the direct selling of services into other countries. We have noted that despite extensive legislation and the subsequent liberalization and deregulation of markets substantial barriers to cross-border activity remain, although certain types of market are more contestable than others. How in practice have such alliances worked out?

Royal Bank of Scotland and Banco Santandar

The alliance between Royal Bank of Scotland (the UK's sixth largest) and Banco Santandar (Spain's fourth largest) is based on a mutual small shareholding. Santandar has a 9.9 per cent shareholding in the Royal Bank of Scotland, the Royal Bank of Scotland a 1.5 per cent shareholding in Santandar.

Each company maintains complete managerial and executive independence and pursues their own overall strategies. The alliance was forged in 1988. At this time both banks were worried about becoming takeover targets and wanted to expand, remain independent, but also enter the wider European market. The banks have similarities but also differences. Both, for example are old institutions well established in their countries. They also have head offices away from the accepted or major financial centres of their respective countries. Management styles, however, are very different. The Spanish bank has a paternal management style based on its close association with a single family who own 3.5 per cent of its stock and hold senior positions. This contrasts sharply with the Royal Bank of Scotland's more collegiate style.

The major achievements of the alliance are:

1 Special treatment of each others' clients in the respective home markets.
2 Joint subsidiary in Gibraltar which handles expatriate banking needs in Southern Spain.
3 Joint shareholding in another Iberian bank.
4 Information exchanges concerning experiences with various products and activities:
   (a) Santandar introduced a high interest chequing account after studying the Royal Bank of Scotland's experience in the same area.
   (b) The Royal Bank of Scotland's Columbus project – a major streamlining of its UK branch network – was based on a study of Santandar's methods.
   (c) A proposal by Santandar to jointly purchase a French bank was turned down by the Royal Bank of Scotland as too expensive. Santandar's subsequent experience with similar acquisitions in Italy and Belgium has shown the wisdom of this move. It has relinquished the Italian stake and closed down its Belgian operation.
5 Possibly the major accomplishment has been the Inter-Bank On-line System (IBOS). Using computer networks they have linked their branch networks and can provide a unique cross-border banking service. Termed 'seamless banking' the network initially linked 1350 Santandar branches in Spain to 800 Royal Bank of Scotland branches in the UK. It has now been extended to include banks in France and Portugal and further links with Belgium, Italy and the USA are planned. By the turn of the century commission from IBOS could account for between 5 to 10 per cent of the two banks' pre-tax income. This development is particularly interest-

ing given a recent decision by the union's single market commissioner. He indicated the existence of barriers to trade and hence competition arising from the high level of costs associated with the international transfer of money. Lack of action by the banks has led to the imposition of a six-day time limit on such transactions and the proposed outlawing of double charging. Other banks will have to follow the lead of Royal Bank of Scotland and Banco Santandar or withdraw from this area of money transmission.

6 Staff exchanges have been fostered between the banks, as have significant managerial and executive contacts. The discussions of Royal Bank of Scotland experiences following the UK's suspension from the ERM and the subsequent rapid fall in UK interest rates shaped Santandar's investment policy in the uncertain days of late 1992. Heavy buying of Spanish bonds and treasury bills in October/November 1992 reaped significant profits in later months as Spanish interest rates fell.

In conclusion, the two banks express themselves extremely satisfied with the alliance. They have profitably swapped information, experiences and expertize leading to product innovation and increased market share. IBOS, possibly the major achievement of the alliance, will be copied and competition in this area will increase, with joint treasury department cooperation likely. However, future developments are still being discussed. The success of the alliance appears to be based upon various factors. Significantly, the two banks do not compete with each other in their respective home markets, thus allowing for a free flow of ideas and information. Both have worked hard to overcome or at least understand and accommodate language and internal differences. Both appear to be benefiting financially from the move.

Banque National de Paris and Dresdner Bank

The link-up between Banque National de Paris (BNP) and Dresdner is an interesting example of an alliance between two of Europe's largest financial institutions. It takes the form of a minority shareholding: Dresdner has taken a 0.9 per cent stake in the newly privatized Banque National de Paris and the French bank has taken a similar holding in its German partner. These holdings may be increased to 10 per cent of each others' capital, as the alliance develops.

Underpinning the move is the problem of low earnings in recession-hit markets and the ensuing need to reduce staff and other running costs. Parallel to this is the growing demand from customers for cross-border banking services in Europe which is forcing banks into cross-border link-ups. Banque National de Paris see the alliance with Dresdner as the core of a Europe-wide banking alliance which could grow into a multinational structure providing uniform services through a European-wide network of participating banks.

Central to their strategy the banks are undertaking joint investments in technology and communications to extend the range of their operations and to lower unit costs. They have also set up subsidiary companies in Switzerland, Hungary, the Czech Republic, Turkey and Russia. They plan to link their computer systems so that each others' customers can transfer money through the branches of the other. They argue that as the single market develops clients will need quick and cheap trans-European money transmission mechanisms.

Both the Banque National de Paris and Dresdner have indicated that they will seek links with other European banks to expand their retail banking activities. The problem for them is that many obvious partners have already forged strong links and Banque National de Paris and Dresdner, although large, are entering the alliance market at a late date. The two banks shrug this problem off, arguing that the Franco-German axis is the most important European link and that others will be drawn into its ambit.

Conclusions

The above case study on the effects of the single market programme on the banking industry in Europe highlights the complex nature of strategic developments within the industry. Some banking developments within Europe can be ascribed to the introduction of the Second Banking Coordination Directive. But in general banks have made little use of the new passport arrangements. This is unremarkable as the market for banking services has always been reasonably open. In addition, few banks were in an expansionary phrase when the Directive came into force, due mainly to factors associated with the European recession and the drive to concentrate on 'core' business. Nevertheless, there has been some movement, often associated with the improvement in cross-border money transmission services.

Many regard the current level of achievement in the banking sector as remarkable, given the powerful vested interests the legislators were up against. Indeed, within the financial services sector as a whole banking is outstanding with slower progress being made in areas such as insurance and stockbroking. In addition, some countries still have derogations stopping access to various areas of their financial sectors; however, firms should be able to compete effectively in all EU countries in the foreseeable future.

References

1   At the time of writing the EEA comprises Austria, Finland, Iceland, Norway and Sweden.
2   Cross-border alliances in banking and financial services in the single market. *Bank of England Quarterly Bulletin*, August 1993.

Questions

1   What are the major remaining obstacles to cross-border alliances within the EU?
2   Compare and contrast the effectiveness of the concept of a single market in banking in the retail and wholesale markets.
3   Outline the factors which have limited the European banks' take-up of the opportunities offered by the single market.

Case 3   Competition policy: the Hungarian experience

Pal Majoros and Laszlo Nyusztay

Economic and political background

Since the political changes of 1989–1990, Hungary, along with other ex-socialist countries of Central and Eastern Europe, has been following the road of overall social-economic transformation. As is often commented by foreign observers, Hungary – of all the former centrally planned economic systems – has made the greatest advances in developing a liberal market economy. Analysis of recent changes therefore, generally describes Hungary not only as 'a peninsula of stability in the sea of ethnic conflicts' of the region but also as 'the first Central European country to be reborn as an economically restructured post-Communist democracy[1].

However pleasing these observations may be, the process of what is called 'systemic change' in Eastern Europe can not be regarded as completed even in Hungary. Political transition has started fairly smoothly, changes have become decisive, a pluralistic parliamentary democracy has been formed, a legal state with constitutional guarantees exists and human rights are protected. However, total economic restructuring may take longer, especially under the conditions of an acute and lasting recession in and outside the country and with the collapse of COMECON and Eastern trade and the revival of protectionist attitudes in international trade relations.

Despite the difficulties, both internal and external, significant achievements have nonetheless been made in Hungary under the rule of the National–Conservative (1990–1994) and the recently elected Social–Liberal (1994–) coalitions. After the first freely elected government came into power in May 1990, the initial two years of its economic programme were devoted to establishing the legal and institutional framework of a market economy, promoting internal economic stability and restructuring the country's foreign economic relations. By the end of 1993, the Hungarian parliament had adopted more than 180 new laws and law-amendments in order to create new market conditions. Prices, wages and imports have been liberalized. The right of free enterprise has been restored. A radical change in property relations has taken place in favour of the private sector. The share of developed market economies in the country's exports and imports has risen above 67 per cent, including nearly 45 per cent with the EU – with which Hungary has had an association agreement since December 1991. Although there has been a fall in demand, GDP and employment, along with a considerable deficit in state budget and balance of payments, inflation has been curbed and kept under control, foreign capital inflow is the highest in the region and foreign exchange reserves have been accumulated to an adequate extent[2]. Among economic priorities of the post-1990 Hungarian government special importance has been attached to the development of a new, favourable business environment, fair competition and curtailing the influence of monopolies[3].

It has to be mentioned at this point that efforts in Eastern Europe as a whole to introduce free competition could rely only on very limited recent experience and relatively underdeveloped understanding of the socio-economic issues. As Dallago[4] correctly pointed out, the outcome of current transitional strategies in Soviet-type systems depends, at least in part, on 'pre-existing factors' inherent in the basic economic and political characteristics of state socialism. These characteristics include soft budget constraints, state interference in the economy, monopoly ineffective incentives, and populist policies. Competition was also hindered by historical and cultural factors such as the absence of market institutions, lack of democratic traditions and, in many cases, direct aversion to market and private ownership[4]. But the two basic factors which exclude the mere possibility of competition from state socialist economies emanated from the very essence of the system: first, the overall shortage of supply, accurately described by the Hungarian Kornai[5]. in his famous study, and second from the very low standard of qualitative trade requirements of COMECON markets in general and the domestic markets of the individual countries in particular. It can be therefore regarded as natural that competition was almost missing from the economies of COMECON countries where the number of market actors was very limited and the overwhelming majority of industrial and service branches were dominated by huge, immobile state-run monopolies and oligopolies.

However, certain 'pre-existing factors' of Eastern European economies can not be evaluated as entirely negative as far as their impact on the business climate is concerned. Dallago, Torok and other researchers attribute considerable significance to the fact that in certain countries private entrepreneurship and business initiatives could, to some extent, develop[6]. Hungary is a good example of this, especially after the mid-1960s. As a comprehensive case-study made by the OECD in 1991 stated, in the period 1964–1989

Hungary moved far away from the traditional central planning model by abolishing compulsory plan-targets and monetary overhang, decentralising decision-making responsibilities to enterprises and introducing profit-oriented incentive schemes along with indirect macroeconomic control through monetary and fiscal means. Important elements of a market economy such as partial price and taxation reforms, new company law and modified banking system were introduced prior to the systemic change[7].

As a consequence of reforms introduced after 1968 and in the 1980s, a 'second economy' emerged in various forms, and by 1988 its share reached 30 per cent in total output, 33 per cent of total working time, 87 per cent in repair and maintenance, 75 per cent in private housing construction[8]. This 'competitive' sector contributed a great deal to the formation of relatively strong 'competitive middle class' of skilled workers, agriculturists, retailers, technocrats and highly qualified intellectuals.

Another post-1968 feature promoting recent transition was the policy of increased access to the world economy. Certain companies with a relatively high level of autonomy and badly needed Western technology, turned to Western partners and made business contacts. Deterioration of the terms of trade and repeated waves of indebtedness in the 1970s and 1980s also necessitated an increase in Hungarian exports to the West. Consequently, the share of trade with COMECON countries fell to 43–44 per cent by 1988, while the proportion of industrialized market economies rose up to the same level, as compared to the respective figures of 70–71 per cent and 22–23 per cent in 1968[9]. This development, which is regarded as unique in the former Socialist bloc, meant a more direct interaction with the world market, a distortion-free evaluation of Hungarian production and business performance thus improving the conditions of the formation and spread of competitive, market-type behaviour patterns.

The new economic policy and competition

The conservative and the social–liberal governments have both emphasized the importance of measures designed to ensure the fairness of competition. As was laid down in the guiding principles of the new economic policy, one of the first tasks of the government was to terminate the practice of state aid that favoured huge undertakings with dominant positions. The government sought to distance itself from the activities of groups of companies which seek to gain an unfair market advantage through central preferences and unjustified liquidity-expansion obtained on the pretext of invigorating the economy or taking a business out of bankruptcy. The government now regulates the operations of surviving natural monopolies, seeking to prevent the inheritance of monopolistic positions and the formation of new monopolies in the privatization process. The new policy envisages an efficient protection of the domestic market and production by introducing rules in conformity with GATT provisions and stresses bringing domestic legal and ethical norms of market and competition into line with those of developed market economies, especially the European Community[10].

Competition policy is thus conceived by the Hungarian government in its broad sense. It extends not only to traditional issues like prohibition of unfair competition, control of concerted practices or merger control but it also covers general economic policy fields such as privatization, deregulation and trade policies including import liberalization. In this approach, particular attention is devoted to venture-incentive policy and special treatment of small and medium companies by the state[11].

Both the concrete measures to promote competition and the results of this policy can be summarized as follows:

1   As regards property relations, the main achievements are the increasing privatization of the state sector and the development of new ventures. Between 1989 and 1993 over 500-state owned ventures have been converted into private businesses, 700 are currently being transformed and 4000 undertakings are pre-privatized (that is, offered and prepared for privatization by State Property Agency). Privatized state property accounts for 21 per cent for all assets of state companies and ongoing privatization affects a further 25 per cent of such properties. As a result, by December 1993 the private sector accounted for a 45 per cent share of GDP as opposed to a 10 per cent share in 1989. Moreover, the corporate structure of the economy has changed fundamentally. In contrast to the former socialist pattern there are around 180,000 business organizations and half a million entrepreneurs in Hungary today, three-quarters of the undertakings employing fewer than 20 people[12].

    The privatization process and new business investment are largely facilitated by the inflow of foreign capital. Direct foreign capital investment in Hungary in the form of economic partnerships has been possible since 1972. Laws passed in 1988 created a stable political, legal and economic environment – attractive to foreign investors – with a high degree of business safety and adequate returns, as well as free repatriation of profits. Since 1989 the number of joint ventures has rapidly increased and the total capital investment has amounted to about USD 7 billion. About 50 per cent of the capital invested in Eastern Europe has come to Hungary. Regarding the origin and the size of foreign capital, the USA, Germany and Austria take the lead. Over 20,000 firms, including GM and Suzuki, have been set up with foreign capital. Foreign capital has played a major role in the development of small scale businesses which had previously been absent from the Hungarian economy but which now constitute the largest market segment in the competitive sphere[13]. Approximately 35–40 per cent of FDI inflow into Hungary has been directed to areas dominated by monopolies, firms with dominant market position and oligopolies.

2   Major achievements have been recorded in improving the business environment and conditions of competition. Their legal foundation was laid down in a package of laws adopted by the parliament in 1987– 1989. Among these laws the most important were the new laws on taxation, the two-tier banking system, acts on Economic Association/ Corporations, Enterprise Transformation and Foreign Direct Investment. New accounting and bankruptcy legislation fundamental to normal business operations came later, after the 1990 general elections. Then prices and wages became almost entirely liberalized and several founda- tions and offices were set up to assist small businesses with financing ('Existence-credit', 'Start-credit', etc.). Bankruptcy law has helped compe- tition and market selection mechanisms to come into existence. Since it came into force some 3900 bankruptcy and liquidation procedures have been initiated including such protected giants of the past as the Lenin Metallurgy Works in Miskolc, Hungarian Shipyard and Cane Works, ORION and VIDEOTON Electronics. RABA or IKARUS Vehicles avoided bankruptcy by transforming themselves into smaller limited liability companies. Within the framework of destatification of the public sector, state subsides to companies have dropped to a level acceptable in a market economy (from 13 per cent to 5 per cent of the GDP) and subsidies to separate state funds have fallen from 13 per cent to 3 per cent[14]. With this the role of the state has considerably been reduced in the competitive business sphere as well as in the redistribution of the national income.

3   One basic element of Hungarian economic policy to promote competition is the liberalization of foreign trade. As early as the middle of the 1980s it had become obvious to Hungarian decision makers that further import restrictions would inevitably hinder not only technological mod- ernization but also any increase in exports, while liberalization could result in equal market position of the actors of the economy and reduce the state role in macroeconomic decisions.

Trade liberalization meant basically two things in Hungary: the liberal- ization of imports and the organizational liberalization of foreign trade.

With regard to the former, imports were liberalized step-by-step, in commodity groups. By the end of 1993, 95 per cent of all imports became exempt from licensing requirement.

As far as institutional decentralization of foreign trade is concerned, as a result of this policy the number of firms dealing with exports and imports rose to 12,000 in 1990 and above 40,000 in 1993, as compared to several hundreds in 1989[15]. Now, two-thirds of companies active in the economy are involved also in foreign trade. Maintaining external trade relations has become a civil right of all Hungarian subjects. The market share of state-run foreign trade enterprises fell back due to the termination of their monopolistic position and the collapse of COMECON and Eastern trade. Many of them have been privatized and a number of small companies with limited liability have appeared in the competitive sphere.

As far as Hungarian experience goes, trade liberalization offers great advantages as well as certain dangers. On the one hand, import liberalisation is good for domestic customers and at the same time offers a more direct contact between the economy and world market standards. On the other hand, as a consequence of the rapid and almost total liberalisation, more than 80 per cent of the Hungarian industrial output has been exposed to competition, with the consequence that a number of previously prospering undertakings have gone into liquidation. Therefore, influential groups of economists now demand a better-considered liberalisation and more efficient market protection. As for newly born SMEs in the trade sector, their performance is also controversial: while they prove to be generally fast and flexible, foreign partners do not always have confidence in them and seek business contacts with traditional, more experienced and wealthier companies.

Competition policy: legal and institutional frameworks

In Hungary, the market and competition became regulated for the first time in 1923, by the Law V. on Unfair Competition, followed by the Anti-Cartel Law in 1931. Prior to 1948, cases of unfair business conduct had been judged mainly by the Jury of the Chamber of Commerce in the framework of ethical (not legal) procedures. Although the Jury had no sanctions, its decisions have served to the present as important legal sources of commercial jurisprudence.

After the 1948 Communist takeover, competition law was not formally repealed but it was deliberately regarded as 'a remnant of capitalist past' and as such, it became totally neglected both in business practice and in education. Since state enterprises had compulsory plan-figures to fulfil, they simply were 'unable' to commit unfair acts between each other. Consequently, malpractices could occur only in the quasi-competitive sphere, i.e. between state companies and private entrepreneurs. As soon as private sectors started to develop after the 1968 reform, the Competition Act of 1923 soon became rediscovered and applied to a limited number of cases. The emergence of *de facto* competition and various forms of advertising by companies accelerated legislation to regulate the new economic phenomena. However, it was not until 1984 that the Law IV. on Unfair Business Practices was enacted by Parliament, followed by the Directives on Advertising Activities of the Ministry of Trade in 1988. The officially declared basic objective of the Law was 'to efficiently counter all forms of unfair market conduct that may occur in the new mechanism of economic direction' such as unfair competition, fraud against consumers, restriction of competition, abuse of a dominant market position and misleading advertizements[16]. But, as was noticed by the Hungarian jurist I. Voros, the 1984 Law was almost a modernized version of the 1923 Law. It reflected the ambiguous approach of the Communist leadership to the market economy and competition by containing a number of compromizes which reduced its significance and use[17].

The Act LXXXVI. of 1990 on the Prohibition of Unfair Market Practices adopted by parliament on 20 November 1990 (hereinafter the Competition Act) came into force on 1 January 1991. It is the first comprehensive basic document in Hungarian economic history to describe competition in terms of the public interest as well as to project justified interests of competitors and consumers.

The Act consists of Preamble, General Provisions and eight Chapters. The Preamble concretizes the principle of the Hungarian constitution on the right to free enterprise and competition. Section 9/2 reads: 'The Republic of Hungary recognizes and promotes the right and freedom of competition[18]. General Provisions declare freedom and fairness of competition and render unlawful all acts and behaviour that jeopardize the legitimate interests of competitors and consumers. This clause, often termed the 'Blanket Clause', has been widely criticized due to the fact that its scope is negatively determined by the scope of the other paragraphs in the law.

Chapter I (Prohibition of unfair competition) protects competitors' reputations and credibility against any kind of defamation and falsification, and prohibits abuse of business secrets. It proscribes the unwarranted use of brands, speculative withholding of goods and tied selling, unfair tendering and auctions and stock exchange dealings as well as other forms of unfair competition. The provisions of Chapter II (Prohibition against consumer fraud) forbid false information regarding basic features of goods or the concealing of faults, misleading comparisons and advertisements, and the use of deceptive labels. Chapter III (Prohibition of agreements restricting competition) imposes a general ban on agreements between competitors excluding or restricting competition and other concerted practices such as market allocation or price fixing. However, it provides exemptions from the prohibition in cases where restriction of competition does not exceed certain levels or the concomitant advantages outweigh the disadvantages. Abuse of market dominance is generally prohibited by the Articles of Chapter IV (Prohibition of abuse of dominant position) including abuse of unjustified advantages by creating disadvantageous market conditions or forcefully influencing decisions of competitors.

For the purpose of preventing undesirable effects of market concentration, Chapter V (Control of concentration of entrepreneurs) regulates mergers and acquisitions by requiring mergers and takeovers above certain thresholds of market share and joint turnover to be approved by the competition authority (the thresholds are fixed at 30% and HUF 10 billion = USD 100 million respectively). All transactions which would have the effect of impeding the formation, development or continuation of competition shall not be authorized. (Article 24, Para (1)).

Chapters VI and VII (Organizational and procedural provisions) fix the rules of initiation of procedures and jurisdiction (with respect to mergers and takeovers). According to these, the procedure may be initiated either upon request of the participating parties or *ex officio*, by the state agency concerned. Cases of unfair market conduct fall under the jurisdiction of the Court. Issues related to consumer fraud are handled jointly by the Court and the competition authority, while all other matters belong to the exclusive competence of the latter.

Chapter VIII of the Competition Act is devoted to the establishment and competence of the state competition authority. As it is stipulated in Article 52, 'the Office of Economic Competition shall perform the duties of supervising competition' in accordance with the provision of the Act and in cooperation with other state agencies. The Office of Economic Competition (OEC) is subordinated to the parliament, its president and vice-presidents are appointed by the President of the Republic on the recommendation of the Prime Minister. The OEC is funded by the state budget and its decisions are subject only to the law.

OEC carries out legal (jurisdictional) and administrative duties. Its authority covers the following basic areas[19]:

- It investigates unfair market practices as stipulated in the Competition Act, prohibits and penalizes abuses and grants exemptions.
- It takes care of preliminary licensing of merger acquisitions.
- It looks after commercial market inspection (but is not authorized to settle contract disputes). Occasionally it investigates the pricing practices of companies (in cases of alleged unfair competition).
- It may contest decisions of government authories if they curtail freedom

of competition, and may initiate civil proceedings in court whenever an activity contrary to the Competition Act is found.

● Upon request of the submitting ministry it will express its views on drafts of new laws which affect competition. The President of OEC attends government sessions with a non-voting status whenever issues concerning competition are discussed[19].

In the period 1991–1993 OEC dealt with about 500 proceedings; the majority of these (85–90%) were initiated on the request of citizens, economic units and other non-governmental organizations and 10–15% *ex officio*. Ninety per cent of these cases were concluded in the year of initiation, by, in 60 per cent of the cases, decision during investigation and, in 40 per cent, by ruling of the Competition Council. These types of cases cover almost the whole scope of unfair market practices described in the Competition Act[20]. A breakdown of the cases concluded by ruling of the Competition Council is given in Table C3.1.

Table C3.1 *Types of cases*

	1991	1992	1993
General clause	11	24	35
Unfair market practices	–	1	1
Consumer fraud	6	24	29
Cartel	5	3	3
Cartel notification	3	2	–
Abuse of dominant position	28	32	26
Merger	5	8	3
Case filed at court	-	1	–
Case transferred by court for imposing fine	1	1	–
Price increase notification	5	6	4
Article 65 ('Old Cartel')	13	–	–
Sum total	77	102	101

Source: OEC, 1993

At the beginning of the period abuse of dominant position led the list, but in 1993 it was outstripped by the deception of the consumer and the general clause provisions.

The appearance of unfair market practices in the Hungarian economy can be attributed to a number of factors of which the following are examples:

164

1   The relative lack of market economy experience. As has already been mentioned, there was no market economy in the history of Hungary and Eastern Europe prior to 1990, apart from some short-lived attempts. This means not only a belated industrialization, backward labour culture and management skills, but also a lack of awareness of the rules and techniques of competition and advertising. As is shown by numerous enforcement actions (mainly for misleading advertizements and consumer fraud) the violation of the law is caused, at least partly, by a lack of competition-mindedness and know-how. This was behind the relatively large number of unjustified initiations of OEC investigations of cases of abuse of dominant position.

There is a very sharp competition in the Hungarian economy with hundreds of thousands of new, hitherto unknown, market actors appearing on the scene with a strong wish to gain customers. Sometimes poor knowledge of rules and limits causes them to use unfair means.

2   The inheritance of the pre-1990 state socialist regime is one of the decisive factors in many aspects. First, to 'manage' in the labyrinth of numerous, often contradictory laws or to evade state rules was not always considered as unfair – rather a virtue or at least a kind of managerial skill. The new mentality of autonomous and responsible market actors has not been formed yet. Secondly, the monopolistic positions usual in state socialist economies have not ceased to exist but have partly survived in a changed form. As recently published empirical research of three markets (taxis, books and flowers) has shown, the oligopolistic market structures that were characteristics earlier have been replaced by a kind of 'monopolistic competition', i.e. price cartels of hugh distribution networks[21]. Thirdly, preserving their experiences from the past, many participants of the economy look at monopolistic positions, cartels or the absence of competition as natural facts of economy and accept the dominant position of their partners as inevitable or still expect the state to solve all their market problems.

3   Under the conditions of rapidly changing economy, long-lasting recession and inflation, free competition is generally hindered and distorted. Under such circumstances as, for example, rapid inflation, it is not easy to distinguish between self-protecting parallel practices of enterprises against external impacts and deliberate concerted actions. Therefore the OEC examines the concrete circumstances of alleged price cartels or other agreements very carefully and imposes fines only in case of concerted anti-competition practices.

4   Problems and malpractices partly emanate from the limited regulation in many areas, for example, on public procurements and consumer protection. As is stressed in the cited report to OECD, important sectoral

165

laws, for example in the field of transport (when enacted), could greatly facilitate the application of Competition Act. The long-awaited Act on Press and Media could make a very special market more transparent and conditions of competition controllable. Finally, the Competition Act itself has certain ambiguites: for a better application of the Act's provisions on mergers, more clarity would be needed in differentiation between market participants (entrepreneurs) and owners as well as between companies registered in Hungary and foreign investors. To put it simply: a further harmonization of competition rules and ownership rights seems to be required[22].

Some future tasks

In the coming period Hungarian economic policy will have to be directed at (1) the furthering of economic transformation processes and (2) adaptation to EU rules and standards.

Furthering economic transformation

Among the macroeconomic priorities of the economic policy of the government an important role is assigned to further market liberalization and competition. Development of an institutional system, ventures and competition mechanisms are especially emphasized[23].

The main objectives of this transformation process are as follows:

- To increase the number of economic actors through accelerated privatisation and increased ownership security as well as legislation on land property, treasury property, etc. The government wants to speed up the privatization of the banking system and other financial institutions and to develop the money market infrastructure. Privatization needs decentralization and better coordination with market competition. Domestic privatization demand has to be boosted by improving privatization supply and introducing new privatization forms (managerial buyout, leasing, special securities, compensation coupons, etc.). Bankruptcy and liquidation procedures have to be accelerated.
- To improve the business climate it has been decided to lift taxation on wage costs, to regulate commodity exchange and to explore business possibilities.
- As 95 per cent of all imports are liberalized, corrective measures seem to be desirable to ensure the necessary protection of market and production. For this, it seems necessary to prevent market-disturbing imports. However, it should be in compliance with international practice and the latest GATT rules. Legal regulation of the agricultural market is also

needed, maintaining export and intervention support in line with prescriptions of the Uruguay Round. A system of health, security and consumer protection as well as environmental protection criteria for import products should also be elaborated.

● The constitutional principles of free and fair competition have to be fully implemented in legislation. For this purpose:

–the OEC should be entirely distinct from governmental activities and should be in co-ordinate relation with the government;

–draft laws on any issue relating to competition should be previously examined by the OEC;

–parliament should annually discuss the operation of the OEC.

● The activity of the OEC is hindered by its close contacts with the state. In East–Central European practice the state is usually an actor of the economy in its two capacities: first as a creator of an economic regulating system, secondly, as an owner. The connection between the state and the OEC is a delicate question: the OEC has to be separated from the government in order to be able to enforce competition law provisions even against the state.

Adaptation to EU rules

An important objective of Hungarian competition policy is the adaptation to legal and other norms of developed market economies, particularly to those of the European Union.

Hungarian competition law is basically modernized, and tends to conform with EU rules. The main problem is that organizational concentration inherited from the socialist system has survived in many fields, hampering the functioning of competition law. Moreover, there are discrepancies between new regulations and the Hungarian practice. The tasks are therefore multiple:

1 In legislation:

–the law needs modernization on the basis of 3–year experience of competition law;

–the law had to be harmonized with EU rules by the end of 1994 (definitions like competition, dominant position, etc., should be clarified, the scope of the law should be extended to acts committed by foreigners against the provisions of Hungarian competition law) and provisions on vertical cartels should be established.

2 In legal practice, legislation that seeks conformity with EU norms has lost touch with actual legal practice and it may take time until synchronicity can be restored.

Competition policy and control over restrictive trade practice have been considered by the EU as issues of great significance since the signing of the

Treaty of Rome. Various Articles of the Treaty of Rome as well as Council documents and European Court rulings cover the main areas of restrictive practices. A number of EC provisions regulate the market position of state-owned and private enterprises and public aid. Community-level market concentration and its potential threats to the competitive environment in the EU fall under the competence of the Merger Control Regulation since 1990[24].

The EU attributes great importance to the issue of competition, especially to state monopolies and state aid, not only in its internal regulations but also in its Europe Agreements concluded with associated countries. The European Agreement with Hungary undertook to introduce measures equivalent to the EC Treaty's Article 85 (dealing with anti-competitive practices), Article 86 (dealing with abuse of a dominant position) and Article 92(state aids)[25].

An Interim Agreement related to the free trade provisions of the Europe Agreement which came into force in March 1992 stipulated five main tasks in the given field, as follows:

1   Rules of implementation of the above-cited provisions of the Agreement have to be enacted to promote competition by 1 January 1995.
2   The position of Hungarian state monopolies with special or exclusive rights has to be revized to ensure that their operation is in compliance with the principles stipulated in Article 90 of the Treaty of Rome and the concluding document of the April 1990 Bonn Meeting of the Conference on Security and Cooperation in Europe, on entrepreneurs' freedom, within five years.
3   As far as state aid is concerned, Hungary was granted a five-year grace for certain undertakings and goods. This period will be renewable for another four years taking into account Hungary's economic situation. To provide the transparency required by the Agreement, annual reports have to be exchanged on the amount and distribution of the aid given upon request or aid schemes. Any violation of the rules is threatened with sanctions of 'appropriate measures' in conformity with GATT rules.
4   The Parties undertook to progressively adjust any state monopolies of a commercial character so as to abolish all kinds of discrimination regarding the conditions under which goods are procured and marketed between their nationals.
5   Rules of accounting, finance, statistics, taxation and fulfilment of contracts have to be adapted to EU norms to provide free and equal business conditions. Hungary undertook the approximation of its existing and future legislation, including competition law. However, this would re-

quire a few years to implement and is likely to be completed by the time of full membership.

Significant cases*

In the three-year experience of the OEC, the variety of cases on its agenda is fairly similar to that in the developed market economies. The main difference is, however, that in the European Union, members of the Competition Council usually deal with cartel and merger cases, whereas in Hungary such cases are rare and most rulings cover consumer fraud and abuse of dominant position. Some of the significant and typical cases will be briefly discussed. The firms involved will be identified by letters rather than named.

Case A

Facts

'A' Limited has performed marketing activity in Hungary in form of mail-order selling of horticultural articles.

In 1992 the company sent its catalogue and direct mail to 650,000 potential Hungarian buyers. The company in its direct mail advertising material announced a competition with a prize of HUF 4 million (approximately USD 40,000, ECU 34,000) and another one of HUF 3 million saying that the winning lucky number had already been drawn and the addressee may be the winner. It encouraged the addressee, ordering being a precondition of winning. The company further promized a wonderful 'jewel' as a gift to each buyer. It enclosed the photo of the gifts to show four gold jewels with precious stones and one brooch.

Legal assessment

In the course of the investigation the OEC found that the campaign was misleading because it concealed the fact that the potential buyer had only an extremely low chance of winning as the competion was not solely nationwide, but a Europe-wide one. Furthermore, all the Hungarian buyers received only the valueless brooch as a gift.

Ruling

The Competition Council of the OEC condemned 'A' on the basis of Article 3 of the Competition Act for its unfair market conduct. It banned the continua-

* This section is based on reports made by the OEC for OECD. The authors express their appreciation to the OEC for having approved the publication of case-studies in this study.

tion of the violation of the law and imposed a fine amounting to HUF 2 million (approximately USD 20,000, ECU 17,000).

Case B

Facts

Company 'B' entered the market at the time of COMECON states and it had a network outside Europe as well. The company advertized its products (mainly slimming drugs and cosmetics) in an aggressive way in the printed press, in periodicals published with a very wide circulation and also collected customers in the form of direct mail. It recommended its products to the addressees in a personalized letter printed by computer. In the case of advertized products it referred to international authorities as well as research institutes to establish that the goods had been recognized by professions in the field.

The company stated that by using some of the products (e.g. a kind of slimming tea and various cosmetics) considerable weight could be lost without regaining the former weight as the products change the metabolism of the user. Drugs of such an effect are classified as medicines, thus registration by the National Pharmaceutical Institute and its permission to market the products would be required. After having received the goods the customers were given inadequate instructions for their use.

Regarding the products which fell into the category 'cosmetics' the Commercial Quality Control Institute stated that they corresponded to the quality of the marketed product performing the same function; nevertheless the advertising of the goods was exaggerated and deceiving as it vested the goods with untrue character (e.g. 'you can become ten years younger in ten days', 'guaranteed rejuvenation', 'effect of self-tanning cream within 24 hours', 'bust measurement increasing cream promizes 5 cm increase in 15 days').

Legal assessment

The Competition Council stated that the advertising of the tea both in the printed press and in the form of direct mail addressed to the consumers contained false information and concealed the fact that goods failed to meet the registration requirements. The company involved violated the law by informing the consumers in a deceitful manner regarding the essential features of the goods, failed to mark the usability date of the goods and generally furnished the buyers with false information.

Ruling

The Competition Council banned the entrepreneur from continuing the violation of the law. The Council obliged the company to pay a fine

170

amounting to HUF 50 million (approximately USD 500,000, ECU 440,000) and to reimburse the costs of proceedings.

The company brought an action against the ruling of the Competition Council before the court; the proceedings are in progress.

Case C

Facts

Company 'C' – of foreign ownership – started its activity in 1993 in Budapest as well as in Hungary as a whole. It carried out its business by mail order, sending circulars to petential customers' homes.

Beside the list of the articles being sold, the consumers were – by a pre-printed sheet – 'officially' informed that they had 'won cash in the first round' draw and that a cheque was to be written out and that the addressee was entitled to participate in the second round draw with a jackpot of HUF 1 million (approximately USD 10,000, ECU 8800). Nevertheless, for this purpose the consumer had to fill in a 'prize request' sheet which at the same time involved completing an order form for at least two products. If the addressee did not complete the order form for two products, he or she would lose the prize already won.

Legal assessment

The confusing wording of the circular of the competition deceived numerous consumers and several of them applied for a remedy to the OEC. On the basis of the investigation carried out by the Office, the Competition Council stated that the request was justified. The behaviour of Company 'C', in that it had informed the consumers falsely about their having won cash in the first round and in tying the realization of their prize demand to ordering two articles, had deceived the consumers. On the basis of the circular even consumers reading the text carefully would be unclear as to in which draw they were participating, how much they had already won and when and how they could obtain their prize.

Ruling

In such a way Company 'C' violated Para. 22 of the Act LXXXVI of 1990 on the prohibition of Unfair Market Practices. The Competition Council banned the continuation of these practices and imposed a fine amounting to HUF 5 million (approximately USD 50,000, ECU 44,000) on the Company 'C'.

Case D

Seventy-eight agricultural cooperatives initiated proceedings against Company 'D' with which they maintained contractual relations and which is the sole manufacturer of their product in Hungary. According to the Applicants, the party involved abused its dominant position when in 1992 it reduced the buying-up price of their products by HUF 2,000 per ton as compared to the 1991 higher price level.

Hungarian competition law provides that it is an abuse of dominant position if in its contractual relations a company possessing a dominant position stipulates an unjustified unilateral advantage or forces its partners to accept disadvantageous terms.

The plant concerned is grown by approximately 800 producers nationwide. Thus, the geographic market should be interpreted on the national level. The overwhelming majority of the total annual yield (approximately 700,000 tons) was bought up by the entrepreneur involved alone, while the rest was exported. Before 1993, exports had to be transacted through agents, as at that time producers could not yet conduct an export activity on their own since exports were subject to a separate permission.

The plant favourably fits in the crop rotation, therefore it can be substituted by other plants. It is entirely at the growers' discretion what they produce. However, in 1992 this option of the growers became only theoretical, as by then the growing of the plants was associated with higher loss. Growers cannot be expected to embark upon growing some other plant which is likely to involve a bigger loss than theirs. In that situation, the dominant position of Company 'D' is indisputable. The conditions were extremely unfavourable for any other buyer-up or processor wishing to enter the market: penetrating the market is practically impossible.

For several years, it had been the normal practice of the entrepreneur involved to set for the producers the basic buying-up price of the crop in the months of November or December. In 1992, Company 'D' did that only in February, when applicants had made the year's final sowing plan and purchased the production equipment necessary for production.

Legal assessment

According to the Competition Council, Company 'D' did not commit an abuse of dominant position, as under the conditions of Hungarian agriculture between November and February no such work can be done in the field which could have suffered by a delay in the company's setting a price.

In 1992, the sowing area increased while the profitability of production decreased with respect to the previous year despite the fact that the general price of the product also tended to decrease in 1992. However, as with the artificially calculated 1991 buying-up price, the price can be compared with 1992 purchase prices only to a limited extent. Namely, the proportionateness of the earlier price can be judged in a reliable manner only in an economic environment which has been stable for a longer time. At the beginning of the 1990s, however, Hungarian agriculture was characterized by substantial changes of the earlier price and cost relations (that had become established under conditions other than those of a market economy).

Despite the initial stage of market development and the unsettled economic environment, Company 'D' concluded a product sale contract with the growers at a fixed price. The growers were paid cash at the time of harvesting. The amounts paid by the company under different titles (weight correction, extra price paid for quality, etc.) and the credit allowance further increased the basic purchased price. Nor can the export price be directly compared with the buying-up price of 1992, as the export price has to be reduced by the additional expenses incurred to the producers (transport, storage, customs examination). As the lowered export price and the increased domestic purchase price showed no substantial difference, a strikingly large value difference between performance and counter-performance could not be established. As no evidence could be produced for the unlawful conduct constituting a breach of the competition law as set forth in the application, the Competition Council rejected the application. This case illustrates the difficulties of making market assessments where a truly free-enterprise economy has existed only for a short time.

References

1 Robinson, A. (1991) The signs are encouraging. In *Financial Times Survey – Hungary*, 30 October 1991, p.1. For details of the transition process see also the Hungary supplement of the *Observer*, 29 September 1991.

2 Monthly Report of the Hungarian National Bank, 11–12, 1993.

3 *Economic Policy 1993–1994 1. Economic Policy and Forecasts*, Hungarian Ministry of Finance, Budapest, 1992. p. 28.

4 Dallago, B. (1994) The Failure of the Soviet-type System and Obstacles to Transition: collective action in the transformation of an economic system, *COST A7 Workshop, Budapest, 28–30 January 1994*, Discussion paper. pp. 20–21.

5 Kornai, J. (1980) *Economics of Shortage*, New Holland Publ. Co. p. 631.

6 Torok, A. (1991) *East European Economies and their Crossroads*, College for Foreign Trade, Budapest, pp. 3–18, and Dallego, *op.cit.*, pp. 20–21.

7 *Hungary 1991*, OECD Economics Survey OECD Publications Service, Paris, 1991, pp. 9–11.

8 Szarvas, L. (1993) Transition periods in Hungary – the Chances for democracy. *Journal of Theoretical Politics*, Sage Publications 1993, Vol. 5, No. 2, 267–276.

9 Majoros, P. (1993) *Magyarorszag kulkereskedelme* (*Hungary's Foreign Trade*), College for Foreign Trade, Budapest. p. 35.

10 *Economic Policy 1993–1994 op. cit.*, p. 28.

11 Sarai, J. (1993) *Competition Policy in a Transitional Economy*, Manuscript, October 1993. p. 1.

12 Nyers, R. (1994) The Economic Strategy of Hungary in the Grasp of the Transformation and Recession, *COST A7 Workshop*, Budapest, 28–30 January 1994. Discussion Paper. p. 5.

13 Majoros, P. (1994) *Opening up to the World Economy and the Single European Market*, Manuscript.

14 *Economic Policy 1993–1994 op. cit.*, p. 5.

15 Vigh-Martonyi (1989) *Verseny-es reklamjogi ismeretek* (*Basic competition and Advertizement Law*), Universitas, Budapest. pp. 9–10.

16 Voros, I (1991) *Verseny, Kartell, ar* (*Competition, Cartel, Price*), *An Explanation of laws*, Triorg Ltd, Budapest. pp. 17–20.

17 *Ibid.*

18 Competition Agency in Hungary, OEC, Budapest, FORKA Publishing Ltd 1993. p. 2.

19 *Ibid.*, pp. 2–5.

20 *Annual Report for the OECD on the 1992 activities of the Hungarian competition authories and the experience gained during the application of the Competition Act*, Budapest, 26 March 1993, Office of Economic Competition, Hungary, Appendix I. pp. 1–2.

21 Szabo, K. (1992) From oligopolies to the monpolistic competition. *Kozgazdasagi szemle* (*Economic Review*), July–August 1992. pp. 667–690.

22 *Annual Report for the OECD op. cit.*, pp. 6–17.

23 *Economic Policy 1993–1994 II. Economic Actions and Legislations*, Hungarian Ministry of Finance, Budapest, 1992. pp. 12–14.

24 For details see Fitzpatrick, E. and Davison, L. (1994). Regulating competition in the EC, In Barnes I. and Davison L., *European Business: Text and Cases*, Butterworth-Heinemann.

25 Europe Agreement establishing an association between the European Communities and their Member States, of the one part, and the Republic of Hungary, of the other part. *Official Journal of the European Communities*, Vol. 36, 31 December 1993. p. 115. Similar principles have been included into the Free Trade Agreement between Hungary and EFTA (1993) as well as in the CEFTA Agreement concluded in 1992 between the countries of the Visegrad-4 group, Poland, the Czech Republic, Slovakia and Hungary.

Questions

1 Hungary wishes to become a full member of the European Union. In your opinion, does Hungary need a separate national competition policy, or should she adopt competition regulation modelled along the lines of the competition law of the Community?

2 In the transition to a market economy, problems for consumers arose in Hungary. Why is this kind of malpractice possible?

3 Are there any grounds for taking exception to the way the so-called 'Blanket Clause' operates in Hungarian competition law?

Case 4 Transforming competition policy: the case of Sweden

Lee Miles

Introduction

Sweden represents a useful case study of an advanced industrialized nation transforming its existing competition policy in accordance with EU competition rules. On 1 July 1991, Sweden applied for EU membership and has become a full member in 1995. Nevertheless, the Swedish economy suffered from declining international competitiveness and a severe recession between 1990 and 1993, which pressured the government to adopt a stronger competitive regime as a means of reviving an ailing economy. Sweden also signed the European Economic Area (EEA) agreement in 1992, obliging it to accommodate EU competition rules. Thus, the purpose of this case study is to evaluate the changes within Swedish competition policy needed to achieve compatibility with EU competition rules and how successful this new competitive environment may be in the future.

Defining the competition problem in Sweden

The Swedish government introduced a new competition policy in 1993 due to a culmination of trends within the Swedish economy.

Structural weaknesses

By the late 1980s, it was apparent that there were severe structural deficiencies within the economy, especially in terms of declining productivity. The extent of these long-term problems were revealed by the disappointingly low level of efficiency in both the private and public sectors[1]. The rate of productivity growth declined after 1970. While labour productivity (GDP per person employed) grew by around 4 per cent between 1950 and 1970, the corresponding figure for the years after 1970 was as low as 1.1 per cent. Between 1970 and 1991 Sweden's GDP per capita growth was consistently around 0.6 per cent below the OECD average and in the manufacturing sector was more than 1 per cent below.

Sweden especially suffered from high labour costs affecting the profitability and competitiveness of firms and contributing to rising prices and inflation. The institutionalized nature of collective bargaining in Sweden allowed for wage inflation to run in 1989 and 1990 into double-digit figures. In addition, a general scarcity of skilled labour in the domestic labour market also helped maintain high wages. Thus, prices in Sweden still remain comparatively high. Most services, such as transportation, restaurants, cafés and hotels are relatively expensive and construction prices are the highest in Europe. Nevertheless, prices of goods in general do not exceed those of neighbouring countries, except for food products, beverages and tobacco[2].

The public sector and level of regulation

From the competition policy perspective, there were two major reasons for Sweden's declining growth rates, namely, the rapid expansion of the Swedish public sector and a corresponding governmental tendency to regulate large industrial sectors of the economy; both of which restricted the nature and levels of competition. The Swedish public sector has remained the largest in the OECD area, accounting for roughly one-third of total employment, but causing severe problems for governments in controlling public expenditure[3]. Consequently, public sector spending rose from 31 per cent of GDP in 1960 to around 66 per cent of GDP in 1982. In 1993, public spending was averaging 73 per cent of GDP. Consequently, the Swedish government has been confronted by rising budgetary deficits, reaching an enormous SEK 217 billion (around 15 per cent of GDP) in 1993 (see Table C4.1).

Furthermore, sectors of the economy, such as the food and beverage industry and the housing sector, have been strictly regulated in order to stifle competition. Although it is difficult to quantify the intensity and scope of the regulatory system in restricting competition, relatively higher price levels for regulated sectors seem to reflect greater inefficiency resulting from limiting competition. For instance, lesser competition in prominent regulated food sectors has resulted in food prices rising 130 per cent more than non-regulated prices during the 1980s.

The case of the pulp industry is also indicative. In practice, there are only three forest-industry owned purchasing companies for pulp-wood (Sydved, Vastved and Industriskog) for the entirety of southern and central Sweden, while in northern Sweden there is a single purchasing cartel (Nordsveriges Virkeskopare), ensuring limited competition and high prices in both instances. In general though, successive Swedish governments have preferred to regulate, rather than outlaw, the existence of cartels. They have viewed cartels as a positive tool for stabilising key markets, provided that they were officially registered with the National Price and Competition Board[4]. Equally, some monopolies were also maintained on the basis of providing a

Table C4.1 *Central government budgetary deficits 1991–1994* (Administrative basis, SEK billion)

| | 1991–92 | | 1992–93 | | 1993–94 | |
	Budget	Outcome	Budget [1]	Outcome [2]	Budget	Outcome [2]
Total revenue	464.6	397.7	382.0	377.5	358.4	322.8
Total spending	470.1	478.5	482.2 [3]	565.0	520.7 [4]	550.5 [5]
Budget deficit	− 5.5	− 80.8	− 100.2	− 187.5	− 162.3	− 217.7
Deficit as per cent of GDP	–	5.6	–	− 13.1	–	− 15.0

[1] Including proposals in the Supplementary Budget of April 1992
[2] Riksvisionverket, October 1993
[3] The budget includes an item 'estimated additional expenditure net' of SEK − 17 billion. This item includes additional expenditures and revenues on which explicit decisions were yet to be taken. In the supplementary budget an additional SEK − 23.6 billion was added to this item
[4] Including an item 'estimated additional expenditure net' of SEK − 0.5 billion
[5] Including an item 'estimated additional expenditure net' of SEK 6.0 billion
Source: Riksrevisionverket, Ministry of Finance, Sweden (1994)

public service or being within the public interest. Two state-owned alcohol monopolies – Vin & Sprit AB (responsible for the domestic manufacture of spirits and the importation of alcoholic beverages) and Systembolaget AB (in charge of retail sales) – were supported by the Swedish government and public on the grounds of public health[5]. An overriding competitive culture does not operate within Sweden and both government and the public support limited levels of regulation.

Levels of state aids

State intervention and regulation is also reflected in the levels of state aids given by the Swedish government. Successive governments have traditionally provided comprehensive support measures for industry, amounting to 11 per cent of industrial value-added in 1983. The bulk of state aids were used to bail out state enterprises (12 per cent of business sector employment), support companies in the Northern regions and preserve jobs in troubled firms and industries, such as mining (LKAB), shipbuilding (Celcius Industrier), iron and steel (SSAB). However, industrial subsidies have been reduced since the late 1980s to less than 2 per cent of industrial value added and are now comparable with most OECD states (see Table C4.2). Ironically, state aids should not prove a large obstacle to Swedish competition policy as most aid schemes have been abolished in order to reduce public expenditure.

Table C4.2 *Government support to industry: Sweden compared with other EC/ EU member states* (Per cent of industry value added)

	R&D[1]	SMEs[2]	Export promotion	Other horizontal aims	Aid to firms/sector	Aid to regions	Total
Sweden (1988–90)	0.26	0.06	0.27	0.57	0.49	0.67	2.3
EC/EU (1986–88)	0.38	0.32	0.37	0.36	1.04	1.37	3.8
France	0.32	0.19	0.92	0.27	1.68	0.28	3.7
Germany	0.46	0.22	0.05	0.21	0.19	1.59	2.7
UK	0.25	0.22	0.23	0.18	0.87	0.83	2.6

[1] Research and Development
[2] Small and Medium Sized Enterprises
Note: The table shows support on the basis of net costs to government
Source: Fair Competition in the Internal Market: Community State Aid Policy, *European Economy*, No. 48, Brussels (1991); Ministry of Industry; and OECD

Market concentration

Yet, even in fully liberalized sectors, the specific nature of the Swedish market has limited the impact of competitive pressures. Although Sweden has a small market (with a population size of only 8.7 million), it is home to a high number of large, export-orientated firms (such as Ericcson, Volvo, IKEA and Saab-Scania) who dominate their respective home markets and act as virtual monopolies. Horizontal concentration has characterized the goods producing and manufacturing sectors, where both the distribution of employment (see Table C4.3) and markets have become dominated by a few

Table C4.3 *Concentration in manufacturing in Sweden. Distribution of employment in manufacturing by enterprise size.[1]* (*Percentage shares*)

	Number of persons engaged		
	20 to 99	100 to 499	More than 500
Sweden (1991)	18.7	25.7	55.6

[1] Only enterprises with more than 20 persons engaged are included
Source: Ministry of Commerce and Industry, Sweden (1992)

producers mainly through mergers and acquisitions. Dominance of the Swedish domestic market in combination with expanding activities abroad have allowed many enterprises to develop into huge corporations. Seventeen of the 500 largest industrial companies in the world are Swedish, which per unit of GDP is twice as many as in Japan and four times as many as in the United States[6].

However, this horizontal concentration has potentially harmful effects in sectors where exposure to international competition is limited. For instance, the three biggest corporations in the Swedish construction industry (which rank among the 20 largest building corporations in Europe) account for half of all domestic building activity. Vertical integration (where firms dominate one or several stages of the production or distribution chain) is also wide-spread. These construction companies also have strong vertical interests, both upwards in terms of housing operations and downwards within the markets for building materials. Hence, vertical integration has accompanied horizontal integration strengthening dominant positions in the Swedish food processing, construction and convenience goods trade.

Thus, from the competition perspective, Sweden was suffering from a damaging cocktail of an overly large public sector, high levels of regulation in the private sector and limited competition in some areas due to the power of large incumbent Swedish firms.

Accelerating the need for action: the onset of recession

However, the severe recession during 1990–1993 and the creation of the single European market (SEM) heightened concerns over the international competitiveness of Swedish industry and its isolation from its European markets. In the past, Sweden's international competitiveness had been maintained through successive devaluations of the Krona. In 1981, a massive 26 per cent adjustment assured that Swedish exports remained competitive. However, the onset of recession in 1990 led to substantial currency speculation resulting in a 20 per cent devaluation of the Krona in 1993 and the abandonment of the Krona's link with the European Currency Unit (ECU). Although, ironically, Swedish exports received a boost from the devaluation, international competitiveness was maintained at the cost of masking stagnating productivity and high labour costs. In addition, the government's deregulation of the Swedish financial markets from 1989 also brought the near collapse of the banking system, severely damaging business confidence. Three banks (Forst SPB, Nordbanken and Gota Bank) were rescued from insolvency after a state injection of funds amounting to SEK 79 billion during 1991–1993. In practice, a new competition regime was required for political reasons as well as economic motives.

The weaknesses of the 1982 competition regime

The Swedish competition regime formulated by the 1982 Competition Act was perceived to be weak in a number of areas. The old Competition Act was based mainly on the principle of abuse control governed by two authorities, the National Price and Competition Board (SPK) and the Office of the Competition Ombudsman (NO). Interestingly, the objective of this legislation was limited to merely promoting 'such competition in the business sector as is desirable in the public interest' (1982 Swedish Competition Act) and not to enhance competition *per se*. Action against restrictive practices could only be taken if it had 'unduly' harmful effects, such as restraining productivity or preventing trade with others. The only two exceptions from this abuse principle were collective tendering and resale price maintenance, which were prohibited by law.

A plethora of cartels

The main practical outcome of this legislation (based upon the abuse principle) was a puny supervisory body and an economic environment in which cartels flourished[7]. Cartel agreements and collusive behaviour among companies not under common control or ownership can hinder competition in the same way as horizontal concentration and vertical ownership links. Yet, formal agreements restricting competition were not illegal in Sweden (except for vertical price maintenance and joint tendering). They were only required to be registered with the authorities on request and could only be prohibited if found against the public interest. In practice, the definition of the 'public interest' proved an elastic one being decided by successive governments[8]. It could therefore include political objections, such as a substantial loss of unemployment. In 1992, the last year of the previous competition regime, there were 1250 formal competitive-restraining arrangements on the Swedish cartel register. Indeed, horizontal price fixing agreements, such as recommended prices and binding price lists between parties, were very common, representing 10–13 per cent of total sales of goods and services[9], while market-sharing agreements accounted for 5–7 per cent of total sales in Sweden. Thus, cartel arrangements did hinder free competition in major sectors of the Swedish economy.

Sporadic enforcement of competition rules

The SPK Board formally monitored the level of competition in the economy, but had no power to take action against restrictive practices. The Competition Commissioner (NO) examined corporate practices and complaints. However, in practice, the SPK had limited manpower (of roughly only 35 full-time officials) to oversee competition rules and enforcement. The number of

181

cases examined declined (from 522 during 1982–1986 to 443 during 1987–1991) as the authorities concentrated their limited resources on investigating larger merger cases (which increased from 53 in 1989 to 70 in 1991). The great majority were settled through negotiation, with only 1–2 per cent of all examined cases reaching litigation.

Failure to remove anti-competitive practices

In practice, the 1982 Swedish competition law was insufficient to abolish anti-competitive practices. The general criterion allowed restrictive practices to be defended on the grounds of public interest, such as efficiency gains in the case of mergers. The difficulties in proving 'undue harmful effects' also meant that a high proportion of cases were abandoned. In addition, the deterrence effect of the legislation was weakened by the virtual absence of any penalties for engaging in restrictive practices. The financial incentives for firms of collaborating were not offset by the threat of draconian action by the competition authorities. There was a general consensus, regardless of the EEA process, that Swedish competition rules would need strengthening.

The 1991 Commission on Competition

A Commission on Competition set up by the Swedish government which reported in 1991 reinforced this view. The Commission investigated 61 different sectors of the Swedish economy, covering more than one third of the country's total GDP. It concluded that over two-thirds suffered from competitive distortions or a lack of a satisfactorily high level of competition. The Commission concluded that more competition needed to be injected into both public and private sectors. Free trade, deregulation, clearer rules for undertakings and more effective supervision of competitive conditions were identified as areas for change. Consequently, once Carl Bildt's non-socialist government came to power in 1991, it sought to introduce a new competition law.

The obligation of the European Economic Area (EEA)

Nevertheless, the single event with the greatest impact on the Swedish competitive environment was the European Economic Area (EEA) agreement, which obliged Sweden to adopt EU competition rules. The Swedish government interpreted EEA membership as opportunity to deregulate and broaden the scope of competitive market operations. The new competition policy was accompanied by broader measures, such as the removal of restrictions on the foreign ownership of Swedish firms and shares under the 1992 Foreign Acquisition of Swedish Companies Act.

A new Swedish competition framework

In December 1992 a new Competition Act was adopted by the Parliament, replacing the previous 1982 Competition Act. The Act became effective on 1 July 1993 and incorporated a set of clearer and more ambitious objectives, stating that:

> The purpose of this Act is to eliminate and counteract obstacles to effective competition in the field of production of and trade in goods, services and other products. (1992 Competition Act, Section 1, p. 1)

Significantly, whereas the previous Act had been based mainly on the principle of abuse control, the new Act was founded on the principle of prohibition. The Act was modelled on Articles 85 and 86 of the Treaty of Rome and established two prohibitions against:

● Anti-competitive cooperation.
● Abuse of a dominant position.

This seemed a logical move on the part of Swedish policy-makers. Given that Sweden is a small but integrated part of the European market and includes a large number of Swedish-based multinationals, these firms rely on foreign markets and investments which are already subject to EU competition rules. Indeed, under the EEA agreement, EU competition rules would also soon constitute Swedish law with respect to trade in the EEA. It was therefore natural to model amendments to the Swedish Competition Act on EU competition rules as this has two main advantages:

1 The system in the EU has already proved an effective instrument in promoting competition in many sectors (see other chapters).
2 Bringing Swedish competition rules into line with those of the EU should ensure consistency and more effective competition in the Swedish market. Swedish undertakings would be subject to one set of rules, regardless of whether they were established in the domestic or the European market.

There is, however, one potential problem with the adoption of rules based on regulating international competition for the Swedish domestic market. In practice, EU competition law aims to strike a balance between the encouragement of efficient distribution and the prevention of isolation of national markets[10]. Yet, as the Swedish Competition Act only intends to achieve one of these goals, namely efficient distribution, it might in certain situations, such as in the case of vertical agreements, be difficult to apply the principles of EU competition policy since the Act does not aim at the creation of a single market. It will not therefore be appropriate to apply in all circumstances the same analysis as the European Court of Justice.

The prohibition of anti-competitive Cooperation

In fact, the prohibition of anti-competitive cooperation is aimed at undertakings that have concluded an agreement with the objective or result of restricting competition. It reflects Article 85 (Treaty of Rome). The prohibition applies both to agreements between undertakings in the same stage of distribution and agreements between manufacturers and their distributors. The Act lists examples of cooperation which are detrimental to competition; for instance, price fixing, restrictions on production and supply, partitioning of markets.

However, the prohibition against anti-competitive cooperation applies only where the cooperation has an appreciable effect on the Swedish market. Cooperation between small undertakings normally falls outside the scope of this prohibition, In principle, undertakings with a turnover not exceeding SEK 200 million are not subject to the prohibition if their combined market share is less than about 10 per cent. This is important given that the Swedish government has prioritized the creation of large numbers of small and medium-sized firms as a way of promoting growth.

The prohibition of abuse of a dominant position

The prohibition of abuse of a dominant position relates to behaviour affecting other undertakings or consumers and embodies Article 86. Dominant positions are consequently not prohibited as such under Swedish law; rather the prohibition applies to uses of such a position that impede competition. The Act also provides examples of detrimental behaviour to competition, namely unfair purchase or selling prices, limiting production and markets, refusing supplies to a trading party. No exemption will be granted from this prohibition.

Prioritising small and medium sized businesses

A central aim of the new Act is accommodate and protect small and medium-sized companies in Sweden. Small and medium-sized companies have been recognized by the Swedish government as important to the Swedish market and as a future vehicle for improved growth in the economy. Therefore, it was deemed important that the new revised competition policy promote their potential for development. The new Competition Act focuses largely on prohibiting behaviour that is especially detrimental to small companies with specific prohibitions laid down in the Act, such as underpricing or refusal to deliver to distributors for the purpose of eliminating competitors. In particular, the position of Swedish small and medium-sized companies is strengthened by the fact that undertakings can be eligible for damages from large firms who breach the prohibitions.

Supplementary elements of the 1992 Competition Act

The new Swedish Competition Act also introduces numerous elements based on EU competition policy rules.

Mandatory disclosure

Swedish companies are obliged to notify the new Swedish Competition Authority on mergers (see later) and must supply the authority with the necessary material to enable it to carry out its investigations. This is a major change for Swedish companies.

Negative clearance and exemptions

Companies that are uncertain as to whether an agreement or practice violates any of the prohibitions in the Competition Act can apply to the new Competition Authority for a 'negative clearance'. Under the 1992 Act, companies can request a declaration from the Competition Authority, stating that an agreement or practice is not subject to the prohibitions (a negative clearance). A 'competition test' will then be undertaken, studying the circumstances in each individual case. However, a 'negative clearance' can only be granted if the 'competition test' reveals there is no hindrance of competitive forces.

Equally, cooperation among undertakings may have positive effects that outweigh their negative impact on competition. Under the new Act, the Competition Authority may also grant an individual exemption where it believes the agreement or practice does not violate the Competition Act, such as where a contribution to improving the production or distribution of goods or promoting technical progress is demonstrated. No exemptions may, however, be granted from prohibitions regarding the abuse of a dominant position.

Nonetheless, the Swedish government has issued nine time-limited block exemptions from the ban on anti-competitive collusion. Eight of these are based on corresponding block exemptions in EC law (such as research and development agreements) as the new authority is still too immature to develop further modifications of block exemptions. Yet, there is a ninth block exemption applying to cooperation within chains of retail trade, which is a Swedish governmental initiative. The Swedish retail trade includes large numbers of chain stores with parallel wholesale and distribution networks. Without an exemption, the structure of the Swedish retail trade would mean it would automatically breach the new competition rules. Thus, the exemption is needed for chains in the retail trade primarily to facilitate cooperation that has favourable effects by allowing small undertakings to compete effectively with larger ones. Only experience will show whether further block exemptions in other sectors in Sweden will be necessary.

Fines and penalties

One of the most useful powers introduced by the Act is the power of the Swedish Competition Authority to threaten to impose or enact sanctions against companies who do not respect the new competition rules. The Act allows for three types of penalties: fines, anti-competitive behaviour charges and provisions for civil sanctions.

In the first place, the Authority can threaten and even terminate infringement of a prohibition by the penalty of a fine. The threat of a fine is intended to induce the undertaking that has infringed the competition rules not to do so again. Should it do, a fine may be levied.

Secondly, under the Act, an 'anti-competitive behaviour charge' may be imposed in order to deter companies from infringing the prohibitions against anti-competitive behaviour and the abuse of a dominant position. The size of the charge depends on the gravity and duration of the offence. Yet, the sanction (Section 27, Competition Act) can be between SEK 5000 and 5 million or an amount that may be higher but not exceed 10 per cent of annual turnover. For very large companies, this could be a significant sum if their turnover figures are high. The Stockholm City Court is responsible for determining the size of the charge at the request of the Competition Authority. Both fines and anti-competitive behaviour charges are intended as a form of punishment.

An additional useful weapon for effective enforcement of the rules is that the Act provides for civil sanctions. Companies are liable for the payment of damages to those harmed by its violations. Hence, the new competition regime introduces a legal framework and a comprehensive array of financial penalties which companies need to be wary of.

Merger control

Swedish Competition policy now includes some element of merger control. Acquisitions and mergers of companies are an important factor in promoting the structural adjustment of sectors and market conditions, especially as competition is keener in many sectors due to internationalization. However, there are still domestic markets with high entry barriers, where mergers result in market domination and the virtual elimination of competition.

The new rules on mergers emanate from, but are less strict than, EU merger policy. Under the new Act, where the parties to the merger have a combined aggregate turnover in excess of SEK 4 billion, the merger must be reported to the new Competition Authority (see later). These potential mergers will then be investigated by the Authority before their actual completion and the Competition Authority can apply to the Market Court for a suspension of mergers until its investigations are completed. To prevent mergers, this 'competition test' must show that competition will suffer. However, in addition, the merger must also have 'significant adverse effects' in the long-term. This is difficult to prove in practice, especially in defining the level of 'significance'. Indeed, there are no fixed criteria either on the competition test or the definition of 'significant adverse effects', and the Authority must rely on the previous decisions of the Market Court and the previous 1982 Act[11]. Indeed, once the merger has taken place, the Authority has no powers or measures at its disposal to break it up. Nevertheless, the system of control is more flexible than previous Swedish arrangements by making a prohibition applicable only to part of a merger deal.

Overall, the Swedish Competition Act does provide a coherent framework for competition policy with a considerable increase in the powers of government authorities in regulating competition and a common system between Swedish and EEA competition policy.

The competition authorities – the Swedish Competition Authority and the judicial process

The Swedish Competition Authority

Perhaps the most effective improvement of the 1992 Competition Act is the establishment of a single, influential supervisory institution to govern the new competition policy. The Swedish Competition Authority (Konkurrensverket) was established on 1 July 1992, replacing the National Price and Competition Board (SPK) and the Office of the Competition Ombudsman (NO). The Authority is organized into three departments, each one responsible for specific sectors of the economy, plus an administrative department and two secretariats (one each for legal and international matters). Significantly, the Authority has increased physical and financial resources, with 125 employees. Although this is still small, given the Authority's increased supervisory and enforcement task, it is still a major improvement on the manpower provision of the previous competition authorities. A Competition Research Council is also affiliated to the Authority, whose main task is to encourage research and development in the field of competition and to ensure that results with relevance to the Authority are brought to its attention.

However, despite the improved resource base of the Competition Authority, it still has a comprehensive set of responsibilities regarding competition policy. It main tasks are summarized in its first annual report into six areas:

- *Surveillance and enforcement of the competition legislation*
  That is, actively intervening against anti-competitive practices as provided for by the Competition Act. This includes the examination of cases and applications for negative clearance or exemptions and the notifications of acquisitions.
- *Propose changes of administrative regulations which restrict competition*
  Its main responsibility here is to investigate distortive effect on competition of public regulations and propose changes and propose deregulations measures that result in greater competition.
- *Enhance competition within the public sector*
  The authority must propose measures aiming at increasing the efficiency and competition in the public sector. This is a critical area given the high level of public sector debt and budget deficits endured by the Swedish government. Liberalization is seen as way of cutting the government's budgetary problems by making the public sector more efficient.
- *Promote a competition-orientated attitude*
  The authority is responsible for disseminating information about rules governing competition and the promoting of attitudes favourable to competition.
- *Stimulate research within the field of competition policy*
  Through its advisory council, the authority will promote research in competition-related matters, especially in the fields of economics, business administration and law.
- *Cooperate with EEA competition authorities*
  The Authority is also the main competition body working with the EFTA Surveillance Authority and the European Commission to enforce the EEA Agreement rules. However, cooperation with the anti-trust agencies in other countries is important in cases where multinational corporations and market conditions are involved. The Authority also participates actively in international agencies such as the Organization for Economic Cooperation and Development (OECD).

The Swedish courts dealing with competition

Two courts of law, the Stockholm City Court and the Market Court, adjudicate cases involving the Competition Act. The Authority's decisions on exemptions, its negative clearance and its injunctions may be appealed to the Stockholm City Court. However, up to now the Court has been keen to uphold the decisions of the Authority as it seeks to establish its new-found role.

The new competition regime in practice

The 1992 Competition Act has introduced a more comprehensive regime, which is virtually identical to EU competition rules except for merger cases. Nevertheless, the new Act has changed the basic principles of Swedish competition policy. The new regime has an ambitious remit of encouraging competition rather than being based on perceptions of public interest and has replaced the difficult policy of abuse control with a workable solution founded on prohibition. Policy is now more transparent and the new rules incorporate a clearer 'competition test' regarding exemptions and the potential imposition of fines and penalties. The prioritising of small and medium-sized enterprises is also a logical progression, given their central importance in fostering growth in the economy. In short, the Competition Authority now has an extensive array of responsibilities and powers, even if its improved resources still remain limited.

Nevertheless, the Swedish Competition Authority has proved to be an energetic and effective organization in its early years. Given its relatively recent birth, the Authority has concentrated its efforts on the surveillance and enforcement of competition legislation and many of its other responsibilities have only been superficially addressed. Yet, regarding surveillance, the Authority has achieved some success. The Authority has been confident enough to actually reject mergers. For example, in April 1993, the Authority took SABA to the Market Court to prevent its takeover of KF Frukt & Grönt on the grounds that SABA was unable to clarify the advantages of the merger for the consumer and the outcome would have a harmful effect in reducing competition within the Swedish fruit market[12].

Generally, Swedish companies have been aware of the constraints of the new competition rules, especially as the Authority can forcefully restrict their activities. For instance, the 'Airtime' advertising collaboration arrangement between the Swedish TV channels, Kinnevik (TV 3) and Nordisk Television (TV 4) was abandoned after action by the Authority. These two television companies had jointly set up a company to sell advertising for both channels, which was deemed as infringing competition by the Authority. After extensive negotiations and the starting of a case against them by the Authority in the Market Court, the companies dissolved the arrangement due to the risk of substantial fines[13]. Thus, the mere threat of action by the Authority is usually enough to bring Swedish companies into line with competition rules on restrictive practices.

189

The position regarding the abuse of a dominant position has also been promoted. The Competition Authority did, for example, initiate proceedings against the Swedish post office (Posten) for anti-competitive behaviour and abusing its position in the deregulated transcription and envelope market for postal services on the grounds of reducing prices to force out new entrants. In 1993, the Market Court decreed that Posten was not to operate some services under the threat of a future fine of SEK 5 million. Thus, the new legislation has proved workable using the new powers to threaten and even impose penalties.

Furthermore, the Authority has tried to prioritize the protection of small and medium-sized undertakings. Its attention in this area has focused on ensuring that small firms are not discriminated against regarding conditions of sale from suppliers when compared to larger firms. In 1993, the Authority supported the case of Cyréns, a small Gothenburg vacuum retailer, who alleged that three suppliers were placing undue pressure on the company to raise prices on sewing machines and vacuums. Under the revized competition law, a trade manufacturer cannot fix a price on its goods without ensuring that retailers maintain the right to lower prices. The threat of action by the Authority enabled Cyréns to secure similar conditions to larger retailers from these suppliers. Hence, the authority has sought to protect the rights of small and medium-sized companies.

The Competition Authority has also promoted deregulation in the Swedish economy and has introduced initiatives in the areas of telecommunications, energy and aviation. The Authority did suggest that the new competition law could allow for structural changes to the telecommunications market and especially the mobile telephone market and this was incorporated into the July 1993 Telecommunications law. Parts of the telecom operations have been broken away from the state-owned telecommunications monopolies, preventing cross-subsidization. Since its liberalization on 1 July 1993, some of the world's biggest telecommunications groups, such as AT & T, British Telecom and France Telecom have entered the market, while new Swedish companies, for instance Tele2, have also been established. The Swedish market has now become one of most liberalized and competitive in the OECD[14]. However, it is difficult to differentiate between the impact of the authority and the implications of the larger and more developed EEA competition rules.

Swedish competition policy – some preliminary conclusions

Sweden does illustrate the case of an advanced industrial nation deciding to transform its competition policy. However, Sweden is unusual due to both its commitment to creating a uniform system based on EU principles at the domestic level and the speediness of its implementation. There are several reasons for this. The severe recession in Sweden created a crisis of confidence that Sweden's large public sector and heavily regulated private sectors would be unable to internationally compete without the imposition of a new competition structure. At the same time, the EEA agreement and later Swedish EU membership offered an ideal opportunity to radically reform Swedish competition policy.

The new competition regime has been welcomed by both government authorities and Swedish business. The authorities have accommodated the new Competition Act as it gives them effective powers of implementation, enforcement and penalty and a more powerful institutional framework to implement competition policy. Large Swedish business viewed the creation of a uniform system between the Swedish and EEA level as beneficial because of the greater commonality and transparency. They now only have to abide by one set of competition criteria whether they are participating in domestic or overseas markets, reducing costs and the possibility of breaching competition rules. For small business, the new Act is also positive as it prioritizes their protection and the maintenance of an operational competitive environment.

However, there are still a number of questions regarding the revized competition policy. First, whether the Competition Authority still lacks resources relative to widened responsibilities. Secondly, the ability of the Competition Act to foster the development of new small and medium-sized firms. Although the Act identifies them as a priority, the relative small proportion of small and medium-sized firms within Sweden (*viz-à-viz* entire Swedish business) makes this is a large task needing considerable resources. Sweden is still dominated by a very large firms and an overarching public sector.

The success of the competition policy regime will depend on its future evolution. The Competition Authority is confronted with the huge task of liberalising the public sector, controlling state aids, removing barriers within private sectors and fostering good relations with other fledgling bodies, such as the Public Procurement Board. The policy must continue to be supported by Swedish business especially with regard to its new competition rules regarding notifications, merger controls and penalties. Overall, Sweden now has a more effective competition policy and a promising future. However, a new era of competition in Sweden will require a mixture of diligence and cooperation between government and industry on all levels.

References

1 Lindbeck, A., Molander, P., Persson, T., Peterson, O., Sandmo, A., Swedenborg, B. and Thygesen, N. (1993). Options for Economic and

Political Reform in Sweden. *Economic Policy*, Vol. 8, No. 17, October 1993, 219–263.

2 OECD (1992) *OECD Surveys – Sweden*, OECD, Paris. p. 68.

3 OECD (1991) *OECD Economic Survey – Sweden*, p. 59.

4 For a more detailed examination see Swedish National Price and Competition Board (1991) *Competitive Conditions in Sweden – A Summary of 8 Investigated Sectors*, SPK, pp. 13–14.

5 When Sweden joins the EU in 1995, this alcohol monopoly will only be retained by retail.

6 OECD (1992) *op. cit.*, p. 72.

7 Commission of the European Communities (1992) *Opinion of the Commission on Sweden's application for membership*, Brussels, SE(92) 1582 Final, 7 August 1992.

8 Interview, *Ministry of Industry and Commerce*, Stockholm, Sweden, 15 September 1994.

9 OECD (1992) *op. cit.*, p. 76.

10 Carle, J. and Simonssom, K. (1993) Competition Law in Sweden. *European Competition Law Review*, 4, ECLR, p. 177.

11 Interview, *Ministry of Industry and Commerce*, Stockholm, 15 September 1994.

12 For more details see Konkurrensverket (1994) *1992/1993 Arsredovisning*, Konkurrensverket, Stockholm. p. 11.

13 *Ibid.*, p. 11.

14 Fierce competition in Swedish market. *Financial Times*, 17 October 1994, p. XII.

Questions

1 Outline the reasons why the Swedish government decided to adopt a new Competition Act in 1992.
2 Compare and contrast the 1982 and 1992 Swedish Competition Acts. To what extent have the post-1993 competition rules improved upon the previous competition policy?
3 How could this revized competition regime be further enhanced?
4 Using this case study and the case study of Hungary in this text, analyse the differences facing an advanced industrialized nation (Sweden) and a command economy (Hungary) in transforming their competition policies to cope with a more competitive environment.

Case 5 Let the Euro 'phone wars' begin

Andrew Mearman and David Gray

Introduction

The telecommunications sector has been identified by leading commentators, for instance US Vice-President Al Gore[1], as a likely major factor in world economic development.

More than 50 per cent of EU jobs depend on information and communications technology[2]. Investment in telecommunications should reduce prices and widen the range of services available. This will alter relative prices and make new investments and increasing employment profitable. In this way, telecommunications, like the railways in the nineteenth century, are viewed as a likely source of a Kondratieff long wave[3] or long-term growth trend. A strong and competitive telecommunications sector therefore offers technological development and growth which is essential for the EU economy to grow.

The European Commission has the aim of achieving a single market in European telecommunications in the long run. However, to achieve this it is required to meet intermediate goals. The first, the standardization of the telecommunications network, will be achieved by allowing alliances or European champions to develop. The second is the goal of improving services on the network. This will also be achieved by allowing such concentrations. However, the creation of concentrations could prove detrimental to the welfare of the consumer. The Commission will seek to avoid this by allowing one company the right of access to another's network. Thus, the European Commission has set a deadline of 1998 for the introduction of competition within the European 'voice' telecommunications services sector.

This case study will identify what is meant by a single market. It will analyse the advantages of a competitive structure from a variety of perspectives and relate this to the nature of the telecommunications industry. This analysis will be placed in a context of the requirements for a successful common market.

The case study will discuss the goals the Commission holds for the telecommunications industry and how it will harness the innovative nature of that industry through the formation of alliances. These alliances will not only be in a stronger position to innovate, but also are able to develop the necessary common standards and technical specifications that can be adopted across the European single market.

The case study will highlight the inherent contradictions within the goals of the Commission for the telecommunications sector. It will reveal, among other things, that the need to create common standards via innovation does not fit well with the aim of a good competitive structure.

The telecommunications industry and its development

The telecommunications sector can be split into three distinct subsectors, although in recent years the division between these parts has become increasingly blurred:

1 Telephone calls (mobile, satellite, cable and hard wire). These can be subdivided into several groups: international, long distance, local loop and interbase or 'outsourcing'.
2 Services which operate along the same wires. These services add value to the original telecommunications services and are called Value Added Network Services (VANS)[4]. Examples of VANS are electronic mail, EDI (electronic data interchange), enhanced facsimile, managed network services and entertainments.
3 Equipment: telephones, facsimile machines, parts of the network infrastructure, etc.

The most significant recent developments in the sector have been in the emergence of new technologies. First, the advance in cellular communications, namely the development of digital systems and the reduction in the price of equipment. Second, the ability to exploit an electronic superhighway[5] – a combination of telecommunications services based on the transmission of information in digitized bits – passed along a single laid fibre-optic cable. The capacity of a fibre cable is enormous. A single fibre, as thin as a human hair, can cope with every single UK phone call on Mother's Day. Thus, a fibre network essentially removes the present capacity constraint upon telecommunications companies.

The digitization of information has permitted existing networks to transmit other complementary services, 'piggy-backing' on existing services. An example of this is that cable companies can run simultaneously telephone and television services[6].

Competition and common markets in telecommunications

The Commission has the stated aim of achieving a 'good competitive structure'. It is usually thought that attaining these benefits involves a large number of firms. However, there are a number of perspectives on competition which can be used to analyse the competitive environment of an industry. In addition, the actions of the European Commission in the development of a competitive structure in the market for telecommunications can be analysed in terms of these perspectives. This will be done later.

However, competition is only a means to an end. It is the benefits from competition that are the long-run goal. One can identify the advantages of competition as: lower cost and price through greater efficiency; the suppression of firms' supernormal profit; innovation, in order to gain a competitive advantage; and better service, for the same reason.

Whenever competition is allowed to flourish, one or more of these advantages will develop. The conditions under which these benefits should be achieved within the European telecommunications sector can be examined from a number of alternative perspectives on competition, three of which will be discussed below.

We then go on to discuss the requirements for a common market in telecommunications. It is in such an environment that competition might be greatest and therefore the benefits of competition maximized.

Alternative perspectives on competition

There are a number of theoretical perspectives from which competition can be assessed. There are clear differences in their analysis of the conditions necessary for competition and it is appropriate to examine more than one. We shall examine just three in the context of the telecommunications sector – the Neo-classical, Austrian and Contestability perspectives. Using these contrasting styles we can assess the criteria for effective competition. Using these perspectives we can analyse the actions of the European Commission in their quest for a competitive telecommunications sector.

The neo-classical textbook analysis can be arranged to form the basis of the structure–conduct–performance approach[7]. The logic of the analysis suggests that the major benefits of competition will be achieved by a market structure comprising many equally-sized small firms. In the neo-classical world this would involve rivalrous rather than collusive price setting, little rather than a great deal of advertising and a great deal of research, although small firms may find this difficult to fund. Good performance

195

requires an industrial structure of many competing suppliers and buyers. Implicitly, monopoly will exhibit poor performance and is hence undesirable. Public policy was traditionally based on this approach.

An alternative approach is Baumol's Contestable Markets Theory[8], which suggests that an industry with a poor market structure can perform well if it is 'contestable'. If a competitor can enter and exit the industry quickly, without incurring irretrievable 'sunk' capital costs, it can extract profits when available and promptly leave when they evaporate – the so-called 'hit and run'. Actual competition is not therefore necessary, the threat of one or more firms entering the industry, attracted by supernormal profit, being sufficient to force the incumbent firm to behave as if it were in a perfectly competitive world. Indeed, in this way, Baumol suggests that the theory implies actual advantages over perfect competition. In a perfectly contestable market there can be only one producer, a monopoly, but still optimal resource allocation, low prices and a quality service.

The Austrian[9] perspective portrays competition as an organic rather than mechanistic process, providing (incremental) product improvements and serving the needs or wants of the consumer. The Austrian has an attitude to profit different from the Neo-classical and Contestability theories appraized above. The central character in this analysis is the entrepreneur. He is both an opportunity spotter and a risk bearer.

In contrast to the neo-classical analysis which makes an assumption of perfect knowledge, Austrians suggest that all parties have only impacted knowledge and that entrepreneurs are constantly acquiring information about consumer tastes by innovating in the market place. Those innovations that are a great success should put the entrepreneur in a temporary monopoly situation, providing their creator with the reward of high profits. Other entrepreneurs see these profits and innovate to improve on existing products and themselves become temporary monopolists. If there are no barriers to entry, other entrepreneurs can enter the market. The consumer is served because he receives better products and the monopolist entrepreneur receives temporary profits as a reward.

Benefits of common markets and of competition

Having discussed the various perspectives on competition we can now further examine the benefits of common markets and of competition. Once the benefits of the common market have been made clear we can then go on to look at the conditions necessary for the establishment of a common market in telecommunications.

Enshrined in the EEC Treaty is the goal of a Customs Union. The Single European Act of 1986 took the EU towards a common market. These are forms of regional economic association with differing degrees of integration between the member states, the essential difference between them being that the latter extends the former to include free movement of capital and labour.

The establishment of a common market should mean that member states' welfare will be increased because of an improved allocation of resources. A common market should allow the exploitation of economies of scale, encouraging greater efficiency and innovation through research and development. In addition, internationally, increased specialization from economies of scale should enhance comparative advantage. Also, significantly, competition in oligopolies should increase which in turn might reduce x-inefficiency[10].

However, these benefits might be achieved at a cost. Larger firms can exploit economies of scale and develop better products through innovation but, without the constraint of competition, real or otherwise, they may gain at the expense of smaller firms and eventually be in a position to exploit consumers. They might also become overmanned and inefficient.

Requirements for a common market in telecommunications

We have discussed perspectives on competition and the various benefits that competition is thought to bring. The aim of a common market in telecommunications is that it should enhance the competitive environment and bring about the above benefits of competition to the consumer. Therefore, we shall now discuss the conditions necessary for the establishment of a common market in telecommunications.

The preconditions under which a common market in telecommunications will prove successful are: the member states are at a similar stage of economic development; and they produce similar products. The EU is at present far from standardized in telecommunications either in terms of technical levels or, as we can see from Appendix C5.1, in terms of competition. This could cause severe problems in the future as certain countries may become impatient and threaten to press ahead alone. Germany made this threat in September 1994[11].

When these preconditions are met, member states must remove barriers to entry which would distort trade and protect sectors from competition. These barriers fall under two headings, technical and market entry restrictions. As far as telecommunications are concerned the key barriers are the differing state norms and technical regulations; market-distorting subsidies; public procurement practices; differing regulation of services and the degree of state ownership within the sector.

Requirements and benefits can be divided into static and dynamic[12]. For the static benefits to be derived a good competitive structure is required. This is linked to the neo-classical analysis. The dynamic effects, for example

197

economies of scale, may be gained but at the cost of some companies going bankrupt, i.e. destructive competition.

Existing situation in the EU

The situation in the European telecommunications sector, as of October 1994, is shown in the Appendix.

Traditionally, telephone (and postal) services have been run by a state monopoly Public Telecommunications Operator (PTO). Until the early 1980s, the EU effectively comprized twelve local monopolies, all of which exclusively provided all services. From Appendix C5.1 it can be seen that the situation has now changed. There are new technologies opening up new market opportunities, such as fibre-optics and digitization providing the basis for the development of VANS. New companies have been licensed to compete with the PTO offering these new services. However, the PTO (or former PTO in many cases) remains the dominant force in all EU countries.

Contestability

Voice telecommunications was traditionally seen as a natural monopoly[13]. However, this perception is changing as it is now recognized that only certain parts of the industry, if at all, constitute a natural monopoly. Yet barriers to entry (licensing, costs of building networks, costs of operating services) remain huge for potential entrants and contestability is low within member states and particularly in cross-border traffic. However, there remains the threat of entry of a large international competitor if they can gain access to the existing network.

The question of how competition will take place is fundamental to the problem being discussed. For example, in the UK there has been a transition from line-leasing to competition between networks. Initially, Mercury bought capacity from British Telecom (BT) and reused it, selling its own service. Unfortunately for both Mercury and the cable companies, their payments to BT for line rental represent their biggest single cost[14]. Consequently, Mercury is building its own network infrastructure. Cable and cellular services are also doing this. In this light, the most effective competition to a PTO might come from competing technologies rather than firms. This will put in place those conditions which ensure the competitive provision of a superior network.

Goals of the European Commission for the telecommunications industry

The central aim of the Commission is the creation of a single market for telecommunications. However in their legislation, several other aims have been stated and others implied.

At the EU level several can be identified:

● The establishment of a single market for telecommunications infrastructure and services. This implies the creation of an environment with a unified access, standards, and cost structure – like in the USA and Japan – where inward investment will multiply. This involves the establishment of common technical standards[15] and operating principles and also of a competitive environment.
● Research and development and innovation within the sector[16]. This is crucial not only to the development of this sector but to EU industry in general.
● Universal service provision at a 'reasonable' price[17] and the end of cross-subsidization and the introduction of cost-oriented services through transparency of accounting[18] and the rebalancing of tariffs[19].
● The financial stability of the sector[20].
● The achievement of economies of scale and the establishment of a (some) European champion(s) able to compete internationally[21].
● Open Network Provision[22].
● European firms to take advantage of the opportunities of outsourcing to multinational companies[23].

At the member state level, the pace of European telecommunications privatization is increasing (see Appendix C5.1), mainly driven by substantial state budgetary pressure. In the dynamic business environment of telecommunications and the single European market (SEM), it may be felt that the 'Austrian entrepreneur' rather than the state-run company is the best agent to capture the opportunities offered by technological change. For example, the compact disc was originally designed by Philips for the use of pictures or pictures and sound but not sound alone. The innovation of targeting sound alone might have been missed by a state-owned company. Privatization itself might not bring about huge cultural changes, but combined with a change in the competitive environment, it could.

Proposed methods of liberalization/standardization

The 1987 Green Paper

The Green Paper of 1987[24] is highly significant as it set the agenda for the liberalization of telecommunications. It had the general objective of the achievement of the liberalization of services, terminal equipment and access to the telecommunications infrastructure. The original timetable for full liberalization of the European telecommunications sector was laid down in the Green Paper.

It covered a number of areas:

- Terminal equipment; standards and their harmonization; VANS.
- Open Network Provision (ONP); ISDN (Integrated Services Digital Network); cost-oriented tariffs; public procurement guidelines.
- The role of Telecommunications Administrations; mobile cellular telephony; satellite communications; and competition.

The Green Paper outlined ten possible positions which the EU could take with respect to the liberalization of the sector. Subsequent action and legislation encompasses many of the positions outlined within, which suggests that these original routes were not strict alternatives but rather answers to different questions.

The Guidelines Document[25]

This document laid out the position with regard to telecommunications companies under Articles 85 and 86, the main aspects of EU competition law. This document is highly significant as it makes plain the Commission's attitude towards competition and its other aims for the sector.

The Commission's attitude can be summarized thus. They have envisaged an EU-wide competitive structure based on a small number of firms. To facilitate technical standardization, the EU feels that cooperation between these firms is necessary. As long as this cooperation does not infringe upon Article 85 or 86, the EU is happy to see it take place. Indeed, the EU can be seen to be actively encouraging it. Once this primary aim has been achieved and standards are common, the EU will begin to create the competitive structure that it desires. This could involve some adjustments to the present structure and certainly easier access to certain markets.

Open Network Provision (ONP)

ONP was explicitly established as a goal of the Commission in the Green Paper of 1987. ONP is the principle of non-discriminatory access to the network in member states, with a minimum guaranteed level of service quality and uniform tariff principles[26].

ONP is essential to the creation of a common and contestable market for services such as facsimile, EDI and electronic mail. Generally, services providers have low sunk and running costs and thus their biggest barrier to entry is the necessity of a licence to gain access. ONP should ensure this.

However, although the Commission has published plans for the liberalisation of services and has witnessed the unilateral liberalization of equipment in many member states, it has made little progress on ONP which in reality has yet to be developed. It remains a proposal which so far has not been implemented.

Additionally, the Commission at present has no plans to liberalize network infrastructure although it plans to publish a Green Paper on this in 1996. It may be eager to liberalize network infrastructure but the more intransigent or less developed Member States are likely to resist this for the foreseeable future. This problem will be exacerbated if ONP for services produces more competition to PTOs which in turn causes them to become less financially stable.

However, in recent months there appears to have been a change in attitude in countries like Spain, Italy and Portugal. Telefonica, the Spanish PTO, has developed international ambitions and is keen to form cross-border alliances. The Italian and Portuguese PTOs have recently been restructured (see Appendix C5.1). They now also seem to want to enter into international activities and alliances.

Actual methods of liberalization/standardization

Standards and outsourcing

The attainment of common operational and technical standards in telecommunications could be achieved by one of two routes. The Commission could lay down a common standard, or they could leave it to the market place (the free market or Austrian approach). There is a history of governments performing poorly when choosing standards. For example, in mobile cellular communications, the EU set the standard, GSM[27], but may have made a sub-optimal choice[28]. As a result, the approach towards the remainder of the sector appears to be different. The market is allowed to determine the standard.

The Commission appears to prefer the 'Austrian' approach to forming standards. In the Guidelines Document discussed above, there was clear indication of the Commission's stance. Telecommunications companies are encouraged to cooperate to develop 'one-stop shops' for VANS, thus establishing a common standard within the group. This means that multinationals need only contact one telecommunications operator for the provision of a series of multimedia services.

The development of the 'one-stop shop' is a positive move towards standardization. However, with regard to the achievement of common standards through innovation, the Commission has sensibly acknowledged that the costs of R&D are prohibitive for a single company, even of the size of, for instance, BT. Therefore, to ensure the provision of effective R&D expenditures, collaboration is encouraged. The Commission has permitted the formation of combinations to provide such services and allowed them access to groups in second and third party European countries.

One of the key drivers to standardization across Europe is 'outsourcing'[29]. This is when a (multinational) company allows telecommunications specialists such as AT&T or BT to bid for the right to run the company's internal telecommunications operations. That is, the company has 'outsourced' or contracted out the telecommunications service they previously provided themselves. The international market for such services is estimated to be worth $10–20 bn/year[30]. This is important to the companies involved but also to the development of the common market in telecommunications and to the attractiveness of Europe as a potential location. Without standardization, non-liberalization would deter MNCs from setting up in EU because of a divergence of national rules/charges[31].

The Commission is keen to see telecommunications groups forming to provide multinationals with dedicated, superior quality networks, through which VANS can be sent. There are three reasons for this:

1　These groups will have to adopt a common standard for network architecture so that all services can operate on all parts of the member sub-networks;
2　The development of superior networks and superior network services can best be developed by large companies with huge R&D budgets.
3　The Commission will be encouraging services to be developed that serve multinationals. This is important as these major employers are to be encouraged to 'add value' in Europe.

At present there are a number of large telephone companies using differing network architectures and standards. The European telephone market comprises four big players, a few medium-sized players and a collection of small players. This puts Europe at a disadvantage compared with the USA, which has several large operators and common standards. The Commission is seeking to achieve common standards across Europe so that telecommunications services can operate on any part of that network.

However, there are problems associated with a multinational enterprise relying on an outside company for the provision of its telecommunications services. The service must be 'resilient' or dependable. The 'outsourcer', providing these services must not be able to take advantage of their status as sole provider. These problems will hinder the outsourcing motive, at least until the services are seen to be resilient. This has led to the practice of 'dual-sourcing'. As there are huge sums involved in international transactions – as much as one trillion dollars can be lost if the telecommunications structure breaks down in any particular financial district for one day[32] – the risk involved in outsourcing is high. It is essential to choose a partner with resilience. Thus, another strategy is to adopt a second, back-up supplier.

The alliances

We have discussed the development of a common market in telecommunications. To achieve a common market, innovation and standardization are required. Research and development is therefore necessary to accomplish this. However, R&D is extremely expensive and requires huge resources. The Commission has acknowledged that to provide these resources, it may be necessary to form alliances of a number of national operators. We shall now discuss the development of these alliances.

In 1993 and 1994, some major and minor players have been allying themselves into groups either as an offensive move, to take advantage of likely future markets, or as a defensive move, to protect the home base against future invasions[33].

Leading the alliance-making pack is BT which took an equity stake in MCI, the second largest US long-distance telecommunications company, in 1993. This has led to the formation of 'Concert', an international companies server, similar to WorldSource discussed below. Later that year France Telecom and Deutsche Telekom, the French and German telecommunications companies, merged their VANS divisions.

The Commission is keen to allow cooperation between telecommunications operators. Similarly, the EU has permitted a leading group of multinationals to act together to bargain with a group of European telecommunications companies to build a new network in an outsourcing agreement[34]. The group of about 50 multinationals includes Rank Xerox, ICI, Philips and ABB. They were looking for telecoms cost savings of 30–40 per cent and a superior cross-border service in return for their business. The Commission also cleared a proposed agreement between twenty-two telecommunications companies (although it failed to go ahead for commercial reasons) because a large degree of standardization was a likely consequence[36].

The consortia of telecommunications companies competing for the above new network are also of significance. The winning group contains Swiss,

Dutch and Swedish telecommunications operators as well as American Telephone and Telegraph (AT&T) and BT. The former three formed Uni-Source, a joint venture (which may become a merger before the year 2000) to provide multinationals with a 'one-stop shop' of telecommunications services. Before this contract was signed they had been in negotiations with AT&T to offer the transatlantic link. AT&T launched 'WorldSource' in 1993. This is a seamless global telecommunications service for multinationals. To do this it needed an EU partner, particularly while the present restrictions on European access remain[36].

The main losers were France Telecom and Deutsche Telekom. They first formed an alliance in 1993 and formed a joint venture called Eunetcom. After this bid failed, they both took an equity stake in Sprint, the third largest long-distance American carrier[37]. This alliance has since been strengthened and is called 'Atlas'.

These moves and the clearance offered to them by the Commission indicated the goals of the Commission and how they were to be achieved. These agreements form concentrations which may be potential problems under Article 86 but may not be an abuse of power. In the first case the deal actually involves what is a 'private network' and is thus exempt from investigation but the other cases are allowed despite possible competitive problems. By implication, the Commission believes clearly that the formations of concentrations actually increases the pace of innovation and standardization of the network despite worsening the structure of competition.

The above provides a strategy for interfirm network improvement but the provision of a fibre network through which residential services within member states are offered is more problematic. It is suggested that domestic consumers would relish home banking, video-on-demand and home shopping. PTOs can finance the transformation of copper to fibre via these services. This is significant as, for example, BT will need a guaranteed return for providing the £10–15 billion[38] to upgrade the network in the UK and this will be true for all the major telecommunications network providers in Europe. The liberalization timetable gives the PTOs the time to upgrade their local-loops and pass the costs on to the consumer.

Analysis

Apparent conflict within the aims of the Commission

Competition and standardization

The EU hopes for competition between standards in the short term with the aim of finding the best standard. This may be a risky strategy, however, for several reasons. If this competition involves the laying of whole networks, competition will cause one technology to lose – destructive competition – and massive amounts of resources will be wasted. A monopoly network operator might result. Also, what if, as in the case of VHS videos, the most popular standard is technically inferior to its less popular competitor?

Competition and innovation

The Guidelines Document suggests the aim of competition but also of innovation through cooperation. This cooperation is allowed up to the point where EU competition laws may be infringed upon. The EU's position is set out clearly in its Guidelines Document where it acknowledges that R&D can only be performed by a small group of undertakings because of the resources required. The document goes as far as to say that 'Cooperation is . . . crucial for attaining the objectives [of technological progress]'[39] and thus should be allowed, in order to facilitate it.

However, there is a clear contradiction between these two aims. Innovation is best facilitated by a concentration of firms but this might be detrimental to competition.

This leads us to the conclusion that the EU is aiming for European champions as opposed to a competitive market structure. There already exists an example in VANS, that of UniSource and AT&T as well as the alliance of Sprint and the Franco-German venture. This movement by telecommunications operators will leave the Commission with little room for manoeuvre with respect to the creation of a competitive structure. Again, these twin aims appear incompatible.

Universal service and the end of cross-subsidization

Universal service is defined as 'one having general coverage and available to all users, available upon request, on reasonable and non-discriminatory conditions'[40].

In the Guidelines, the EU recognizes the need for cross-subsidy. Where a service is a natural monopoly line which might be loss-making and would otherwise not be provided, firms are allowed to cross-subsidize from other more profitable services. If the company is privately owned, the cross-subsidy comes from profits. However, if the firm is state-owned, tax revenue is used.

Liberalization of services and the cherry-picking of profitable services by competitors, together with widespread privatization, will alter the behaviour of the PTOs and is likely to reduce their willingness to provide a public service.

Universal service and cost-oriented services

The dual aims of cost-oriented services and low-cost universal service are laid out in 93/C 213/01. This means that both the cost of business calls should fall and residential calls should remain 'reasonable', i.e. cross-subsidisation and price discrimination should end. These goals seem to be contradictory. If the price of business calls were to fall to truly reflect cost levels, this would result in a revenue loss for the firm. To compensate for this would require an increase of some magnitude in the price of residential calls. Even if residential call charges remained 'reasonable', any significant rise in price may be politically unacceptable and would be avoided if possible.

Universal service and competition

Many of the governments in Europe have socialist or social democratic leanings and will maintain a commitment to an inexpensive and guaranteed universal service. This might require some cross-subsidization from the profits of operators. Newly-privatized PTOs might be unwilling to provide this service while facing competition.

The EU has attempted to resolve this problem. Under Resolution 94/C 48/01 there is provision for all operators in a state to form a pool of resources from which uneconomic lines would be subsidized. This is important as it is an advantage for the existing monopoly PTO. However, this might discourage entry and therefore competition as potential competitors might feel unfairly disadvantaged.

Competition and financial stability

When liberalization occurs and competition intensifies, the less-efficient firms of the sector will be under the most severe pressure and will become less financially stable. This would involve destructive competition in that these weaker firms would be driven out of business. This is a possible dynamic effect of liberalization. This could lead to state intervention in the form of subsidies even though this would be illegal under Article 92 of the Treaty of Rome (1957).

Competition and economies of scale

The first response by telecommunications operators has been a tendency to concentration, partly in its desire to take advantage of outsourcing. The large operators have been looking for smaller (but sometimes bigger) partners within Europe, an obvious example being the Franco-German venture. This applies not only to the indigenous firms but also to US rivals.

Aims stated in the Guidelines for a 'strong competitive structure' and firms 'reaching the necessary economies of scale . . . to become competitive not only on the Community market but worldwide' appear to be contradictory. Additionally, it seems that only the second of these aims is currently occurring. Indeed, the proposed UniSource merger is an indicator of this[41].

The Commission appears to have a 'trade-off approach'[42] to mergers or cooperation, i.e. the benefits of increased efficiency from economies of scale and also in terms of innovation versus the possible costs of the concentration. This applies equally to all sectors of the industry. An example would be that a business, possibly a multinational, would be able to go 'one-stop shopping' in Europe rather than engaging in contracts with several separate operators.

European champions and competition

Another clear goal of the Commission is the creation of companies large and powerful enough to compete in the European and international markets with large non-EU firms like AT&T. This movement towards large groupings is forcing those companies outside the existing groups to reassess their position. Several small operators, for example Telecom Eireann, are attempting to join the large players like BT and UniSource.

The economies of scale that could be gained within European firms might lead to the rationalization of the industry. For instance, since four firms (BT, France Telecom, DBT and Telecom Italia) provide 80 per cent of services in Europe[43], they are most likely to flourish. This would involve the dissolution of some less efficient, smaller former state-monopoly PTOs. This may be unacceptable on political and security grounds to the member states involved.

Competition and the 'Noah's Ark' approach

The Commission has a 'Noah's Ark' approach – it wants two competitors in each sector such as cellular, cable, long distance and local-loop. This is a behaviourial idea. Two firms can (happily) be allowed to jointly dominate a market as long as they are not tempted to abuse this position. If they did so, they would be acting contrary to Article 86. To further safeguard against abuse, the Commission is ensuring contestability through ONP and by allowing the formation of groups financially capable of breaking into others' markets such as UniSource and WorldSource. This again reflects the EU's discretionary approach in this field.

Harmonization and a multi-speed Europe

The goal of harmonization of standards and access is central to the common market in telecommunications. However the Commission recognizes that Europe is diverse in terms of technology, liberalization, ownership and economic development, and that harmonization will take longer for some traditionally protected PTOs. This could cause problems. It is for this reason that there is a timetable for liberalization.

The Commission realizes the need, at least in the short term, for a multi-speed Europe. Consequently, there have been derogations granted to certain countries: Spain, Portugal, Ireland and Greece; and allowance for distinct national regulatory regimes. Only recently has the EU set guidelines for uniform regulation of operators[44]. Nonetheless, the EU has pressed on with aspects of access harmonization, including the mutual recognition of telecommunications licences. Mutual recognition should allow all telecommunications companies to operate anywhere within Europe.

This development is important given the disparate levels of technology in Europe. In France, the extent of digitization in 1987 was over 70 per cent while in Greece it stood at only 7 per cent[45]. It would also appear logical to encourage harmonization and structural readjustment in telecommunications in the light of the desire to create a common market for telecommunications. This means that member states with poorer quality services will need a longer period of adjustment. Therefore despite mutual recognition in some liberalized services (see Appendix) access will still be limited in these States. Additionally, these poorer states have licence to pass on the costs of improvement to the consumer without the fear of intrusive competition.

EU interpretation of competition

A comment which can be passed about the EU legislation is that although the tenor of the legislation is competition oriented, this appears to be only a veneer. After closer examination of subsequent legislation, the impression gained is one of tolerance towards concentration as long as there is some benefit derived in terms of either external competitiveness or innovation. That is, if cooperation is necessary to achieve these significant technological gains, then it is to be allowed.

This can be explained by the existing EU laws which are the framework for liberalising telecommunications, particularly Articles 3(f) and 85–94 of the Treaty of Rome (1957). The EU has a pragmatic approach to competition in that it assesses the behaviour of a firm rather than simply its competitive position. For example, Article 86 refers specifically to the abuse of a dominant position. This means that even a monopoly can be acceptable as long as it does not restrict entry and if it encourages social cohesion. Therefore the Commission is not necessarily concerned with concentration if it acts in a positive way. This view is expressed clearly in the Guidelines Document (above).

Appendix C5.1

Country	Services liberalized [1]?	1989 Number of competitions	1994 Number of competitors
Belgium	VANS	RTT Benelux analogue	Belgacom[2], Belgacom analogue
Denmark	VANS	TeleDenmark TD analogue	TeleDenmark[3] TD analogue and GSM, Sonofon GSM
France	VANS Mobiles	France Telecom, SFR analogue	France Telecom[4], SFR analogue and GSM
Germany	Mobiles	DBT DBT analogue	DBT[5], DBT analogue, E-Plus PCN, DBT (GSM) (Mannesmann)
Greece	Mobiles	OTE	OTE[6], Panafon GSM, STET Hellas GSM
Ireland	VANS	Telecom Eireann	TE[7], Eircell analogue ITL[8]
Italy	VANS	STET, IRI (Government) SIP analogue	Telecom Italia[9], Government[10]
Luxembourg	VANS	PTO	PTO, PTO GSM and analogue
Holland	VANS	KPT	KPT[11] KPT analogue
Portugal	VANS Mobiles	CPRM, CTT, TLP, TMN analogue	Portugal Telecom[12], TMN GSM and analogue, Telecell GSM
Spain	VANS	Telefonica Telefonica analogue	Telefonica[13], Bell South analogue Telefonica GSM and analogue
UK	ALL	British Telecom, Mercury[14], 3 cellular-Vodafone, Cellnet, Rabbit[15]	3 + 2 hard wire[16], 4 cellular[17], cable TV

[1] Services do not include equipment. Equipment is liberalized in all EU member states.

[2] State-owned private equipment.

[3] Privatized May 1994.

[4] Publicly-owned company. The issue of privatization has been raized but faces domestic trade union opposition.

Notes to Appendix C5.1 (*continued*)

[5] Deutsche Bundespost Telecom. To be privatized in 1996 but a monopoly position to be maintained until 1998.

[6] Hellenic Telecommunications Organization. Privatization planned for 25 per cent sell-off in October 1994.

[7] State-owned company. No plans to privatize but state has allowed investment by Cable & Wireless.

[8] International Telecommunications Limited. International calls only.

[9] Created on 19 May 1994. Privatization planned. Telecom Italia is the amalgamation of SIP, SIP cellular analogue, Telespazio (satellite communications), SIRM (maritime telecommunications), Iritel (long distance) and Italcable.

[10] The government provides various services through its departments, ASST, DCST and DCSR.

[11] Privatized along with the postal services in June 1994.

[12] New company. Amalgamation of TLP, which served Lisbon and Porto, and CTT which served the rest of Portugal. CPRM is still responsible for international calls.

[13] State-owned company. No plans to privatize or liberalize. The company provides analogue and GSM mobile cellular services in addition to its normal role.

[14] There is also the case of Kingston Communications (Hull) that operates in its local area. It remains from the pre-Post Office era.

[15] Now defunct – users transferred to Orange.

[16] There are three in operation: BT, Mercury Communications Limited and Energis. There are several more planned.

[17] The three operators in 1989 are still in the market although Vodafone and Cellnet now offer both analogue and GSM services, while Hutchison Telecom has replaced its Telepoint system with a PCN network. Mercury offers a PCN service.

Glossary

MNC A multinational company – one that has sites in many different countries and thus one with its own international telecommunications network.

one-stop shop The facility of a large firm seeking to improve its internal network to approach a single telecommunications operator in order to complete this. This represents a significant saving to the firm in terms of time and cost.

ONP Open Network Provision – The scheme proposed by the EU for improving access onto European telelcommunications networks for firms wishing to provide services (VANS).

Outsourcing The process whereby a company – probably a multinational – allows a specialist telecommunications operator to operate the company's internal network.

PTO Public Telecommunications Operator – until recent years, these were state-owned monopoly operators of telecommunications networks and services.

VANS Value Added Network Services – services such as facsimile and electronic mail which can be added on to the existing network. Such services can be provided by any small telecommunications operator.

References

1 Gore, A. (1994) Plugged into the world's knowledge. *Financial Times*, 19 October 1994.
2 Clarke, H. (1992) Resistance in Europe, *Financial Times International Telecommunications*, 15 October 1992.
3 Kondratieff, N. (1926) The long waves in economic life. Reprinted in *Lloyds Bank Review*, No. 129, July 1978.
4 Sometimes called VASs (Value Added Services) or VANs (Value Added Networks). These are not identical but are essentially the same: the extension of functions beyond the basic provision of the network and of telephone calls.
5 Cassidy, J. (1993) Bell rings multimedia revolution. *Sunday Times*, 17 October 1993.
6 *Financial Times Telecommunications In Business*, 15 June 1994, pp. 6–10.
7 See, for instance, Thompson, A. A. and Formby, J. P. (1993) *Economics of the Firm, Theory and Practice*. Prentice Hall.
8 Baumol, Panzar and Willig (1982) *Contestable Markets and the Theory of Industry Structure*, Harcourt, Brace, Jovanovich.
9 This generally means the work of, for instance, Boehm-Bawerk, Mises and Schumpeter.
10 Lack of internal efficiency because of a lack of competitive pressure.
11 Parker and Adonis (1994) Germany ready to defy EU on telecom (sic) liberalization. *Financial Times*, 13 September 1994.
12 For further discussion of Customs Unions theory, refer to Robson, P. (1987) *Economics of International Integration*, Unwin Hyman.
13 For further discussion of natural monopolies, see, for example, Laidler and Estrin (1991) *Introduction to Microeconomics*, Philip Allan.
14 Horton, M. (1994) Hurdles for new contenders. *Financial Times Telecommunications in Business*, 15 June 1994, p. IV.
15 Refer to Council Resolution 88/C 257/01 in which the European Telecommunications Standards Institute is established.
16 Council Recommendation 91/C 233/01.
17 Council Resolution 94/C 48/01.
18 See also Council Decision 92/13/EEC.
19 See also Council Resolution 94/C 48/01.
20 See also Council Resolution 93/C 213/01, the review of the sector.
21 Refer to Council Recommendation 91/C 233/01.

22 Commission Directive 90/388/EEC and also Council Resolution 94/C 48/01.

23 Council Recommendation 91/C 233/02.

24 Com (87) 290, 30 June 1987.

25 Council Recommendation 91/C 233/02.

26 Council Resolution 94/C 48/01.

27 Groupe Speciale Mobile. One may see GSM defined as other things.

28 It is now felt by many good judges that Personal Communications System (PCS), the format favoured by the USA, is superior and should have been adopted. However, the USA feels that the EU may have an advantage in having adopted a common standard.

29 Linked to the idea of Virtual Private Networks where companies rent private network space from the PTO.

30 Adonis, A. (1994a) Wind blows both ways. *Financial Times*, 15 June 1994, p. IV.

31 Adonis, A. (1994b) Prices hamper Europe's competitiveness. *Financial Times*, 23 February 1994.

32 Adonis, A. (1994c) A crucial role in companies large and small. *Financial Times Telecommunications in Business*, 15 June 1994.

33 Further discussion of motives for the formation of alliances and joint ventures like the ones discussed can be found in Dunning, J. (1993) *The Globalization of Business*, Routledge.

34 Adonis, A. (1994d) BT and US-Euro consortium win pioneering telecoms deal, *Financial Times*, 11 April 1994.

35 Council Recommendation, 91/C 233/02.

36 See Council Resolution 93/C 213/01 para 32.3 pt. 7 which states clearly that access to the EU may be affected by demands for reciprocity.

37 It is worth noting that despite the size of its market, Italy is noticeably absent from this activity. Telecom Italia may well change this, however.

38 Adonis, A. (1994e) Monopoly walls breached. *Financial Times Telecommunications in Business*, 15 June 1994, p. IV.

39 Council Recommendation 91/C 233/02 para A23.42.

40 Council Recommendation 91/C 233/01 A23.47.

41 Adonis, A. (1994f) Telecoms alliance may turn to merger. *Financial Times*, 16 August 1994.

42 Hughes, A., Mueller, D. and Singh, A. (1980) Competition policy in the 1980s: the implications of the international merger wave. In Mueller (ed.) (1980) *The Determinants and Effects of Mergers*, Oelschlager, Gunn & Hain.

43 do Carmo Seabra. M. (1993) Telecommunications, *European Economy*, No. 54.

44 Com (92) 247.

45 IFO Institute, BIPE, Prometria, Cambridge Econometrics and NEI (1991) *Europe in 1995.*

Questions

1 To what extent is there a contradiction in the goals of the European Commission for a Common Market in telecommunications?
2 Examine the necessary preconditions that must be achieved for a common market in the European telecommunications sector to exist.
3 Is it possible to reconcile an Open Network Provision while precluding cross subsidy, expecting improvement in quality of service and the maintenance of a universal service?

Case 6   Europe's energy sector

Debra Johnson

Europe's energy markets have been highly resistant to the introduction of competition. The reasons for this are complex and various. First, energy was neglected for many years. It was omitted from the 1985 Single Market White Paper and the first serious assessment of the barriers which needed to be removed to open energy markets to competition was not made until 1988 when the Internal Energy Market White Paper was published. It was also not until 1987 that the European Court of Justice ruled that the the Treaty of Rome's competition rules applied to energy.

Secondly, the objective of greater energy competition often conflicts with two other key energy policy objectives – environmental protection and supply security. The lower costs and prices resulting from greater competition in energy markets will increase energy demand. This in turn will harm the environment and reduce security of supply. On the other hand, increased competition can work in tandem with other aspects of energy policy. Competition from greater access to and extension of transmission and distribution networks, and eventually from the working of the Energy Charter, will increase the number of energy suppliers to the European Union and thus increase supply security.

Thirdly, the introduction of competition into energy includes not only competition within individual sectors of the energy industry such as gas, electricity, coal, and crude oil and petroleum products but also inter-fuel competition. The wide diversity of the energy sector in terms of fuels, forms of industrial organization and the sheer extent and variety of trade obstacles ensures that the liberalization process is highly technical, complex and drawn out.

Fourthly, there has been strong resistance from some member states and energy utilities to the freeing up of the gas and electricity markets in particular. The resistance to change of the energy producers is much stronger than the support for the proposals from energy-intensive industries – i.e. the consumers who are the potential beneficiaries of the liberalization.

Increasingly, the importance of energy to the Union is being recognized and the opening of energy markets to competition is firmly on the EU's policy agenda. The trans-European Network initiative and the Energy Charter Treaty, signed in December 1994, support this liberalization. In addition, the inclusion of a chapter on energy in the Treaties is high on the agenda for the 1996 Intergovernmental Conference which will review the Maastricht Treaty.

Characteristics of Europe's energy markets

The European Union accounts for approximately 15 per cent of world primary energy consumption but is responsible for only 8 per cent of world primary energy production. Consequently, the EU is a major net importer of energy.

Import dependency is increasing for the three primary fuels and this trend is forecast to continue. Supply security concerns will therefore move up the energy policy agenda during the next few years. The estimates of import dependency in Table C6.1 are based on moderate GDP growth assumptions and on continuation of the existing trend of declining energy intensity. If growth exceeds these moderate levels and/or there is a reversal of energy intensity trends, the import dependency of the European Union will exceed the Commission's estimates.

Table C6.1 *Import dependency by fuel* (%)

	1985	1990	2000	2005
Coal	26	33	54	61
Oil	68	78	80	81
Gas	32	39	47	50
Total	43	50	56	58

Source: European Commission

The natural resource endowment of individual member states varies considerably and helps shape the attitude of member states towards energy policy. The UK accounts for 34 per cent of the EU's primary energy production, followed by Germany (23%), France (17%) and the Netherlands (11%). The other eight member states account for the remaining 15 per cent of total primary energy production. Table C6.2 shows EU energy balance.

Petroleum

Supply security issues have dominated Europe's policy towards oil. The two oil price shocks of the 1970s demonstrated Europe's vulnerability to the vagaries of oil supply and demand. The emphasis of policy in individual member states and at European Union level, therefore, has been on energy

Table C6.2 *1993 Energy balance (million tonnes of oil equivalent)*

	EU	B	Dk	Ge	Gr	Sp	F	Ir	It	L	N	P	UK
Primary production	624	11	12	145	7.5	29	106	3	27.3	0	67		1 215
Total imports	890	62	17	209	21	73	137	8	152	3.8	100	19	88
Stock change	4	0.2	1	0	−0	0	1	0	1.4	0	0.1	0	0.5
Total exports	293	20	11	20	3.7	12	22	1	23.3	0	88	3	89
Gross consumption	1246	53	20	334	25	90	221	10	157	3.8	80	17	215

conservation, greater fuel efficiency, diversification into other sources of energy and reduction of the dependence on Middle Eastern suppliers.

This approach has been successful to a certain extent and the cycle of constantly escalating oil consumption growth appears to have been broken. However, crude oil consumption still accounts for 43–44 per cent of primary energy consumption (down from over 50% in the early 1980s). The potential for fuel switching is limited in the short term. Almost half Europe's oil consumption is by the transport sector; although the development of alternative motor fuels is under way, their commercial exploitation is a long way off. Consequently, it is the household sector (20% of the market), where oil is primarily used for heating purposes, which provides the most scope for fuel switching.

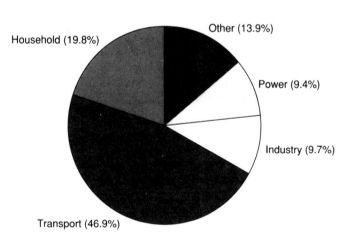

Figure C6.1   Oil consumption in the European Union (%)

Significant increases in EU oil production, which accounts for about 20 per cent of EU oil crude oil consumption, can be ruled out. EU crude oil production is dominated by the UK which accounts for 80 per cent of the EU's domestic crude production. Other EU oil producers include Denmark (6.2% of EU oil production), Italy (3.2%) and the Netherlands (3.3%). Production from traditional EU sources will decline in the coming years and, although exploration is under way in previously unexploited parts of the Union's territory, the outlook for new sources compensating for the decline in the old is not good.

The EU imports most of its crude oil requirements from non-EU sources. The Middle East remains the EU's single biggest source of oil imports (38%), followed by Africa (33%), and is expected to increase its share. From the mid-1980s, after the initial oil price shock, the oil markets experienced several years of historically low real oil prices. The surpluses of the mid-1980s were a direct result of the high oil prices which had encouraged exploration and production in previously unprofitable areas of the world. The exhaustion of these high-cost supplies plus rapidly increasing demand in the developing world have given rise to speculation that oil prices will rise again and that Middle Eastern producers will regain their previously dominant position over world oil supplies.

Gas

Natural gas accounts for about 20 per cent of the European Union's gross primary energy consumption but consumption patterns vary dramatically throughout the Union. Greece and Portugal, both without indigenous gas resources or connections to the European gas grid, do not consume gas. Approximately half of energy consumption in the Netherlands, on the other hand, is of natural gas.

Demand for natural gas is growing more rapidly than that of other energy sources. Since 1980, the annual growth rate of gross inland natural gas consumption has been 2.8 per cent. This contrasts with total inland energy demand growth rates of 1.5 per cent p.a., hard coal growth rates of less than 0.1 per cent and crude oil growth rates of -0.6 per cent. Most energy commentators expect continuing strong demand growth for natural gas in Western Europe and forecasts of a 50 per cent increase in natural gas demand in the twenty years to 2014 are commonplace.

Such increases have security of supply implications. In 1993, 50 per cent of European Union natural gas demand was met by European Union sources, notably by the UK and the Netherlands, who together supplied 38 per cent of total EU gas consumption. Extra-EU imports of natural gas are predominantly from the former USSR (44.8%), Algeria (29.5%), Norway (23%) and Libya (1.7%). If overall gas demand does grow as expected, indigenous EU suppliers will meet a falling share of EU gas demand. The EU will become increasingly dependent on existing third country suppliers and on new suppliers. These will be in the Middle East where several countries are potentially large exporters of natural gas and in the longer term, if prices begin to reflect the costs of long haul transportation, in West Africa and Latin America.

Thus the 'dash for gas', which will be accelerated by movements towards greater competition in Europe, will increase supply security concerns. The shift to gas, which has environmental advantages over competing fuels and great potential for power generation, will support the environmental pillar of Europe's energy policy.

Electricity

Although a homogeneous product, electricity is produced via a number of different fuels. Electricity generated from traditional thermal fuel sources (i.e. coal, oil and, increasingly, gas) comprized 53 per cent of total electricity production in the European Union as a whole in 1993. The equivalent figure for nuclear power was 36 per cent and hydroelectricity 11 per cent.

The situation varies widely from country to country. Half the member states (Denmark, Greece, Ireland, Italy, Luxembourg and Portugal) have no nuclear power stations whatsoever whereas almost 80 per cent of electricity in France comes from nuclear power stations. Belgium's electricity sector is also dominated by nuclear generation (60% of total production). In the Netherlands, Ireland and Denmark, on the other hand, over 90 per cent of electricity generated comes from conventional thermal sources. Hydroelectric power makes important contributions to electricity generation in Spain, Portugal and Greece.

In the coming years, the balance of electricity generation in Europe will change. Bad publicity for nuclear generation has stalled nuclear programmes in several European programmes and gas-fired power stations will become more common. Cross-border trade in electricity exists already but is limited with only France and Germany engaging in significant exchanges. If the proposals for a single market in electricity outlined below come to fruition, there is much unfulfilled potential for cross-border trade.

Coal

Coal, the driving force behind Europe's industrialization, retains an important but declining role in Europe's energy portfolio. Solid fuels (coal and lignite together) accounted for 40 per cent of EC energy production in 1980. This had fallen to under 30 per cent by the early 1990s. This decline in coal consumption is expected to continue in view of increasing competition from natural gas in power generation, coal's largest market in Europe, and concern over the environmental impact of coal.

Coal consumption is declining but the share of imported coal in Europe's coal consumption has risen from under 20 per cent in 1980 to over 40 per cent in the early 1990s. Rising import penetration will also continue as subsidies to high-cost European producers are reduced and competition from lower cost mines in Australia, South Africa and North America gathers pace.

The challenge for the European Union as the coal industry adjusts to the new world of competition in the energy industry is to handle the social and regional problems which will occur as the result of the decline in the coal industry.

Obstacles to competition

The Commission's 1985 White Paper *Completing the Single Market* set out the grand plan for the introduction of competition throughout the Community's economy. This exacting programme provided for the removal of all barriers restricting trade and competition over the following eight years. Although the White Paper did not directly refer to the energy sector, the following general provisions applied to energy as much as to other sectors:

● Harmonization of rules and technical norms.
● The opening up of public procurement.
● The removal of fiscal barriers.
● The application of Community law.

However, many energy-specific trade barriers also existed and were not mentioned in the 1985 White Paper. In order to combat the remaining 'considerable barriers to trade in energy products' [Brussels European Council meeting, 11–13 February 1988], the European Commission drew up an inventory of the obstacles which inhibited the development of a more integrated energy market. This inventory, *The Internal Energy Market* [Com (88) 238], was published in May 1988 and formed the basis of subsequent proposals to eliminate these obstacles by the end of 1992. The proposals have met with varying degrees of success.

Electricity and gas

The following obstacles were identified by the 1988 White Paper as the main barriers to free trade and competition in the electricity and gas sectors.

Price transparency

Gas and electricity are sold to the majority of consumers in line with published tariff schedules. However, this is not the case with large industrial consumers. In the UK and Germany, for example, gas suppliers conclude

219

individual contracts with such customers. Even in countries with official tariff schedules for large industrial consumers, special tariffs are often negotiated. The absence of price transparency makes it impossible for large consumers to make rational purchasing decisions and inhibits the workings of competition.

Grid-interconnections

Gas and electricity grid interconnections between member states have existed for some time but are inadequate. In other cases, they are non-existent: at the time of the 1988 White Paper, the UK, Ireland, Spain, Portugal and Greece were not connected to the European gas grid. A similar situation exists in the electricity market. Such shortfalls could hamper potential growth in gas and electricity trade in a liberalized energy market and prevent the emergence of the full benefits of competition. The whole issue of trans-European networks has moved to the top of the European integration agenda during the 1990s and is discussed below.

Tax harmonization

In 1988, VAT rates on gas varied from 0 per cent in the UK to 22 per cent in Denmark. Although the rates have shifted since then, substantial differences remain in natural gas taxation rates. Other specific taxes on gas and electricity in some member states have also resulted in discrimination among consumers.

Technical standards

The 1988 Energy White Paper did not stress differences in technical standards in the gas and electricity sectors but the European Commission has subsequently taken a closer look at this matter. The First Progress Report on Completion of the Internal Energy Market concluded that standardization in the energy sector was crucial for the completion of the single energy market and would assist the development and dissemination of advanced energy technology. In relation to electricity and gas, standards relate to production, transportation and distribution equipment. A 1992 Commission Communication [SEC (92) 724] on this topic indicates that the Commission intended to place more emphasis on the harmonization of technical standards in the energy sector.

Public procurement

In the late 1980s, European Union gas and electricity undertakings purchased billions of ECU worth of pipelines, storage facilities and gas terminals. The purchasing practices of member states favoured national producers. However, the inclusion of the energy sector in the public procurement directive which was implemented in 1990 brought an end to this practice and the fragmentation of the European market for energy equipment. In the medium term, this should encourage the emergence of strong European energy equipment producers.

Exploration and production

Member states have widely varying requirements for granting licences for the exploration for and exploitation of natural gas and oil resources. Many of the regulations require, to a greater or lesser degree, the participation of national enterprises in the venture.

Imports and exports

In 1988, all member states exerted some control on the export and import of natural gas. Member states used a variety of methods, including the operation of a state monopoly, the conditions of granting transport licences and, in the UK, the requirement to obtain the permission of the Secretary of State to export gas (a requirement subsequently dispensed with).

Storage and transportation

Monopolies in the transportation industry and rights to use the gas and electricity grids are probably the single biggest obstacle to the development of competition in the electricity and gas industries. More extensive discussion of the measures the Commission has introduced to rectify the situation are outlined below.

Crude oil and petroleum products

The crude oil and refined petroleum product sectors are the most open of all the energy markets in Europe. Although state-run companies and restrictions do exist, the presence of international oil companies and a large number of operators allow the forces of competition to operate more fully in the oil markets than in any other parts of the energy sector. Excess refinery capacity within Europe and increasing refinery capacity within the territory of major crude oil producers have also fostered competition. Unlike gas and electricity, which rely on networks for their transportation and require controversial legislation to open them to competition, crude oil and refined petroleum products can be transported by tanker, inland waterway, rail, road and pipeline and do not depend on highly complex third party access proposals to ensure competition is achieved.

Despite this relative openness, the 1988 Single Energy Market White Paper identified a number of barriers in the oil sector, including:

● The reservation of certain exploration rights to national oil companies.

- discriminatory exploration licensing procedures.
- Oil field development conditions which obliged or encouraged companies to purchase services and equipment from national suppliers.
- The use of oil production taxation to promote the development of certain fields and thus distort competition.
- Obligations in Italy and the UK to land crude oil produced offshore at a port within their jurisdiction.
- Restrictions on the import of crude oil and petroleum products from non-Community countries.
- Obligations on Spanish and French refiners to accept crude oil purchased by the state.
- The obligation to use national flag shipping for the carriage of crude oil and/or refined petroleum products by sea.
- Refining monopolies in Portugal, Spain, France and Greece.
- A marketing monopoly for Spanish company Campsa.
- Differences in technical norms and rules applying to petroleum products. These increased costs of production, storage and transportation, especially for those companies hoping to supply several countries from one refinery.
- Differences in compulsory storage arrangements.
- Price controls in seven member states.
- Differences in VAT and excise duties on oil products.

Approximation of taxation, which was a prominent feature of the 1985 White Paper on the Single Market, was identified as a priority. Other elements regarded as ripe for action included the different technical norms applying to petroleum products, obstacles arising from the existence of oil monopolies and obstacles to internal transport.

Single energy market progress

Electricity and gas

Three stages of liberalization were envisaged for the gas and electricity industries. Phase one was relatively uncontroversial and comprized measures to improve price transparency of gas and electricity prices and the liberalization of gas and electricity transit.

The price transparency directive, which was agreed in 1990, established the principle of price transparency for the final consumer of gas and electricity. Most gas and electricity prices were already transparent but contracts between gas and electricity utilities and large industrial consumers often were not. The price transparency directive required member states to make available to the Commission price data relating to such contracts, while still preserving commercial confidentiality. The publication of such information is regarded as an important guarantee of competition, enabling large industrial consumers to make rational decisions on their supplies of electricity and gas.

The Commission has concluded, in its Second Progress Report on the Internal Energy Market [Com (93) 261], that the data provided as a result of the price transparency directive underlines 'the need for increased competition in order to achieve an efficient internal market in which prices accurately reflect costs so as to allow more efficiency to be introduced into the system and the necessary price adjustments to be made.' In other words, once further competition is allowed into the gas and electricity sectors, the price transparency directive will really come into its own and facilitate rational purchasing decisions by large industrial consumers.

The directive on the transit of electricity was adopted in October 1990 and that relating to the transit of natural gas in May 1991. The provisions for gas and electricity transit broadly parallel each other and were designed to encourage trade in both energy products. The directives allow transmission companies to use grids in other member states to transmit gas and electricity to third countries on payment of a negotiated charge. The Spanish electricity network operator, for example, if required, would have to negotiate terms for the transit of French electricity to Portugal.

The directives require the parties to inform the Commission about requests for transit, the conclusion of a contract and of reasons for failure to reach agreement. In the case of disagreement between the parties, either may request that the conditions of transit be subjected to a conciliation procedure by a body set up and chaired by the Commission.

The transit proposals were opposed by gas companies and several member states. Resistance was not based on opposition to transit, which already existed extensively among the core gas producers of Continental Western Europe, namely Belgium's Distrigaz, Gaz de France, Gasunie of the Netherlands, Ruhrgas of Germany and Italy's SNAM, but stemmed largely from the fear that the directives represented the first step in allowing the European Commission regulatory powers over the industry.

Phase two in the construction of the single gas and electricity markets has proved more controversial and, despite softening of the proposals, is still far from complete. These proposals outlined 'Common Rules' for the gradual introduction of single market principles to the gas and electricity sectors. The main elements of the Common Rules, proposed in 1991, were:

● The introduction of a transparent and non-discriminatory system for

223

granting licences for the construction of electricity production facilities and of electricity lines and gas pipelines. This should boost competition in the sector by providing production and transport opportunities for independent operators.

● The separation, or 'unbundling', of the management and accounting of production, transmission and distribution operations within vertically integrated undertakings. The aim is to ensure transparency of operations, especially costs and profitability, thereby enabling potential market participants to assess the costs of the network operators.

● The introduction of limited third party access (TPA) for large industrial consumers to transmission and distribution networks at reasonable rates and within the limits of available capacity.

TPA is the key to the introduction of competition into the gas and electricity markets. In one sense, the licensing provisions and unbundling of accounts, albeit competition enhancers in their own rights, are facilitators and prerequisites for achievement of TPA.

Although highly complex and technical in its implementation, TPA, as defined by the European Commission in its original proposal [Com (91) 548 final], is relatively simple. TPA is:

> a regime providing for an obligation, to the extent that there is capacity available, on companies operating transmission and distribution networks for ... gas/electricity to offer terms for the use of their grid, in particular to individual consumers or to distribution companies, in return for payment.

The underlying rationale is that by opening the gas and electricity networks, gas-to-gas and electricity-to-electricity competition will increase among the major players in the market; consumer choice will increase; gas and electricity prices will fall and the competitiveness of European industry will improve.

Phase two TPA proposals were limited to large consumers and distributors. These included:

● Large industrial users with consumption of electricity in excess of 100 GWh or 25 million cubic metres of gas on a site. The Commission estimates that the eligibility criteria will cover roughly 500 electricity-consuming companies in the aluminum, metallurgical, chemical, construction material and glass industries and a similar number of gas producers in fertilizer and electricity production.

● Distributors who supply at least 3 per cent of electricity or 1 per cent of gas consumed in their member state. Distributors not reaching this threshold can band together to qualify. The European Commission anticipates that about 100 electricity and 100 gas distributors will qualify for TPA.

The original draft directive on common rules proposed implementation by 1 January 1993. Stage three of the single market in gas and electricity was envisaged by 1 January 1996. Stage three was dependent on stage two and involved extending the provisions of third party access to smaller consumers. However, in view of the resolute resistance of the network owners themselves, opposition from member states (with the exception of the UK) and of a highly critical report from the European Parliament, the European Commission has been unable to carry its proposals through the Council of Ministers. Consequently, the Commission brought forward revized TPA proposals at the end of 1993 in an attempt to break the deadlock.

The original proposals set out regulatory mechanisms for access to networks. The amended proposals enable producers or transporters of gas or electricity to supply directly large industrial consumers through the network on a negotiated basis. Negotiated rather than regulatory access is intended to provide greater flexibility to network access and to reduce the bureaucratic load. Member states will have the responsibility of providing an appropriate dispute settlement procedure. The Commission has stressed that the amendments do not, in any way, prevent companies applying to the courts to apply Community law as set out in the Treaty of Rome.

The modifications retain the unbundling of accounts for both gas and electricity in relation to their main activities such as production, transportation and distribution. However, the unbundling of management is no longer required. In the electricity sector, however, the administrative independence of the network manager must be maintained.

The revized proposal is also more explicit on the issue of public service obligation than the initial draft. The draft Directive states that the imperatives of supply security and consumer protection imply some public service obligations on utilities which cannot be ensured by the exercise of competition. Member states are therefore authorized to impose public service obligations with regard to security, quality, price and regularity of supply on gas and electricity companies.

Subsidiarity has prevailed and member states are free to determine what constitutes public service obligations and to use them to refuse TPA. The Commission hopes to avoid member states using public sector obligations as a pretext for avoiding the requirements of TPA by requiring them to define the obligations within the framework of Community law and to be explicit about the obligations for the purposes of transparency and legal security.

The Commission has deliberately referred to 'public service obligations' rather than used the more general phrase 'general economic interest' which would have allowed member states too great a scope for seeking exemption from the directive's provisions.

The Commission brought forward its amendments in December 1993. By the Energy Council of May 1994, the member states had still not completed their discussion of the technical aspects of the revized proposal within COREPER and were not ready to embark upon a political discussion of the draft. Consequently, although views were aired at the Council meeting, no conclusions were reached and COREPER is continuing its work with a view to achieving more substantial results at the Energy Council to be held under the German presidency later in 1994.

Meanwhile France, one of the more unenthusiastic member states about TPA, has put forward alternative proposals. This option, known as 'sole purchaser', would allow countries where there is a sole purchaser to keep to the arrangement provided competition is introduced through a tender system. The Commission has indicated it is willing to consider this alternative approach if the following conditions apply:

- Public service obligations must be fulfilled.
- The sole purchaser must be independent of the commercial and economic interests of the sector, especially the producers.
- Appeal against the sole purchaser's decisions must be possible.
- The sole purchaser must be an intermediary only and not an import or export monopoly.

Such a solution, on the face of it, would appear to fly in the face of the rationale of liberalising the energy markets and it is difficult to envisage how it would work in a way which does not undermine the single market philosophy.

Oil and petroleum products

The need to harmonize petroleum product standards is as great as ever. New European environmental regulations on the emission from motor vehicles have prompted some member states to introduce their own standards and require changes in both engines and fuels. Following the adoption of a European standard on unleaded petrol in 1987, the European Commission charged the European standards body, CEN, with the task of drawing up five new standards. These are yet to come into force. The Commission has acknowledged, however, the need to take account of the link between fuel quality, engine technology and exhaust emissions in any standard which is passed.

In the area of oil and gas exploration and production equipment, the intention, as set out in the public procurement directive, is to adopt American Petroleum Institute standards as the appropriate standards.

In view of the restrictions on equal access of companies to the exploration and production of oil and gas (described above), the European Commission brought forward a proposal [Com (92) 110] to establish common and open licensing rules. The directive requires member states to grant authorizations for the exploration and production of hydrocarbons in line with non-discriminatory, transparent and objective procedures. All interested parties are allowed to apply for authorization and the criteria on which decisions are to be made must be set out by the competent authority in advance.

The directive was adopted at the Energy Council of May 1994 and will come into force in 1995. The proposal allows member states to retain their sovereignty over their natural resources but this sovereignty must be exercized in line with the principles of the single market. In other words, the directive lays down the general principles for such rules but allows member states the scope to devise the most appropriate rules for their own operating conditions and resource management plans. Member states will be able to decide which areas are to be open to exploration and exploitation and when and also to decide the level and rates of tax and other royalties.

Trans-European networks

Given that the general single market programme has largely come to fruition (even if the internal energy market is still beset with problems), the integration emphasis of the EU has switched from the removal of regulatory barriers to competition within the European Union to the construction of a European infrastructure to enable business to take advantage of its new freedom. The energy, transport and telecommunications industries are at the heart of this initiative. Article 129 b–d of the Maastricht Treaty reinforces this priority which fits squarely within the aim of achieving open and competitive markets.

The rationale behind the push for genuine trans-European energy networks is that existing gas and electricity grids have been developed from a national perspective and ignore the wider European dimension. The single energy market programme, as described above, stresses the enhancement of competition through the end of special and exclusive rights to network access in particular. However as the Commission's Communication *Electricity and Natural Gas Transmission Infrastructures in the Community* [SEC (92) 553] maintains:

The proposals [i.e. Common rules] will only be effective in promoting intra-Community trade in gas and electricity if transmission infrastructures are strengthened and integrated at Community level.

In order to bring the infrastructure project to fruition, the European Commission has published a series of guidelines on the attainment of trans-European networks in the energy sector and has identified eight priority projects for the first stage.

The guidelines identify the main challenges to the network projects as:

- The need to bridge the remaining discontinuities at the interfaces between national networks;
- To increase the capacity of the interconnections.
- To connect isolated or underequipped countries to the European gas and electricity networks.
- To ensure that there is interoperability of networks at European level in terms of continuity of supply, stability of voltage and frequency.

The Commission envisages that trans-European network development will be the result of a partnership between itself, member states and the private sector. It sees its role as the identification of projects of common interest and the development of technical, administrative, legal and financial measures to provide the framework for completing the networks.

Energy charter

In 1990, Ruud Lubbers, the Dutch Prime Minister, proposed the negotiation of a European Energy Charter. The Charter, which was a response to the collapse of the Soviet Union, was intended to serve a number of ends. By facilitating the export of energy from the former Soviet Union (FSU) and foreign investment in the FSU, the Charter would improve the energy security of the European Union; provide a market in the FSU for the sale of much-needed Western equipment; and boost transparency, and hence security, for Western energy investment in the FSU. The energy-producing ex-Soviet republics would benefit from much-needed investment in their run-down oil and gas industries. The energy industries provided the best prospect for earning badly needed foreign exchange.

In December 1991, the text of the Energy Charter was formally agreed. The Charter was not a legally binding text but a statement of principles and intentions which were the basis for negotiations which took place between 1992 and 1994 to transform the aspirations of the Charter's fifty signatories into legal texts.

The ambitions of the Charter have an unashamedly competitive, liberal, anti-monopoly flavour. The Charter envisaged an area covering the whole of Europe and the former Soviet Union which entailed:

● An open and competitive market for energy products, materials, equipment and services.
● Access to energy resources, and exploration and development thereof on a commercial basis.
● Removal of technical, administrative and other barriers to trade in energy and associated equipment, technologies and energy-related services.
● Promotion of the development and interconnection of energy transport infrastructure.
● Easier access to transport infrastructure for international transport purposes in line with the principles of open and competitive markets for energy products.

In short, the principles of the Energy Charter mirrored the principles of competition used by the European Union in attempting to develop its own internal energy market. Not surprisingly, in view of the difficulties encountered in the attempts to obtain the agreement of the twelve member states to their own internal energy market and the domestic economic and political problems of the republics of the FSU, the reality of the Energy Charter Treaty fell somewhat short of its competition aspirations. In order to achieve any agreement whatsoever, the process was divided into two stages. Stage one was agreed in 1994. Over the subsequent three years, negotiations will take place on the more controversial aspects of the Charter Treaty such as national treatment and access to natural resources.

Despite these problems, the Energy Charter is important in several respects. First, it represents an imaginative attempt by the European Union to develop a mutually beneficial policy beyond its borders. Secondly, the potential for improving political and economic stability in the former Soviet Union extends the implications of the Charter far beyond the technical requirements of oil and gas production and transport and into the area of international relations and politics. Thirdly, the Charter reinforces the commitment of the European Union to the attainment of free and open competition within the energy markets.

The future?

As the 1996 Intergovernmental Conference to review the Maastricht Treaty approaches, the debate is hotting up about the steps which need to be taken to enhance the effectiveness of European Union policy. Energy policy will take a central role in this process. A Green Paper on Energy will form the basis of the debate about future energy policy and strong attempts will be made to accord energy its own title in the Union's treaties.

European Union energy policy priorities after the 1996 Conference will look familiar. The introduction of competition will remain a key theme. Even if agreement is reached on the first phase of third party access, which is far from certain, the struggle to extend TPA to smaller consumers and distributors will only just have begun. Achievement of competition objectives will become even more crucial if the trans-European network initiative is not to be stifled. The Union will also be attempting to maintain the balance between the attainment of competition and other policy priorities. Diversification of energy suppliers will remain high on the agenda as will environmental protection.

As the twenty-first century unfolds, the requirement to adjust for eastern enlargement will become pressing. The challenge will be particularly strong in relation to energy as the drive increases to build up networks with Central and Eastern European countries, to extend access (and hence competition) and to improve energy efficiency in that region.

Questions

1 How might the different resource endowments of member states affect their approach towards energy policy?
2 There are three pillars of energy policy – competition, security of supply and protection of the environment. These pillars can and do conflict. Suggest circumstances in which such a conflict could occur and decide which pillar you think should take priority. Be prepared to justify your choice.
3 In what ways are the policies of Third Party Access, Trans-European Networks and the Energy Charter Treaty mutually reinforcing?
4 To what extent will the introduction of competition into Europe's energy markets bring the expected benefits?
5 How can the push towards greater competition be reconciled with public service obligations?

Case 7   EU railways: open access or natural monopoly?

Brian Milner

Introduction

The introduction of competition has been a key theme of EU policy in all transport sectors. The railways are no exception. This preoccupation with competition plus environmental concerns and a growing appreciation of the efficiency of high speed train services have moved the development of railways up the EU policy agenda in recent years. The effects of greater competition will operate not only within the rail sector itself but also increase inter-modal competition: high speed routes over long distances will increase competition between railways and airlines, for example.

Continuing and, in some cases, increasing subsidy to railway undertakings has become a financial burden to most member states. The creation of a competitive market will not only reduce these costs but will also improve services to the customer. This case study investigates these issues both from the point of view of member states and of the EU, analysing the differing rail policies of EU governments and considering what is likely to emerge as a common policy.

At the moment, the amount of subsidy to and investment in railway organizations varies considerably between member states. 300 km/h routes are being developed in some states whereas in others little or no development is occurring. Differences in signalling systems, power supply systems and the loading gauge limit interoperability of rolling stock. This is important when considering the development of trans-European rail networks and competitive services that may run on them.

National governments are becoming concerned at ever-increasing exchequer costs and are considering privatization as a possible solution. A number of models have been developed and will be considered. The UK model provides for the introduction of competition into every area of railways and will be considered in depth. Passenger, trainload freight, wagonload freight and parcels services are being separated from each other and from the ownership of track, trains and stations. A difficulty here is that although competition between operators is a desired objective, those organizations within the private sector that have shown an interest are demanding sole monopoly access to the routes for themselves alone.

Another particular difficulty is that track, stations and trains have a very long life whereas the impact of competitive forces is felt very strongly in the short and medium term. The creation of large European train leasing companies is a possibility but technical differences between railway systems are likely to prove a general constraint on the movement of rolling stock.

The key question for railways is: 'Is it possible to create contestable markets in this industry or will railway systems always involve monopoly?'

EU railway policy

Over the past few years, the EU has published a number of important papers regarding railways. Perhaps the most important of these concern the separation of infrastructure from operations and the provision of limited open access to independent railway operators. This should enable competition to take place between train operators instead of the monopoly situation which generally exists today.

Another important development has been the growing appreciation of the importance of the trans-European transport networks: in the past such networks were generally developed from a national perspective only. Among the many benefits of such networks are increased inter-modal competition and the boost to the EU's competitiveness resulting from a more efficient transport system.

The EU is generally neutral on the subject of privatization (unlike member states) but the Council has proposed a Directive on the licensing of railway undertakings and a further Directive on the allocation of railway infrastructure capacity and on the charging of infrastructure fees.

Access to Europe's rail networks

On 29 July 1991, a Council Directive was published on the development of the Community's railways. Known as Directive 91/440, it has caused considerable change to occur in the railways of the European Union. The Directive came into force on 1 January 1993 when limited rights of access to national rail networks were made available for private companies.

The main provisions of the Directive are as follows:

● Railway undertakings must hold assets, budgets and accounts which are separate from those of the state and must be managed on commercial grounds, the latter also applying to the undertakings' public service obligation as defined by the state. The public service obligation details those non-profit making services which the state is prepared to subsidize.

- Accounts concerning business relating to the provision of transport services must be kept separate from those concerning business relating to the management of railway infrastructure. Aid paid to one of these two areas may not be transferred to the other. Member States may provide for this separation by the creation of separate divisions within one undertaking or by the creation of a separate organization to manage the infrastructure. The *infrastructure manager* shall charge a railway operator a fee for the use of the infrastructure, the scale of fees being defined by the Member States. The fees should take into account matters such as mileage, speed, axle load and frequency.
- Member States must take steps to reduce the indebtedness of railway undertakings.
- International groupings shall be granted access and transit rights in their own states and transit rights in other Member States. Infrastructure managers must make non-discriminatory agreements with these international groupings.

Railway infrastructure includes track, stations and signalling systems. Other matters that an infrastructure manager will be responsible for include safety issues and the production of working timetables.

The concept of the separation of railway infrastructure from railway operations is relatively new. Although it seems perfectly natural for lorry, bus and car owners not to own the infrastructure on which they travel (the road system), the opposite has always been true as far as railways are concerned. Throughout the world, the operators of railway services have almost always been the owners of the track on which they travelled. Some would argue that this ownership has led to the infrastructure more closely matching the needs of the customer whereas others would say that it produces monopolies that are unlikely to provide for the needs of the market.

The directive also allows for competitive open access to international groupings. The Eurostar project linking Britain with France and Belgium is a good example of an international grouping. EPS (the British operator – European Passenger Services), SNCB (Belgian national railways) and SNCF (French national railways) constitute this grouping. This organization owns and runs the passenger trains and markets the services. So far, no competition has emerged for this service.

When a larger grouping, including NS (Dutch national railways) and DB (German national railways) attempted to set up overnight services between Britain and the Continent, the EU suggested that they were creating a cartel and excluding competitors. The latter was inconsistent as Hotelzug AG had been set up by DB, OBB (Austrian national railways) and SBB (Swiss

233

national railways) to provide overnight services between the three countries without any difficulty. In due course, after discussion between DGIV and DGVII, the EU was satisfied; the joint venture European Night Services Limited are planning to begin services in late 1995. This will itself increase competition with the existing services across the Channel. The EU had made the point that access to other operators must be real in terms of traction and other resources.

Common transport policy (CTP) White Paper

On 2 December 1992, the European Commission published a White Paper on common transport policy. Much of the White Paper lies outside the scope of this Case Study because it concerned all transport modes but there are many matters of direct interest to railways.

The main objective of the CTP is sustainable mobility for the community as a whole. Other concerns of the CTP include:

- Reduction of the environmental damage caused by transport, especially road vehicles through carbon dioxide emissions.
- The improvement of transport infrastructure in the regions and the development of trans-European transport networks.

On the subject of railways, the White Paper notes that significant change has occurred. Urban and inter-city traffic has increased while traffic in old industrial areas has declined. Insufficient investment has produced a number of saturation points. Some surplus capacity has been created with the introduction of high speed lines although the surplus capacity is sometimes not where it is most needed. Rolling stock has been significantly reduced with little or no spare capacity now available for new traffic or an increase in traffic. The paper suggests that further development of the high speed network will release more capacity on existing lines which, with limited investment, could then be used for services such as long distance freight.

The paper notes that previously transport networks were designed largely from the national point of view and often with only one mode in mind. In the future, intermodal and international traffic is likely to become far more important.

It states that further action is needed towards liberalization as discussed in Directive 91/440. Criteria for access to and charging for rail infrastructure and for the setting up of railway undertakings should be made at the EU level. Without this, liberalization will be uneven and in some cases may not take place at all.

An inventory of state aids to different transport sectors will be set up. This will make transparent the levels of subsidy provided and may provide an important indicator of unfair competition in the provision of international services.

The development of the trans-European transport network

On 7 April 1994, a proposal for the development of a trans-European transport network was published by the Commission. The intention is to complete a single trans-European transport market by identifying necessary infrastructure requirements to provide for sustainable mobility for people and goods across the EU. It will also change the competitive position between transport modes.

The trans-European rail network, of 70,000 km, will include 23,000 km which will form the High-Speed Rail Network. Of the 23,000 km, 10,000 km will be new lines designed for speeds in excess of 250 km/h, the remainder being upgraded existing lines capable of about 200 km/h. It will provide links between the main European towns and cities. The paper gives the reason for setting up the high speed train network as the provision of greater mobility for Europeans with less impact on the environment than other modes. The rest of the 70,000 km network will be used for access to the regions, to ports and airports and for combined transport.

The proposals discuss the investment of ECU 400 billion over the next 15 years with ECU 220 billion to be implemented by the year 2000. It is suggested that partnership projects between the public and private sector may be necessary to complement public investment.

The railway network is expected to play a more important part in the transport market in the future; it will be adapted to meet its particular market, that is the rapid large-capacity transporting of passengers and the carriage of large volumes of goods especially over long distances. Rail will also play a key role in a combined transport network which will consist of corridors and well-developed intermodal platforms for the efficient trans-shipment of goods between rail, road, inland waterways and maritime shipping.

In centrally-situated countries, numerous bottlenecks will need to be eliminated whereas in peripheral countries improvements such as replacing obsolete equipment, electrifying lines and completing missing links will be necessary. Bearing Directive 91/440 in mind, schemes aimed at technical harmonization of infrastructure, rolling stock and control systems will be considered favourably from the point of view of funding.

Trans-European priorities

At the EU Council of Ministers meeting in Corfu at the end of June 1994, eleven priority projects were presented by the Commission for consideration. Of the eleven, eight were for the rail network.

The eight rail priority routes are as follows:

- The London to Paris, Brussels, Cologne, Amsterdam corridor.
- Capacity expansion in the Munich–Brenner–Verona corridor, including construction of the Brenner Pass tunnel. Subsequent extension from Munich to Berlin via Leipzig is planned.
- France's TGV Est to Strasbourg and on via Appenweier to Karlsruhe in Germany and other links. Later routes should be completed from Paris to Berlin and Leipzig.
- The Lyon–Turin high speed line including a new transalpine tunnel. This is likely to allow shuttle operation of drive-on/drive-off trains for road vehicles and may have links from Geneva and Lausanne.
- The high speed lines from Madrid to Barcelona to Perpignan to Montpellier and from Madrid to Vitoria to Dax. This will connect Spain with the French TGV network.
- The Betwuwe freight line from Rotterdam to the German border.
- Improved rail links between Cork, Dublin, Belfast and the Larne–Stranraer ferry.
- The Oresund link between Denmark and Sweden.

It was surprising that, apart from the link to the Channel Tunnel, the UK did not feature in these priorities especially since UK lacks any 300 km/h routes. After considerable pressure from local authorities, the UK government decided to ask for the West Coast Main Line (WCML, linking London with Birmingham, Manchester, Liverpool, Edinburgh and Glasgow) to be added to the priority list. A feasibility report, produced jointly by the pubic and private sectors in December 1994, suggested a 1996 start to the £500 million project.

A disappointing omission was the direct link to Stranraer from the WCML which was closed in the 1960s but could be reopened with relatively little expense. Pressure from the MEPs for South of Scotland and Ulster did not meet support from the Scottish Office. Instead it was proposed to add a road connection across Wales and Southern England (to link Ireland and the Channel Tunnel) to the list of priority routes.

The initial tranche of priority routes is estimated to cost ECU 68 billion. ECU 5 billion per year has been earmarked from the EU budget, the rest to be found within the member states. In November 1994, Economic Affairs Commissioner Henning Christophersen announced that of the rail priorities, only Cork to Larne and the Oresund link had finance in place. It was reported that Britain was resisting new forms of financial support for the outstanding projects.

Limitations on interoperability

Significant investment is necessary to ensure compatibility between rail networks. Motive power for Eurostar, the trains operating between London, Paris and Brussels, has been complicated because of the requirement to allow for three different power supply systems. In all there are five supply systems in Europe. Signalling is even more diverse with ten different cab signalling systems in operation (some countries do not have cab signalling). Loading gauge also differs between countries. The British gauge is much smaller in cross-section than the Berne Gauge which is common in Europe – the German gauge is bigger still.

The effect of these differences will be to limit the interoperability of EU rolling stock. International competition between train operators will be limited and combined transport, where lorries are transported on other modes such as trains, will be more difficult to introduce. Technical differences make the creation of trans-European rolling stock leasing companies unlikely. They will also limit competition with other modes. For example, rail freight may penetrate the South East of England but not easily go further.

The licensing of railway undertakings within the EU

Each member state is required to set up a *licensing authority* which will grant railway operating licenses. To ensure independence, the authority must not be associated with the national railway undertaking of the state. A railway undertaking, meeting the requirements of the directive, will be entitled on a non-discriminatory basis to receive an operating licence which has validity throughout the Community – this will enable competition between train operators.

By derogation, member states may exclude railway undertakings which are solely concerned with the transport needs of a region including urban, suburban and cross-country services as well as preserved and museum railways. The proposal is not clear as to the meaning of the term 'region' but clearly the derogation would not be allowed for routes of trans-European importance.

Requirements of suitable railway undertakings are as follows:

● As far as financial fitness is concerned, it must be able to show that it will be able to meet its actual and potential obligations for a period of twelve months.
● The applicant must be able to demonstrate that it will be in a position to provide appropriate rolling stock including traction and maintenance arrangements so that it can operate services safely and efficiently. Its personnel, equipment and organization must be able to ensure a high level of safety and staff, such as drivers, must be fully qualified for their work.

● The applicant must have made arrangements for insurance cover in case of accidents concerning passengers, luggage, freight, mail and third parties.

The licensing authority may review a new licence after one year and, in any case, the situation will be reviewed every five years. A licence will continue to be valid as long as the undertaking fully meets the requirements of the directive. If suspension or revocation is necessary, other member states and the Commission must be informed.

If a railway undertaking wishes to significantly change its activities, then the licensing authority must ensure that all requirements are met as far as the new services are concerned. Precise details of these changes, such as a change or extension of service or a proposal for a takeover or merger, must be given. It remains to be seen whether this will limit entrepreneurial flair between competitors.

It is intended that the Directive will apply from 1 January 1996. A transitional period of six months will be allowed from that date assuming that requirements for safety have been complied with.

The allocation of railway infrastructure capacity and the charging of infrastructure fees within the EU

To enable fair charges to be raized to competing train operators, it is proposed that:

● Each member state shall establish an *allocation body* responsible for the allocation of infrastructure capacity ensuring that infrastructure is allocated on a fair and non-discriminatory basis and that the allocation procedure is efficiently organized applying market principles.
● If the member state's infrastructure manager (see the discussion of Directive 91/440) is not also a train operator, it may also become the state's allocation body. Again, to ensure fair competition, the 'allocation body' must not be linked to a train operator.
● Priority will be given to public service transport in general but where infrastructure has been constructed or upgraded for specific services, such as high speed or freight lines or lines for combined inter-modal transport, the specialized types of operation will have priority. As usual, train paths on such specialized infrastructure must be allocated on a fair and non-discriminatory basis.

The infrastructure manager may finance infrastructure development and may make a return on such capital employed. Fee charges must be 'reasonable' and will be notified to the allocation body.

These Directives will enable competitive trans-European rail services to begin operating. This will be a major change since, previously, almost all rail services have been provided by national railway undertakings. If member states wish it, the Directives can also apply to regional services, providing for competition generally.

Comparisons between EU railways

Having examined EU railway policy, we now turn our attention to comparisons between the different national railways in the period prior to the introduction of competition. We will consider financial performance, market share and investment.

Table C7.1, which gives financial performance data for some of the major European railways, indicates the relative level of subsidy that they require. When considering rail operations only, none of these companies were able to cover their operating costs let alone their total costs from receipts. Only SBB in Switzerland and DSB in Denmark were able to cover their operating costs when including non-rail aspects.

Table C7.1 *European railways in 1990*

		Receipts/ total costs		Receipts/ operating costs	
		Rail only	Rail and non-rail	Rail only	Rail and non-rail
UK	BR	0.82	0.85	0.87	0.90
Sweden	SJ/BV	0.59	0.73	0.72	0.88
Switzerland	SBB	0.51	0.89	0.64	1.11
France	SNCF	0.50	0.68	0.64	0.57
Norway	NSB	0.49	0.51	0.54	0.57
Netherlands	NS	0.46	0.58	0.54	0.68
Ireland	IE	0.46	0.46	0.51	0.63
Denmark	DSB	0.45	0.78	0.63	1.10
West Germany	DB	0.44	0.58	0.52	0.69
Spain	RENFE	0.42	0.60		
Austria	OBB	0.35	0.72	0.39	0.81
Portugal	CP	0.34	0.73	0.42	0.90
Belgium	SNCB	0.27	0.49	0.31	0.57
Italy	FS	0.16	0.27	0.20	0.33
Mean		**0.46**	**0.63**	**0.53**	**0.75**

Source: *Railway Gazette International*, July 1994

BR in the UK comes out very well from this analysis while FS in Italy is exceptionally poor. BR is outstanding especially in the area of rail-only business. Much non-rail business has previously been privatized and exposed to competition – road haulage, buses, shipping, station catering, train construction and much maintenance. When the costs of train services became more visible, it was necessary to become more efficient. This was achieved without competition as only one nationalized organization was involved. The reader should note that continuing pressure is being placed on costs as subsidy to the UK's railways is projected to fall dramatically in real terms over the next few years.

The subsidies provided to other member states' protected undertakings are major reasons for the movement towards competition and privatization within the EU.

Table C7.2 was included in the same journal. In this table, the UK is the only country to show an improvement in receipt/cost ratio over the years from 1977 to 1990. In 1990, UK has the best receipt/cost ratio but this has been achieved at the expense of market share, especially in freight. BR's market share of both the freight and passenger business was lower than the majority of other countries shown. Some predict that increased transaction costs following deregulation will worsen this situation although the existence of the Channel Tunnel may improve it. Note however the performance of FS in Italy. Here market share dropped by more than BR's but the resulting receipt/cost ratio was twice as bad as before.

Table C7.2 *Trends in key indicators between 1977 and 1990 for selected European railways*

		Market share freight (%)		Market share passenger (%)		Receipts/costs rail only (%)	
		1976	1990	1976	1990	1977	1990
Netherlands	NS	4.9	4.6	6.4	6.9	56	46
Sweden	SJ/BV	44.6	42.5	5.4	6.1	83	59
Belgium	SNCB	22.1	17.8	11.4		50	27
UK	BR	16.8	9.9	6.5	5.4	71	82
Denmark	DSB	15.0	16.0	7.3	7.1	61	45
West Germany	DB	26.1	20.6	6.4	6.3	61	44
Norway	NSB	23.2	14.3	5.6	5.1	60	49
France	SNCF	34.1	26.7	11.0	9.2	55	50
Italy	FS	18.2	10.1	12.1	7.1	32	16
Mean		**22.7**	**18.1**	**7.6**	**6.7**	**59**	**46**

Source: *Railway Gazette International*, July 1994

Another very important indicator is long-term investment. The UK has a long history of under-investing in its railways. Table C7.3 gives an indication of current plans.

Table C7.3 *Comparison of European railway investment plans during the 1990s*

		Spending (mECU)	Length (route-km)	Rating (mECU/kmN)
Netherlands	NS	8689.1	2798	3.105
Switzerland	SBB	6516.7	2982	2.185
Belgium	SNCB	6470.3	3466	1.867
Germany	DB	62,463.2	45,706	1.367
Denmark	DSB	1372.1	2344	0.585
France	SNCF	20,019.4	34,322	0.583
Norway	NSB	1933.2	4027	0.480
Spain	RENFE	5940.4	13,060	0.455
Portugal	CP	1541.1	3910	0.394
Sweden	BV	4080.5	10,970	0.372
UK	BR	4386.5	16,588	0.266
Finland	VR	737.1	5853	0.126

Source: Rail Business Report, 1994

Details of each of these plans are given in the Rail Business Report. Note that only Finland has a lower rating than the UK in this table, although Italian figures were not available. One of the reasons for the UK's low investment is that the government believes that major programmes should be financed by the private sector. A good example of this, apart from the Channel Tunnel itself, is the high speed link between the Tunnel and London. In comparison with the SNCF link from the Tunnel to Paris, which was completed early, the UK link is unlikely to be completed until the 21st century. Until then, international trains will be required to travel on the essentially suburban South Eastern Main Line. President Mitterand made clear how amused he was at this situation when the Queen and he opened the Tunnel on 6 May 1994.

An unfortunate side-effect of this policy is that the privatized railway supply industry is in severe decline in the UK – most companies are declaring redundancies in 1994 and some may not survive. This is in contrast with the rest of Europe where expansion is the order of the day. European manufacturing plants can tender anywhere in Europe but so far British plants have had few successes. Perhaps a stable home market is an important element of success.

We have looked at some of the key differences between the EU railways in this section. We now turn our attention to policy for the future especially in terms of privatization and infrastucture allocation. Because the UK's plans go further than those of any other EU state, UK policy will be considered in depth, later.

Current trends within the EU on the Continent

As noted earlier, many member states are becoming concerned at the level of subsidy required by national railway undertakings. In response to this, some are proposing privatization to inject competition while most are moving toward separation of infrastructure from train operating, as required by Directive 91/440.

Sweden is perhaps the most advanced in this regard. The country's 1988 Transport Act created a new national track authority, Banverket, run on the lines of the Swedish national roads authority. Charges for use of the track, incorporating both fixed and variable cost elements, have been agreed but these are not intended to cover all track costs any more than road users pay all road costs. Support for transport investment comes largely from government and there has been a sharp movement towards investment in railway infrastructure in recent years. One of the primary aims of the separation of infrastructure from operations in Sweden was to ensure that infrastructure investment was shared out fairly between rail and road after the consideration of socio-economic and environmental issues. In terms of privatization, organizations may compete with the national train operator (SJ) but so far only some local passenger services have been privatized. The intention is to allow fair competition and if SJ is the best, then it will continue to run services. Often, these decisions are made by regional authorities.

In both Germany and the Netherlands, the national railway system is being reorganized into a holding corporation containing a small group of companies. It is intended that train operating companies will involve an increasing amount of private finance and management. One company within the group is responsible for control and maintenance of the infrastructure while a separate organization manages track allocation and planning. In the Netherlands, infrastructure will be provided free of charge at least until the year 2000. In both countries a major expansion of the rail system is taking place. Responsibility for developing local services is being devolved to regional level, supported by substantial funding from state level.

In Austria, Denmark, Finland, Italy, Norway, Portugal, Spain and Switzerland the management structures of the national railway organizations are being reorganized to separate operations from infrastructure. In some cases, for example in Denmark, these changes are purely for accounting purposes which is the minimum required by Directive 91/440. In all cases, however, significant new investment is taking place in the railway infrastructure.

In France, private capital has played a major role in the securing of investment funding for some years, with some investment being made by regional councils. The Haenel report published in mid-April 1994 envisages that administrative regions will be given both the power and the money to decide the level and fares of their passenger services. Bearing in mind the EU single market, it is believed that all key regional centres should have access by fast rail links to the rest of the Community and modernization of these links to 200 km/h standard 'should not be dependent on profitability'. For the trans-European Network, France is continuing to develop and extend its very successful 300 km/h TGV routes and services. A recent National Assembly commission of enquiry proposed changes in infrastructure owner-ship, subsidy and capital investment but was rejected by the Transport Minister and Unions. Privatization has not yet been considered by the government.

UK policy

Since the UK's railways were nationalized on 1 January 1948, they have been subject to many changes in government policy. There have been long periods of neglect with occasional periods of considerable investment in track, signalling and rolling stock. As we have seen earlier, subsidy and investment are among the lowest of the EU. Despite this, the UK's railways provide the best receipts against costs quotient and are generally regarded abroad as being one of the most cost-effective and innovative in the world. This is not reflected in opinion at home – the Prime Minister, John Major, in discussions about the Railways Bill described the UK's railways as one of the worst managed in the world.

This extraordinary efficiency has been achieved through continuous cost reduction and by targeting the product and price as closely as possible to the customer. One of the major moves in this direction has been the *Organising for Quality* (OfQ) programme. It took ten years to complete and the moment it was finished, reorganization for privatization began. Many within the industry believe this continuous change to be destructive – it is easy to forget the customer when so much change is taking place.

Under OfQ, all resources within the British Railways Board (BRB) were allocated to a business sector. This included track, signalling, maintenance, train operating and retail services. This vertical integration moved away from the production-led style of management which, traditionally, railway

243

organizations portray. The business sector became all-important – total costs dropped and service to the customer improved.

These efficiency gains were made by good management and cooperation within the industry. They were achieved without the core businesses being opened up to competition or privatization.

Many expected the privatized railway to follow the OfQ model. It was something of a surprise, therefore, when the proposals were published.

Privatization policy

The government decided to separate the constituent parts of the BRB into nearly one hundred organizations which were to be privatized separately. At a stroke, the vertical integration of OfQ was to be abolished and, since the train-operating parts of the business sectors were to be privatized as subsectors, much useful lateral integration was to be lost also.

One reason for this decision was that EU policy requires the separation of infrastructure from operations and the provision of open access, at least for international services.

The primary reason for the planned organization, however, appears to be the creation of a contestable market; *competition* is required at every level. Train operators are not allowed to own rolling stock or track or signalling or maintenance facilities, so their start-up costs should be very low.

Roger Freeman MP, then Minister for Public Transport, commented as follows in a keynote address given to the Institute of Civil Engineers on 10 March 1992:

> The construction of new track involves enormous sunk costs and therefore new players have not been able to enter the rail market. There is nothing we can do to alter this hard fact; what we can and will do is legislate to open up the infrastructure to allow new and fresh services to come into being. At present there exists a public monopoly in the provision of rail services. We think it is important not only to privatize, but to end this monopoly. Our policies of privatization and liberalization are twin forces working to produce incentives for better services to customers.

The new organization as from 1 April 1994

In order to facilitate contestability, the UK government created the following new organizations to work with the BRB:

- Railtrack
- Franchise Director
- Rail Regulator

Railtrack was set up as a government-owned organization to work completely separately from the BRB. It owns all track and signalling systems together with around 2500 stations and employs 12,000 staff. It is also responsible for the production of working timetables and will publish a national public timetable if train operators decide not to do so. Railtrack is Britain's infrastructure manager. It has set track access charges for passenger train operating units, local authorities and freight operating units. These charges are based on current replacement cost asset values and an initial return of 5.1 per cent. In general, these charges are considerably greater than previously required. For example, Greater Manchester Passenger Transport Authority was charged an additional £22.3 million or 147 per cent in one year. After much negotiation, the government agreed to underwrite these increases in the short term but future uncertainty remains. Some have suggested that these high charges are designed to enable the early privatization of Railtrack. Major stations will be privatized separately but the remaining organization is likely to be large enough to be included in the FT-SE 100 Index.

The **BRB** continues to be responsible for passenger train services, freight trains, rolling stock maintenance, passenger train leasing, infrastructure maintenance. It is planned that these remaining responsibilities will be privatized as follows: twenty-five passenger train operators, five freight train operators, seven rolling stock workshop companies, numerous rolling stock depot companies, three passenger train leasing companies, twenty infrastructure maintenance and design companies, two parcels and mails companies and dozens of small support organizations. Prior to privatization, contracts are being set up between the nascent businesses. For example, each passenger train operator is required to lease all locomotives and coaches from one or more of the three leasing companies.

Total subsidy to the railway industry will continue to decline in real terms. However, to provide Railtrack with a significant return, it will be necessary to subsidize all passenger train operators, including the previously profitable Inter City routes. If Railtrack is privatized then profits will go to shareholders and total subsidy will almost inevitably increase, unless services are to be lost.

The **Franchising Director**, Roger Salmon, is responsible for the privatisation of the twenty-five passenger train operating units. With very few exceptions, these units operated as subsectors under OfQ. For example, it is intended that all local services from Grimsby to the Scottish Border, East of the Pennines, will be privatized together. In this area, long-distance Inter City services will also operate on some routes but most routes and most stations will be served by the single monopoly operator – clearly this will not provide for open access or competition. Nationally, potential franchisees will bid for subsidy for each of the 25 operating units. In November 1994,

Mr Salmon estimated that half a dozen companies will be privatized by the end of 1995 with more than half of the passenger railway services in private hands by April 1996.

The following train operators have been selected by the government for early privatization:

- Gatwick Express
- Inter City East Coast
- Inter City Great Western
- London Tilbury and Southend
- ScotRail
- South West Trains

These are a very varied selection and will prove interesting cases in themselves.

The **Rail Regulator**, John Swift QC, is responsible for licensing and access agreements. There are four types of licence:

- Network Licence (issued to Railtrack only)
- Passenger Train Operating Licences
- Station Licences
- Light Maintenance Depot Licences

In issuing a licence, the regulator must consider the financial probity of the licensee and ensure that the Health and Safety Executive has approved its safety case.

The role of the Rail Regulator includes ensuring fair competition including provision for open access and fair charges from monopoly organisations such as Railtrack. He has expressed concern at Railtrack's 8.0 per cent return on capital from 1997–98 and at the use of modern equivalent asset value for these capital calculations. He has also suggested a RPI-% basis of charging in subsequent years to reflect expected cuts in infrastructure maintenance costs. Until March 1996, the Rail Regulator is controlled by the Ministry of Transport – it has been suggested that this is to ensure that the sale of Railtrack is not affected by reduced revenue figures.

Concerns of franchisees

A number of operators have shown an interest but, at the time of writing, all are concerned at the lack of control over the infrastructure, rolling stock and maintenance facilities. The Director of a management buy-out team commented that a significant strike such as the signallers' dispute of

Summer 1994, over which a train operator would have no control, would cost more in reduced revenue than the annual profits of the organization.

A different concern is that of entrepreneurs such as Richard Branson. Virgin Rail planned to run premium services on a number of routes but appears to have lost interest with the complexity and uncertainty of the privatization process. Train operating companies are insisting on monopoly franchises of at least seven years to ensure that revenue is not abstracted by competitors, providing services at peak times only. If accepted by the Franchise Director, this is likely to stifle individual enterprise and will not provide open access or competition.

Potential franchisees are primarily concerned with uncertainty. It is not clear in the long term either what the subsidy will be or what the infra-structure and rolling stock costs are likely to be. The government state that competition will reduce charges but monopoly situations will continue to exist. Railtrack is a natural monopoly and all rolling stock for passenger franchises will be owned by three leasing companies. In some cases, rolling stock required for a particular route is only available from one leasing company and virtually all spare rolling stock was scrapped under OfQ. In most towns and cities, stations are also in a monopoly position. An additional concern is the possibility of a change of govern-ment – the Labour Party has promized to renationalize the railways if they come to power.

Despite all these concerns, planning for privatization continues. Rail privatization has been described as the biggest legal task in history. An example of the task concerns Railtrack's 2500 stations. It is understood that each of these stations requires the following: a 42 page lease, a 196 page station access conditions document and, for each train operator, a 26 page collateral contract and a 31 page station access agreement. These are simply examples of the massive transaction costs involved. Consider also the complexity of legal and financial relationships between train operators, train leasing companies and light maintenance depots.

Open access for special passenger trains and railfreight

At the end of 1994, the only privatized passenger service in Britain was the small operator Special Trains. This was purchased by Pete Waterman, the millionaire record producer, for an undisclosed sum. Surprisingly, he was allowed to purchase the rolling stock and maintenance facilities as well as operate it. Special Trains is primarily concerned with day and weekend tours and has open access throughout Britain. It deals with the leisure market and is very different from all other passenger train operators which provide regular services.

Open access was provided for rail freight in Britain as from 1 April 1994.

Private owner rolling stock, such as oil tankers and iron ore carriers, has been common since the 1960s and Mendip Rail has been operating its own foreign-built locomotives with British Rail drivers for some years. National Power began to run its own trains early in 1994 and built a suitable maintenance facility in Ferrybridge, Yorkshire

The BRB's Trainload Freight was separated into three companies geographically based in the South-East, North-East and West respectively but encouraged to compete throughout Britain. Increases in track costs have taken their toll in this area too and much business has been lost although subsidy for flows transferred from road to rail is promized for the future.

Freightliner, BR's loss-making container train operator, is likely to be the first freight train operator to be privatized. With the exception of a management buy out team, no potential bidder has shown an interest in the locomotives required by the operation, leading to concern that it is the customer list which they want and that the business may be transferred from rail to road.

Conclusion

At the time of writing, the future of railways in the UK is unknown. A single unified organization is being replaced with dozens of organizations with perhaps only one thing in common, to make profits for their shareholders. The alternative view is that the imagination of entrepreneurs and the spur of competition will create wonderful new services which will herald a great new world for railways.

Perhaps the greatest concern is that of investment. Privatization appears to have been rushed and most of the players in the game are uncertain of its outcome. Rolling stock and infrastructure lasts for decades and uncertainty is not conducive to long-term investment.

General conclusions

This case study has provided a glimpse of the very varied situation of EU railways and how they are changing for the future. Within the EU, policy has been devized for the separation of infrastructure from operations, the licensing of railway undertakings and the allocation of infrastructure capacity. This is to provide a competitive market and, hopefully, a reduction in subsidy and expansion in services. The efficiency of the different national railways, prior to this introduction of competition, varies very considerably. The UK introduction of quality management led to the most cost effective railway in the EU, although low investment provided no new routes this century. Current UK policy, to provide a contestable market at every level, brings with it high transaction costs but with possible efficiency gains.

On the Continent, investment in high speed routes continues, competition is being introduced at a slower pace and generally with the agreement of regional authorities.

Bibliography

Journals:

European Parliament News, September 1994
Journal of Common Market Studies, June 1994
Modern Railways, 1980–1994
Rail, 1990–1994
Rail Business Report, 1994
Railway Gazette International, 1990–1994
Today's Railways, 1994

Newspapers

Financial Times, 1991–1994
Independent, 1991–1994
Independent on Sunday, 1991–1994
Observer, 1991–1994

Report

Rail Privatization – Deregulation and Open Access, The Institution of Civil Engineers (1992).

EU Communications

L 237/25 (91/440/EEC) *Council Directive on the development of the Community's railways*, 29/7/91.
COM (92) 494 final *The Future Development of the Common Transport Policy*, 2/12/92
COM (94) 106 final *Proposal on Community guidelines for the development of the trans-European transport network*, 7/4/94
COM (94) 316 final *Proposal on the licensing of railway undertakings* and *Proposal on the allocation of railway infrastructure capacity and the charging of infrastructure fees*, 14/7/94

Questions

1 Discuss whether UK railway policy is likely to be successful in providing for competition in train operating.

2   Discuss the major competition implications of separating infrastructure from operations.
3   The Trans-European Rail Network will provide the infrastructure necessary to underpin competitive rail services. Discuss.

Index

Accor/Wagons-Lits acquisition, 69
AEG Telefunken, 49–50
Aer Lingus, 127
  state aids, 138
Agreements, anti-competitive, 48–53
  Swedish competition policy, 184
  tolerance of, 47
  see also Treaty of Rome, Article 85
Agriculture, state aids, 34
Air France, 127
  access to Orly, 132–3
  financial performance, 128
  state aids, 136–7, 138–9
  see also Air transport industry
Air transport industry, 10, 125–40
  barriers to entry, 129–34
    congestion, 129–30
    slot allocation, 130–1
  financial performance, 127–8
  liberalization of routes, 125–6
  productivity, 128–9
  state aids, 134–9
  structure, 126–7, 140
Airbus consortium, 39–40
AKZO case, 56
Articles, *see* Treaty of Rome
Austria, competition policy, 88
AUTOMEC case, 47

Banco Santandar, alliance with Royal
  Bank of Scotland, 151–3
Bank for International Settlements (BIS),
  145
Bank of England, 150–1
Banking Act 1979, 148
Banking industry, 143–54
  barriers to single market, 147
  competition in practice, 149–51
  cross-border alliances, 151–4
  directives, 145–9
  passport system, 143–4, 148
  single market legislation, 145–9
Banque National de Paris, alliance with
  Dresdner Bank, 153–4
Basle Ratios, 145

BAT case, 60
Baumol's Contestable Markets Theory,
  196
Belgium, competition policy, 82–3
Bilateral agreements with non-member
  states, 120
BMW, 48–9
Border control removal, 9
BPB (plasterboards), 55
Bretton Woods system, 5
British Aerospace (BAe), VSEL bid, 63–4
British Airways, 127, 131
  financial performance, 128
British Gypsum, 55
British Rail, 239–42
British Railways Board (BRB), 243–8
British Telecom (BT), 198
Building Societies Act 1986, 148

Capital Liberalization Directive, 145
Cartels, Sweden, 181
Cassis de Dijon decision 1979, 9
Cecchini Report, *The European Challenge*,
  9, 12
Channel Tunnel, 241
Civil Aviation Authority (CAA), 131–2
  Airline Competition in the Single Market,
  128, 129
Coal:
  market characteristics, 218–19
  state aids, 34–5
  see also Energy sector
Collective dominance, 57–8
COMECON states, 156–8
Comité des Sages, 128–31
  Expanding Horizons, 128, 129
  state aids and, 137–8
Commission on Competition 1991
  (Sweden), 182
Common market, *see* Single market
Common Rules for the Allocation of Slots
  at Community Airports, 131
Common Transport Policy, 10–11
Competition:
  benefits of, 13–14

role in single market, 4–5, 8, 24
  mechanisms, 12–14
telecommunications industry, 195–8
Competition Act:
  Denmark (1989), 84–5
  Hungary (1923), 162–6
  Sweden (1982), 181–2
  Sweden (1992), 183–7
  United Kingdom (1980), 87
Competition Directorate DG4, 134
Competition policy, 14–17, 24, 77–90
  advent, 78–9
  external dimension, 112–21
    European dimension, 112–19
    impact on non-member states,
      109–21
    international dimension, 119–21
  Hungarian experience, see Hungary
  in member states, 82–8
  merger control, 17
  rationale for convergence, 79–81
  state aids, 16
  state monopolies, 15–16
  Sweden, see Sweden
  see also under names of constituent
    institutions
Concentration with a Community Dimension (CCD), see Merger Control
  Regulation
Consten, 52
Continental Can, 60
Cooke Committee, 145
Cooperation, anti-competitive, see Agree-
  ments, anti-competitive
Court of First Instance (CFI), 45

DB (German national railways), 233
De Havilland case, 66, 119–20
Denmark, competition policy, 84–5
Directives, banking industry, 145–9
Dominant position abuse, 15
  collective dominance, 57–8
  identification of, 55–6
  merger control and, 68–9
  oligopolistic dominance, 69–70
  relevant market identification, 56–7
  Swedish competition policy, 184, 190
Dominant position abuse, 86
  see also Competition policy; Treaty of
    Rome, Article 85

Dresdner Bank, alliance with Banque Na-
  tional de Paris, 153–4
Du Pont/ICI acquisition, 69
Dyestuffs case, 50–1, 111

Eastern Europe, competition policy influence, 117–18
Economic climate, European integration
  and, 5–8
Economic Competition Act 1956 (Netherlands), 85
Economic growth, 5–8
  wage costs and, 98–100
EFTA, see European Free Trade Association
EFTA Surveillance Authority (ESA), 115–
  17
Eire, competition policy, 82
Electricity:
  market characteristics, 218
  obstacles to competition, 219–21
  single market progress, 222–6
  see also Energy sector
Energy sector, 214–30
  characteristics, 215–19
    import dependency, 215
  Energy Charter, 214, 228–9
  obstacles to competition, 219–22
  single market progress, 222–7
  trans-European networks, 22–4, 214,
    227–8
  see also Coal; Electricity; Gas; Oil;
    Petroleum
Environmental policy, 21–2
European Authorized Institutions (EAI),
  149
European Commission communications:
  Communication on the Operation of
    the Internal Market After 1992 –
    Follow-up to the Sutherland Report,
    17
  Completing the Internal Market, 3–5, 7
  Electricity and Natural Gas Transmission
    Infrastructures in the Community,
    227–8
  Growth, Competitiveness, Employment –
    the Challenges and Ways Forward into
    the 21st Century, 17–18, 46, 92
  Reinforcing the Effectiveness of the Inter-
    nal Market, 17

The Way Forward for Civil Aviation in Europe, 129
European Community:
  growth, 5–8
  benefits of competition, 13–14
  single market goals, 3–5
European Court of Justice (ECJ), 45
  influence on non-member states, 110–11
European Economic Area (EEA), competition policy, 114–18, 182
European Free Trade Association (EFTA):
  competition policy, 88–9, 114–17
  transfer of states to European Union, 111–12
European Passenger Services (EPS), 233
Eurostar project, 233
Extra-territoriality, 110–11

Fibre-optic cables, 194
Fifth Medium Term Economic Policy Programme, 6–8
Financial services industry, *see* Banking industry
Finland, competition policy, 88–9
First Aviation Package, 126
First Banking Coordination Directive, 147–8
Fiscal barriers, 11
Foreign Acquisition of Swedish Companies Act 1992, 182
France:
  competition policy, 86
  railway policy, 243
French/West African Shipowners' Committees decision, 46
Frontier control removal, 9

Gas:
  market characteristics, 217–18
  obstacles to competition, 219–21
  single market progress, 222–6
  see also Energy sector
General Agreement on Tariffs and Trade (GATT), 120
Germany:
  competition policy, 86–7
  railway policy, 242
Givenchy, 50

Global influences of competition policy, 119–21
Greece, competition policy, 84
Green Paper 1987 (telecommunications), 200–1
Grid interconnections, electricity and gas, 220
Grundig, 52
Guidelines Document (telecommunications), 200–1

Heathrow Airport congestion problems, 130–1
Holdersim-Cedest, 67
Holiday entitlement as labour cost, 102–3
Hualon Corporation, 38–9
Hungary, competition policy, 155–73
  background, 156–8
  case studies, 169–73
  future tasks, 166–9
    adaptation to EU rules, 167–9
    furthering economic transformation, 166–7
  legal and institutional frameworks, 161–6
  new economic policy, 158–61

Inflation as economic indicator, 6
Inter-Bank On-line System (IBOS), 152–3
Internal market, *see* Single market
Irish Competition Act 1991, 82
Italian Flat Glass, 57–8
Italy, competition policy, 83

Joint ventures, merger control, 70–3

KLM, 127, 133–4
  financial performance, 128

Labour costs, 97–100
  economic growth and, 103–4
  indirect costs, 102–3
  minimum wages, 100–2
Large Exposure Directive, 148
Lauda Air, 133
Law in Defence of Competition and the Market 1990 (Italy), 83
Law on Protection of Economic Competition 1991 (Belgium), 82–3

Lufthansa, 127
  financial performance, 128

Maastricht Treaty, 4
  energy policy and, 229
  environmental policy, 21
  Social Protocol, 21, 92, 94
Market Court, Sweden, 188–9
Market economy investor principle
  (MEIP), 136
Mercury, 198
Merger Control Regulation, 4, 17, 60–
  75
  application, 65–9
    dominant position assessment, 68–
    9
    reference market definition, 65–8
  external dimensions, 113–14
  joint ventures, 70–3
  oligopolistic dominance, 69–70
  procedure, 64–5
  scope of, 61–4
  Sweden, 186–7
Minimum wages, 100–2
Monopolies, 15–16
  air transport industry, 139–40
  Sweden, 177–8
Mutual Information Directive, 10

Nestlé bid for Rowntree, 110
Nestlé/Perrier acquisition, 69–70
Netherlands:
  competition policy, 85
  railway policy, 242
NO (Office of the Competition Ombuds-
  man, Sweden), 181, 187
Non-member states:
  EU competition policy impact, 109–21
  European Court of Justice influence,
  110–11
North American Free Trade Area
  (NAFTA), 121
NS (Dutch national railways), 233

Oil:
  barriers to competition, 221–2
  consumption, 216
  market characteristics, 215–17
  single market progress, 226–7
  see also Energy sector

Oligopolistic dominance, 69–70
Olympic Airways, state aids, 138–9
Open network provision (ONP), 200–1,
  210
Organization for Economic Cooperation
  and Development (OECD), 119
Orly airport, access to, 132–4
Outsourcing, telecommunications, 202–
  3, 210
Own Funds Directive, 148

Paris, Orly airport access, 132–4
Passport system, banking industry,
  143–4, 148
Pasteur-Merieux/Merck, 72
Petroleum:
  barriers to competition, 221–2
  market characteristics, 215–17
  single market progress, 226–7
  see also Energy sector
Philips/Thompson/Sagem, 47, 72–3
Picat and Zachmann's analysis, 68–9
Plasterboards, 55
Porter's Five Forces approach to competi-
  tive structure, 74–5
Portugal, competition policy, 85–6
Price transparency, electricity and gas
  sectors, 219–20
Productivity growth, 103–4
Prohibition of Unfair Market Practices
  Act 1990 (Hungary), 162–6
Protection of Competition Act 1989
  (Spain), 83–4
Public enterprises, state aids and, 35
Public Telecommunications Operator
  (PTO), 198, 210

Quinine Cartel case, 48

Railtrack, 244–6
Railways, 11, 231–49
  comparisons between national railways, 239–42
    financial performance, 239–40
    investment, 241
  current trends, 242–3
  EU policy, 232–9
    access to rail networks, 232–4
    allocation of infrastructure capacity,
    238–9

common transport policy, 234–5
interoperability limitations, 236–7
licensing of railway undertakings, 237–8
trans-European network development, 235
trans-European priorities, 235–6
United Kingdom policy, 243–8
franchisee concerns, 246–7
open access, 247–8
organization, 244–6
privatization, 244
Recession:
European integration and, 5–7
Swedish competitiveness and, 180
Restraints upon Competition Act 1990 (Germany), 87
Royal Bank of Scotland, alliance with Banco Santandar, 151–3
RTE case, 56

Sabena, 127
state aids, 137
Santandar, alliance with Royal Bank of Scotland, 151–3
Second Aviation Package, 126
Second Banking Coordination Directive, 145, 148, 149, 154
Second Banking Directive, 10
Shipbuilding industry, state aids and, 40–1
Single market, 3–24
achievements, 17–19
background, 5–8, 78–9
barriers, 8–13
banking industry, 147
benefits of removal, 12–13
fiscal, 11
physical, 9
technical, 9–11
development of, 19–24
environmental policy, 21–2
relations with third countries, 19–20
social policy, 20–1
trans-European networks, 22–4
European Commission campaign, 3–5
mechanisms, 12–14
telecommunications industry, 195–8
Slot allocation, airports, 130–1

Small and medium sized enterprises (SMEs), Social Charter and, 104–5
SNCB (Belgian national railways), 233
SNCF (French national railways), 233
Social Charter, 21, 92–4
economic basis, 96–7
opting out, 105–6
small and medium sized enterprises and, 104–5
United Kingdom and, 94–6, 105–6
Social policy, 20–1, 92–107
see also Social Charter
Sociétié Téchnique Miniere, 51–3
Solvency Ratio Directives, 148
Spain, competition policy, 83–4
SPK (National Price and Competition Board, Sweden), 181, 187
Standards, technical, 9–10
energy sector, 220
mutual recognition, 10
telecommunications, 201–2
Stanford Research Institute, A European Planning Strategy for Air Traffic to the Year 2010, 130
State aids, 16, 26–42
air transport industry, 134–9
Comité des Sages and, 137–8
control of, 40–1
EC Treaty and, 32–5
agriculture, 34
coal, 34–5
steel, 34–5
transport, 34
monitoring of, 35–41
political economy, 27–31
case against, 29–30
international economy and, 39–40
justification for, 28–9
national politics and, 38–9
politics of, 30–1
public enterprises and, 35
role of EU-wide policy, 31–5
Sweden, 178–9
State monopolies, see Monopolies
Steel, state aids, 34–5
Steetly/Tarmac merger, 62
Stockholm City Court, 188–9
Subsidies, see State aids
Sutherland Report, The Internal Market After 1992 – Meeting the Challenge, 17

Sweden, 89, 176–91
  Commission on Competition 1991, 182
  Competition Act 1982, 181–2
  Competition Act 1992, 183–90
    anti-competitive cooperation and, 184
    dominant position abuse and, 184, 190
    fines and penalties, 186
    mandatory disclosure, 185
    merger control, 186–7
    negative clearance and exemptions, 185–6
    prioritization of small and medium sized businesses, 184–5, 190
  defining the problem, 176–80
    market concentration, 179–80
    public sector and regulation, 177–8
    recession, 180
    state aids, 178–9
    structural weaknesses, 176–7
  EEA agreement impact, 182
  railways policy, 242
  Swedish Competition Authority, 187–8, 191
  Swedish Courts dealing with competition, 188–9
Systembolaget alcoholic beverages (Sweden), 178

TAP, state aids, 138–9
Tax differences and competition, 11
  electricity and gas sectors, 220
Technical standards, see Standards
Telecommunications, 14, 193–211
  alliances, 203–4
  common markets in, 195–8
  competition in, 195–8
    analysis of, 204–8
    EU interpretation, 208
    existing situation, 198
    glossary, 210–11
    goals, 199
    industry structure, 194
    liberalization methods, 200–4
      Green Paper 1987, 200
      Guidelines Document, 200
      open network provision (ONP), 200–1

    standards and outsourcing, 201–3
  trans-European networks, 22–3
Telecommunications Law 1993 (Sweden), 190
Third Aviation Package, 126
Third countries:
  agreements with, 113–17
  relations with, 19–20
Third party access (TPA), gas and electricity markets, 224–6
Trans-European networks, 22–4
  energy sector, 22–4, 214, 227–8
  telecommunications, 22–3
  transport, 22
  railways, 235
Transport:
  state aids, 34
  trans-European networks, 22
  see also Air transport industry; Railways
Transport Act 1988 (Sweden), 242
Transport Directorate DG7, 134
Transposition of directives, 18–19
Treaty of Rome, 3, 14–17
  Article 85, 15, 17
    alignment of national and Community law, 46–7
    exemption, 53–4
    generalized application, 46
    interpretation of, 48–53
    scope of, 44–5
    see also Agreements, anti-competitive
  Article 86, 15, 17, 54–8
    alignment of national and Community law, 46–7
    generalized application, 46
    interpretation, 55–8
    scope of, 45
    see also Dominant position abuse
  Article 90, 15–16
  Article 92, 16

Unemployment:
  as economic indicator, 6–7
  wage costs and, 98–9
United Brands, 56, 57
United Kingdom:
  competition policy, 87–8
  railways policy, see Railways

Index

Social Charter and, 94–6, 105–6

Value Added Network Services (VANS), 194, 202, 211
Vereeniging van Cementhandelaren, 52
Vin & Sprit alcoholic beverages (Sweden), 178

VSEL, bid from BAe, 63–4

Wage costs, *see* Labour costs
White Papers, *see* European Commission communications
Woodpulp case, 51, 111, 120